John William Martin

Roach, Rudd & Bream Fishing

Being a Practical Treatise on Angling with Float and Ledger in Still Water...

John William Martin

Roach, Rudd & Bream Fishing
Being a Practical Treatise on Angling with Float and Ledger in Still Water...

ISBN/EAN: 9783337143664

Printed in Europe, USA, Canada, Australia, Japan

Cover: Foto ©Lupo / pixelio.de

More available books at **www.hansebooks.com**

ROACH, RUDD & BREAM FISHING.

Being a Practical Treatise on Angling with Float and Ledger in Still Water and Stream.

Including a Few Remarks on Surface Fishing for Rudd and Roach.

By J. W. MARTIN.

The "Trent Otter."

A Working Man Angler's Experiences; written expressly for the benefit of his brethren of the Craft.

ALL RIGHTS RESERVED.

PUBLISHED BY
THE ANGLER LIMITED, AT THE OFFICES, SCARBOROUGH,
AND 279, STRAND, W.C.
1896.

Preface.

IN the preface to the first volume of this little work, I pointed out that in scores of big towns and cities there are thousands of factory and other workers who dearly love a day's fishing, and when the workshop bell or steam buzzer at noon on Saturday's signalled a cessation of the week's toil, these workers were soon after wending their way, rod in hand and basket on back, to their favourite river, drain, canal, or reservoir, as the case might be.

The great majority of these men are, as I said then, bottom fishermen, pure and simple; and I may say also without fear of contradiction, that by far the largest number make Roach and Bream the special objects of their quest. It was this consideration that made the Publisher of this little effort of my pen decide to issue it in two volumes—1st, dealing with Barbel and Chub; and 2nd, Roach and Bream.

In the little volume now before you, I have most carefully noted the difference between stream fishing and still water fishing for Roach and Bream, giving full details of the outfits, the tackle and methods of shotting and using it, with the ground baits and hook baits; each style separate and distinct from the other, so that the youngest and most inexperienced angler can hardly make a mistake.

If there is a special feature in this small volume, that feature will be found in Chapter V., where I treat a distinguished member of the Roach family at greater length, from a practical standpoint, than I think it has ever been treated before in a work on bottom-fishing.

I must also tender my best thanks to the two or three gentlemen, whose names I have mentioned in the following pages, for the great trouble they have taken in answering my queries, and giving my readers and myself the benefit of their valuable advice on certain vexed questions.

Roach fishing has been for many years a favourite pastime of mine, and I have also had the distinguished advantage of calling "friends" some of the most expert and observant roachers that are to be found in the kingdom, and I thankfully acknowledge the valuable experience I gained from the companionship of these friends.

I should like to repeat what I said in the preface to the volume on "Barbel and Chub Fishing," that the principles I lay down are those of economy, based upon a practical knowledge and experience extending through many years, and under peculiar advantages. I know what it is to have a working-man's pocket, because, brother working-man angler, I am one of yourselves ; and have not the least hesitation in saying that a careful study of this part of my subject will be a saving to you of many shillings during a single season.

And now, Mr. Critic, I must again remind you, when picking out passages that are badly expressed, or sentences that are not exactly in accordance with the Queen's English, that I left school at the early age of ten, and most of my learning and experience have been picked up by the wayside, riverside, and hedges.

This little volume I also dedicate to my brother working-men fishers, and await the result of their verdict with the greatest confidence.

JOHN WM. MARTIN
("The Trent Otter").

December, 1896.

Contents.

PART III.—ROACH, RUDD, AND BREAM.

CHAPTER I.—ROACH AND ROACH FISHING.

Roach fishermen—Ancient v. Modern Roach—Shyness of Roach—Fecundity of Roach—A Remarkable Incident—How did they get there?—Description and peculiarities of Roach—Habits and haunts of Roach—Food of Roach—Weight of Roach—Good bags—Roach fishing—The Sheffield style—The Nottingham style—Still water Roaching—Striking with a wobbly rod - - - - - - - - - 1

CHAPTER II.—THE ROACH *(continued)*.
ROACH FISHING IN STILL WATERS.
(ON ROACH BITES AND THE OUTFIT).

Choosing a Roach Rod — An Ouse pattern — The Author's Roach Rod — A bit of sound advice — Rod-rings—The Reel and Line—Gut Lines and Gut Hooks—Roach Floats—What is a Roach bite?—A born Roacher—Sucking in, and blowing out, the bait — Striking the fish — "Missed him"—The reason why—The Bleak nuisance—Slow v. quick sinking baits—Those small tormentors - - - 10

CHAPTER III.—THE ROACH *(continued)*.
ROACH FISHING IN STILL WATERS.
(ON GROUND BAITS AND HOOK BAITS).

Still-water Roachers—Ground Baits—How to ground bait, and how not to do it—Mixing the ground bait—Roving for Roach—Creed wheat as a Roach bait—Ringing the changes—How to cree wheat — Plumbing the swim — Feeding in mid-water—Stale v. fresh wheat—The postman's knock—Malt — Gentles or maggots — How to breed, and how to prepare them—Gentles in the winter—Paste, plain and coloured—King's bait—The cockspur worm—The weather and its deception - - - - - - - - 20

CHAPTER IV.—THE ROACH *(continued).*
    STREAM AND DRAIN FISHING FOR ROACH.
    (THE NOTTINGHAM AND SHEFFIELD STYLES).

Stream *v.* drain fishing—The stream fishing rod—The Outfit—Floating the line—Floats and Tackle—Ground baiting the streams—Baiting the hook—Fishing the swim—A strange ground bait—A flooded water—"Stret pegging"—The Nottingham style—Finding the depth—Casting out the bait—Ledgering for Roach—Undercurrents—A heavy stream—The Sheffield style—Shrimps as bait—A killing style—Experiences on the Avon and Frome - - - 36

CHAPTER V.—THE RUDD.
    RUDD AND RUDD FISHING.

Rudd and Rudd Fishing—A little known fish—Characteristics of the Rudd—Weight of Rudd—Habits and Haunts of the Rudd—Luring them out—Food of Rudd—Baits for Rudd fishing—"Fine and far off"—The outfit—Floats—Gut lines and gut hooks—A slowly-sinking bait—Fishing the runs—Playing the fish—Dr. Norman's experiences—The Norfolk style—Fly fishing for Rudd - - - 55

CHAPTER VI.—THE BREAM.
    BREAM AND BREAM FISHING.

Bream fishing—White Bream—Carp Bream—Weight of Bream—Distribution of Bream—Peculiarities of Bream—"On the flit"—Antiquity of Bream—Bream in the frying-pan—The Trent style—The Ouse style—A rustic breamer—A picture drawn from life—Night fishing—The outfit—Ground-baiting for Bream—A Bream bite—The hook and crutch—The weather in connection with Bream fishing—Special precautions—Lake Bream—An extraordinary ground bait—Hook baits—Ledgering for Bream—"*Au revoir*" - - - - - - - - - - 71

PART III.
THE ROACH.

CHAPTER I.
ROACH AND ROACH FISHING.

*Roach Fishermen — Ancient v. Modern Roach — Shyness of Roach— Fecundity of Roach—A Remarkable Incident—How did they get them?— Description and peculiarities of Roach—Habits and haunts of Roach— Food of Roach — Weight of Roach — Good bags — Roach fishing — The Sheffield style—**The** Nottingham style—Still water Roaching—Striking with **a** wobbly **rod.***

"The Roach, whose common kind to every flood doth fall."

Bottom fishermen, and their name nowadays can be called legion, dearly love a day's roach fishing. It hardly matters whether they make a speciality of chub, or barbel, or bream; they are nevertheless always ready for a bit of roaching. There is also a large class of anglers who confine their attention exclusively to this branch of fishing; they are never tempted to try any other, and I have fancied more than once that they rather prided themselves on the fact. But there is one thing certain; a successful roach fisherman stands on the very highest rung of the angling ladder. He must be possessed of great skill, patience and ingenuity, and also of a thorough knowledge of the habits of the fish. He must also be able to detect the places where roach are likely to be found, and know what places they avoid; he must pay particular attention to a number of the most minute details, a good swim must be selected, and then it must be fished at the exact depth; a very fine tackle must be used, and in hooking a roach the angler must have the orthodox roach trick, and do it

B

in the twinkling of an eye. Dame Juliana Berners, writing of this fish, says: "the roche is an easy fysshe to take." Perhaps it might have been four hundred years ago when that good old lady wrote of fish and fishing. Even coming down a little later, we find Izaak Walton speaking of the roach in these terms: "he is accounted the water sheep for his simplicity or foolishness." These two old writers were perhaps justified in making those remarks, but nowadays the well-fed, good-conditioned, and aldermanic roach of any well-fished river are not to be caught by any tyro, as soon as August gets in, at any rate. They are then amazingly shy of the hook, and appear to be pretty wide-awake, perhaps taking stock of the angler and his proceedings. They seem to be very highly educated during the autumn months, and cannot stand a reckless stamping by the angler up and down the bank, or splashing about with heavily-weighted tackle. To be a successful roach fisherman, the motto must be "Fine and far off." Keep out of sight as much as possible, use suitable tackle, proper baits, and be in a good swim, and if the roach are not what you could call well on the feed, you still stand a chance of deceiving a few of them; even when they are "on," it is necessary to pay attention to a number of minute details, or else they will very soon be driven "off." Roach, in a pond where they are small and ill-fed, might perhaps allow themselves to be caught by any sort of bait and tackle; even river roach during June are sometimes perfectly reckless, allowing themselves to be caught by dozens with the cad-bait when the milk has been running from them; but these cases are exceptions.

The roach is one of the most plentiful of all freshwater fishes. Hardly any stream, lake or pond (of any size) but what contains it; indeed, it not infrequently happens that there are quantities of them in some sheet of water where even their very existence was not known, and if by any chance the fact was discovered, the owner of the water was at a loss to account for their presence. In connection with this question I once read a very remarkable instance. A writer, in one of the sporting journals said: "I know of a small lake that was emptied of water and fish. The lake is about three acres in extent, and did not exceed six feet in depth. The water was run off by means of a sluice. the bottom of the lake was fairly level and pretty firm; a crop of rye grass was sown on it, which yielded an enormous crop. For three successive seasons the same thing was done. Under these circumstances it is certain that no fish could have been by any possibility left, there being no water except an occasional shower of rain or a fall of snow for the whole of the three years referred to. After cutting the grass for the final time, the water was let in through a fine grating, and in the depth of winter. The water, in addition, came from a spring supplied by a well on the hillside, in which there were no fish. Thus no roach, or indeed fish of any kind, could have found their way into the lake, and yet three years afterwards the place literally swarmed with roach. Can anybody give me an idea how this could have happened?" This question seems to me to be a poser. I could hardly accept the theory put forward by the writer of the letter just quoted; he thought that probably water-fowl might have carried the spawn there sticking to their legs, or that the same fowl might have swallowed the spawn and passed it out again without being digested. If I might offer a theory, I should say, perhaps the impregnated ova or spawn is capable of lying on the ground or among the roots of the weeds for years at a stretch without vivifying into life, the same as the chrysalis of certain insects will; the advent of the fresh water into the lake forming the starting point of the swarms of roach that had created such surprise.

The roach is also a member of the carp family, his specific name being "Cyprinus Rutilus." When in good condition he is a very handsome fish. Yarrell thus describes him: "The colour of the upper part is dusky green with blue reflections, becoming lighter on the sides, and passing into silvery white on the belly; the irides yellow, cheeks and gill covers silvery white; dorsal and caudal fins pale brown tinged with red; pectoral fins orange red; ventral and anal fins bright red; the scales are rather large, marked with consecutive and radiating lines; large eyes, the circles of which are of a gold colour and the iris red.

Their scales are very smooth except during and just after spawning time, when they feel to the touch like a nutmeg grater." From this it would appear that our roach is possessed of considerable personal beauty, which I, for one, do not intend to deny. Indeed, an October roach, when in condition, is a lovely fish, and a dish of a dozen pounders is a splendid sight, and one that any angler, no matter how clever and experienced he is, will be mightily proud of, more especially if he himself happens to be the lucky captor. A roach has a small head and a hard mouth, with a peculiar top lip; this lip, if you take hold of it, raise it, and bring it forward, shows to you that it has the power of elongation, and that it is shaped something like a hood. This power of the roach to alter the shape of its mouth goes to prove that he can feed in a variety of ways, grope along the bottom like a barbel or gudgeon, take a bait in midwater, and even from the surface like a dace. Perhaps this telescopic mouth may have something to do with the roach's power of so promptly blowing out a suspicious bait, which act puzzles the novice more than a little; but more of this further on. These fish may very readily be confounded with others of an apparently similar character, but which, on closer observation side by side, are widely different. When I was secretary and weighing-in officer of an angling club, certain members would some odd times bring in to be booked as roach two and even three pounds chub, under the idea that they had got hold of an extra-fine specimen of the "rutilus" family.

Roach spawn about the latter end of May, and are wonderfully prolific, as many as 125,000 eggs being counted in the ovum of a pound fish. For some little time after this operation they are very dirty and slimy, and have a lot of rough white pimples on their scales. About this time t'ey retire among the weeds, and feed a good deal on those weeds and the insects found among them. As soon as July gets well in they leave the fastnesses of the weed beds and take more to the open water and the gravelly swims, and are then found in large numbers in such places, and the clear runs by the side of rushes and flags. In another week or two, say by the latter end of July or the beginning of August, the weed gets out of them, and the very slimy coat they wore quite wears off; their scales are smooth and bright, and their fins nice and clear. Now they begin to get very shy indeed, and it requires an artist in the business to take them. These fish prefer a clean, sandy bottom, and don't like a muddy one, being in my opinion a very clean fish. The baits have to be sweet, and no suspicion of tobacco juice or dirt about them, or he will have none of them. Roach are very fond of a lazy eddy by the side of a swift stream, but being a bulky fish are not found much in very strong and rapid waters; they like the slow, lazy curls under bushes, the quiet lay-byes or corners away from the main stream; swims that flow at the rate of not more than two miles an hour, or in the curls, eddies and dimples in the vicinity of a weir, or in the immediate neighbourhood of an old wooden bridge, and sometimes in the shallows of a mill tail. These are the principal places to look for roach in a swiftly flowing river. In slow rivers, broads, and lakes, that abound with these fish, they can be found nearly anywhere, provided the bottom is all right and the locality suitable; but I shall divide the subject into two parts, one part treating of still water roaching, and the other stream fishing, in the following chapters. The food of roach consists of weeds, cad-baits, grubs, flies, worms, fresh-water shrimps, insects, spawn of other fish, etc.; while as baits he will take gentles, paste, bread, malt, wheat, pearl barley, et hoc genus homme. As a fish for the table, he is several degrees better than either the barbel or the chub; nicely fried in plenty of lard, and browned, he is not at all bad faring; in fact, I am very fond of a good-conditioned autumn roach out of a gravelly river. I should think the top weight of our English roach can be put down at 3lb., and even this would only be reached on very rare occasions. I can only remember seeing two caught of that weight, and they were got in the salmon net as mentioned in the chapter on barbel. A 2lb. roach is considered a very good one indeed, and thought worthy of a glass case. The Hampshire Avon, I am told, contains the largest roach, specimens from two to two and a half pounds, or even a little over, being frequently taken.

The Ouse in Huntingdonshire has some splendid roach in its waters, one angler that I know frequently getting individuals up to two and a half pounds in weight. I don't know how it is, but out of the thousands of roach I have killed in one river or another, I never got one of two pounds to my own rod. Once I thought I had reached the goal of my ambition, and landed a veritable two-pounder; but, alas! a careful weighing-in only made him 1lb. 15½oz.—very near it, in all conscience, but still not the one. From one and a half to one and three-quarter pounds I have had in plenty. I once picked a dozen fish out of a very large bag I made in the Ouse that scaled eighteen pounds. My two best bags of roach taken in the Trent contained among others fifteen fish weighing fourteen pounds, and seventeen fish weighing fifteen pounds. Taking things all round, I may say that a half-pounder is a sizeable one, a pounder is a good one, a pound-and-a-half fish ought to make any honest angler's heart rejoice, while if he did get a two-pounder, his mission on earth is fulfilled.

And now just a few words on the various styles of roach fishing that I have seen during my piscatorial wanderings. The rivers and waters are very varied in this character, even in one particular district. Some of the rivers are slow and sluggish in the extreme, others again are streamy and shallow, whilst others widen out into meres, broads or lakes, with sometimes a considerable depth of water; yet, again, the waters of others are nothing but artificial drains, rather narrow, with no stream at all; but one thing is certain about these fen waters, it hardly matters which class of water it is, they all contain vast quantities (more or less) of splendid roach. There appears to me to be at least three different schools of roach fishermen on the banks of these waters, each one fishing in his own particular way, and each separate style is adapted for the class of water operated upon. On some of the narrower canals and drains, where the water is not above six feet or so deep, and very still, the more successful roachers follow what is sometimes called the Sheffield style. The outfit used is of the very lightest possible build: the rod is a little ten-foot weapon, weighing probably about as many ounces, fairly stiff, and with a strike about it that is sharp and at once direct from the point, so that if a cunning old roach, who is endeavouring to quietly suck a bait from the hook without moving the float, makes the very smallest of errors and betrays his presence by only a tiny quiver of the said float, he is himself sucked in in consequence of the strike of the rod top being so prompt and accurate. The wooden reel also used by these men is a very light three-inch one, fairly easy running; the plaited silk line is nearly as fine as can be procured, the float in many cases is only a little porcupine quill, carrying not more than three very small split shots. Sometimes this float is only a tiny crow quill, with one shot, while the bottom tackle itself is a yard of the very finest drawn gut, hardly visible to the naked eye when held a few yards away, and yet the ease and certainty that pound roach and upwards are played and landed on even that frail tackle is something marvellous to the uninitiated. Another class of roachers operate on the more streamy, shallower rivers by what is known as the Nottingham style. This style requires a heavier set of tackle than the one just noted, and is in my opinion the very style par excellence for killing roach in the heavier streams, where the water runs somewhat faster than it does in the generality of fenland rivers. The tackle used by these men is nearly as fine as can be; when I said just now that it was a little heavier, I meant the float was a little bigger one, say a small swan quill carrying some half a dozen medium-sized shots on the tackle. This style of fishing also requires a light and stiff rod, about eleven feet in length will be the best, and it must also be smart and prompt in its actions, so that it would respond promptly at the will of the user, and hook a roach in an instant, even if the angler's float happened to be twenty yards away down stream. The roach that inhabit these streamy places, where the water runs with a rather swifter current, take a bait somewhat different to their brethren in the very quiet waters. As just hinted, these latter are sly and cunning to a very remarkable degree, robbing the hook of the novice time after time without so much as giving him the slightest hint as to their presence. Stream roach, on the other hand, must of necessity betray their bite; the baited hook is gliding down the stream, the fish must attack the bait somewhat quickly, and if the float is a correct one and properly weighted some idea of this bite is communicated to the angler.

But by far the larger number of these roach fishermen ply their craft in very deep and sluggish water, ranging from ten to fifteen feet in depth, with a stream so quiet that the float scarcely travels down it at all. For successfully fishing this class of water it is necessary to have a rod somewhat different to those already mentioned. Bank anglers will find that the majority of these slow running and deep rivers are fringed with reeds, and generally have a weed bed all along the margin stretching some four or five feet into the stream. A judicious application of the plummet will in many cases tell our roach fishermen that just over these weeds the bottom is level and clear with an uniform depth of say ten feet. In order to fish these places properly the rod should be fourteen feet in length, stiff and light; this length of rod is required in order to reach comfortably over the weeds, and more especially is it required if the water should chance to be, as I have found in scores of good swims, nearer fourteen or fifteen feet deep than ten. This rod should also be one that is prompt and sharp in its action, because in this class of swim the roach are as sly as can be, and the bigger the fish the slyer they are. In biting, the float only moves the very slightest, and as quick as can be; the strike must be on the very instant or it will be too late. I have seen rods in the hands of certain fen anglers that would not hook two roach out of every dozen bites; they wobbled down to the very hand, and in striking, instead of switching the point upwards, the point would even, if held a yard above the surface, duck downwards and strike the water before the stroke could take effect and the fish be hooked. This action on the part of your rod would be fatal to your success as a roacher in these very deep and quiet waters. Any angler who feels a little doubt as to the truth of this statement should try a little experiment at home. If he has a fourteen foot roach rod which might be described as moderately stiff and not very wobbly, let him put it together and take hold of the butt as if he were fishing; hold the point eighteen inches above a table and strike gently, as though responding to a roach bite, and the chances are that in nine cases out of ten the point of the rod will first duck downwards and touch the table before it strikes upwards to hook the imaginary fish; and if this would even happen in using a fairly good and stiff rod, what must it be in a very limber one? I shall have occasion to refer to this subject again, so will leave it for the present. Briefly, the foregoing remarks give a few hints and some idea of the various styles of roach fishing in vogue in different waters. I will try to explain them all in detail as I proceed.

CHAPTER II.

THE ROACH *(continued)*.

ROACH FISHING IN STILL WATER.

(ON ROACH BITES AND THE OUTFIT).

Choosing a Roach Rod—An Ouse pattern—The Author's Roach Rod —A bit of sound advice—Rod-rings—The Reel and Line—Gut Lines and Gut Hooks—Roach Floats—What is a Roach bite?—A born Roacher —Sucking in, and blowing out, the Bait — Striking the fish — "Missed him"—The reason why—The Bleak nuisance—Slow v. quick sinking baits—Those small tormenters.

When the young tyro, or even the would-be roach fisherman of mature years, walks into a tackle dealer's shop for the purpose of choosing his rod, in nine cases out of ten he selects one that is made up of a number of short joints, say from two to three feet long each, because his first consideration is that it is nice and handy to carry about, and also he perhaps considers that it can be carried out of sight under his coat, as if he were ashamed of his occupation. Now this portability is the only good feature these short-jointed rods possess; when the angler has to travel by train to his sport, his rod can be packed up in a small compass, without being a nuisance to any of his fellow-passengers, and he will not be in danger when boarding a railway carriage of poking one end of it into the eye of somebody sitting inside, or doubling up another who happens to be standing on the platform behind him by a blow in the stomach with the butt end, as he would be if each joint was six or seven feet long. But here the practical usefulness of these many-jointed rods cease; they are not a success when operating against the shy old roach of these deep still waters, the wobbly action, as noticed in the last chapter, is very much pronounced; besides, the extra joints and ferrules represent so much extra weight that ought if possible, to be dispensed with. A roach rod from eleven to twelve feet long should not have, under any circumstances, more than three lengths, while one of fifteen feet should have no more than four, and this will allow the necessary stiffness for the sharp and prompt strike that is absolutely indispensable in a good roach rod. The rod should be built with plenty of timber or cane in the lower half of it, and should have an accurate taper up to the fine point in the top end half; indeed, if the angler can manage it anyhow, his rod for still water roaching, even if fourteen feet long, will be all the better for strike, balance, and weight, if it has no more than three lengths to it. One of the nicest roach rods, as far as practical work went, that I ever saw was not a very handsomely got-up affair. It belonged to an angler who lived close to the river Ouse, and had no ferrules or joints in it at all. It was a single stick of beautifully tapered East Indian cane, with about a yard of lancewood, spliced, glued, and whipped firmly on the top end. It was fairly thick at the butt end, was a trifle over fourteen feet long, and was a perfect treat to handle; it would respond on the very instant, and hook a roach in a twink. The owner assured me that it had killed some thousands of roach and bream during the six years he had had it. Unless the angler lives on the banks of these deep still waters it is not advisable to have a rod in a single length like the one just described; its extreme awkwardness in travelling or carrying about precludes its universal adoption.

Personally, I have had many a try, and wasted many a good bit of cane and lancewood during my endeavours to make myself a really first-class fourteen-foot roach rod, but I succeeded at last, and the one I finally experimented on, and pronounced satisfactory is a composite weapon of rather peculiar build. The butt is a length of East India cane six feet long, fitted with the usual ferrule, safety rings, winch fittings, and butt cap. The centre joint is also East India cane, five feet long, with rings and ferrule, and the top is lancewood three feet long only, ringed as usual. This rod, when put together is what I call a perfect fourteen-foot roach rod, and by being built in different lengths for each joint, gives the necessary stiffness without extra weight, and the shortness of the tapered top gives it the sharp, prompt, and accurate strike so beloved by a first-class roacher.

My object in being so particular in this matter of a rod is to give the tyro or youthful angler a bit of sound advice which is the result of many years' experience, and also my anxiety to save him unnecessary expense in the matter of purchasing a rod. He might pick one out of stock that for the moment took his fancy, only to find, after a few trials by the riverside, that it was not at all suitable for the purpose, and another expense would be necessary. When selecting a roach rod for these deep still waters he must carefully eschew rods that have a lot of play in them nearly down to the butt. Never mind what any shopman may advise, select the rod that has the fewest joints (no more than four at the outside); see that it is light in hand, and above all nice and stiff, with a strike that seems to be a sort of a switch direct from the end of the point, and I might again add, no material in my opinion is so good for a long roach rod as East India cane and lancewood. The rings, too, of the rod should be carefully looked at; the loose lay-down pattern should not be had at any price. They should be stiff stand-up rings, either "Bells Life" or safety for the lower two joints, and snake rings for the top. It must be clearly understood that the rod, reel, line, floats and tackle I describe and recommend in this chapter are for use in deep quiet waters. Tackle suitable for fishing down streams will be touched upon in the chapter on "Stream Fishing for Roach."

Some roach anglers discard a reel altogether; they simply have a few yards of silk line, and tie one end of it about halfway down the rod; of course, when this plan is adopted every fish must be played and killed with a tight line. Now, I am decidedly in favour of a reel and a few yards of extra line, because it is necessary to fish with the very finest gut that is drawn, and if a very good roach is hooked a sudden plunge when at full length of the tether might result in breakage, whereas if a reel and running line is employed this danger is nothing near so apparent; besides, the angler can swim his float if there is a gentle current a few yards lower down stream, where very often the biggest roach lie. This reel need not be very large, nor yet very expensive : a plain, easy-running wooden one about three inches in diameter, and costing no more than from two to three shillings, will be plenty good enough ; but one thing the tyro ought to observe, and that is, the reel should have a strong crossback to it ; the brasswork on the back should be fitted right across and in four opposite directions. This arrangement prevents the wooden back under the brasswork from twisting, warping, or sticking, and helps to keep the reel in proper running order. Twenty yards of line will be ample, and this should be of undressed silk, plaited, and fairly fine in substance. This line is, of course, wound on the barrel or centre portion of the reel just noticed. The next articles our roach fishermen require are a few lengths of good gut, and I recommend most strongly for this purpose drawn gut lines, two yards in length, tapered from one X at the top end down to three X at the bottom end. There is a loop tied at each end of these gut lines, that at the stoutest end being to fasten the silk line to, and the one at the finest end to loop the gut hook itself in, as already indicated in previous chapters.

With regard to hooks for roach fishing, anglers are not agreed as to which is or is not the best shape. Some swear by sneck bends, others by round bends, while others again favour the crystal bends. Personally, I prefer the latter, as I find by careful practise that they hook and hold their fish much better than either round bends or snecks. This class of roach fisherman would do well to procure three dozen of these hooks tied to the very finest drawn gut, say a dozen No. 11 (Redditch scale), on four X drawn gut for creed wheat and paste fishing ; another dozen No. 10 on three X drawn gut for maggot fishing, or small red worms ; and another dozen No. 9 on two X drawn gut for tail end of lobworm, when water is a trifle flooded. A box of split shot, a few porcupine floats, a light plummet, and a disgorger, completes his outfit.

On second consideration of the above lines, I fancy it will hardly be advisable for the young tyro to invest in these very finest four X drawn gut hooks for a start ; they are so very, very fine, and require delicate handling. Some considerable skill and patience is required in landing roach from 1lb. to 1½lb. on this very frail tackle, so perhaps until our novice has had some experience in the matter, it will be advisable to begin with three X drawn gut, and work up to the finer size as he feels more confidence in himself. A sudden bite when he was hardly prepared for it might make him feel a little flurried, and cause him to strike harder than necessary. If he were using the very finest tackle, and the roach a good one, a smash would be nearly a certainty, and his swim and sport spoiled for an hour or two afterwards. I need not say, I suppose, that it is necessary to fish as light as possible in these deep, quiet, or semi-quiet waters. The float is one of the most important articles in the roach fisherman's outfit, and should be of such a character, and shotted in such a manner, that it will indicate the very smallest nibble. I find, as already hinted, that a porcupine quill is as good, in fact better, than any other that can be used, and the size of it and number of shots on the gut line will depend on the character of the water operated upon. In some waters it is necessary for the bait to be a slowly sinking one, while in others it must sink quickly for reasons that will be stated and described directly. I have seen all sorts of roach floats in use, some of them a mixture of quill, cork, and wood, but many of them are liable to become water-logged, and this is not desirable, even in the smallest degree, especially for roach fishing in still water.

The novice now finds himself confronted with a very simple question, and one which at the first glance seems easy to answer. It is this: What is a roach bite? I ask the tyro this question in all sincerity. In all probability nine out of ten will answer straight as a dart, with a little laugh at being asked such a very simple question, "Why, when a roach takes the bait in his mouth and pulls the float clean down out of sight." Yes, this is one kind of a roach bite, I will admit, but it also is one that the angler does not very often get. At odd times, when he seems to be perfectly reckless in his feeding, and will quietly suck down the bait at nearly every swim, any tyro can scarcely miss them. At these odd times that answer will apply, but, fortunately for the roach, the chances do not often occur. The roach bite more generally met with, especially where they are very shy and constantly fished for, is nothing more than the very smallest quiver of the float, or again a slight tilt or stoppage of the said float, or yet again, and this is the bite that can be most easily perceived, a very small and instantaneous dip of the float of not more than one-eighth of an inch, and the time occupied in this dip is not more than one-fifth of a second. Now and again small roach, bolder and more hungry than their larger brethren, will pull down the float in a much more decided manner, but, generally speaking, the half-pounders and upwards proceed in a much more cautious way. When the roach are fairly on the feed, and their natural caution has for an hour or two forsaken them, the bite is a more prolonged affair: the float suddenly dips, and instead of coming up again, as it will when they are coming shy, the float is held down for a much more considerable space of time. This sort of bite is what an old friend and Ouse roacher calls "a dweller," and is the very easiest to respond to. Again, there is a roach bite that is neither seen nor felt. Strange as this statement may seem, it is, nevertheless, perfectly true. A very old friend of mine, a whitesmith he was by trade, once told me that a good roach fisherman was born one, no amount of practice could make him a perfect roacher. He might fancy he was up to all the moves on the board as far as roach fishing was concerned, and even be a very successful one, but there will come odd times when even he, clever as he is, will be at fault. He knows the roach are there, and that they are on the feed, but do as he will his basket gets no heavier—he cannot perceive the bite. It is at these odd times that our born roacher proves his superiority. I have stood, or rather laid down, behind my old friend the whitesmith, and have seen him hook and land big roach one after the other, when I have been prepared to swear before any court of justice that his tell-tale float never moved in the slightest degree. Other good anglers who were fishing some few yards away without any luck would also come behind to view this strange phenomenon, and like me marvel greatly at it. He declared that he had a sort of inward feeling, the strike and hooking the fish came natural to him, without any movement of his float to indicate the presence of the fish; but whether this was so or not I must admit that he was about the very cleverest roach fisherman I ever knew, and I have known a few during my wanderings after sport. He could tell as soon as he looked out of doors in the morning if the day was likely to be favourable or otherwise for roach fishing, and his judgment was rarely at fault. But I must get back to my roach bites. The novice may have noticed when fishing with gentles that when a roach is hooked and landed, his previous bait is blown some four, or even six, inches up the gut away from the hook, and wondered however on earth it managed to get up there. He may learn a lesson from this circumstance; this is one peculiar feature of a roach bite. If he can blow a bait out of his mouth so far up the gut, when that same bait is carefully and firmly threaded on the shank of a hook, it sands to reason that he can eject a loose bait with considerable force. We will suppose the young angler is trying a pill of paste, and sees what he supposes to be a tiny nibble, the float just gives a momentary bob, scarcely perceptible to any but a practised eye, so tiny and quick is this bob that our angler thinks (if he notices it) that the fish is only just touching the bait with his nose end, and waits a second or so, all intent for another and more decided bob of his float before striking; perhaps a fraction of time after the first little bob of the float there does come a second and more decided one, and our novice now thinks to himself: "Now, my lad, I have got yer!" and strikes promptly, only to find to his great astonishment that his bait has gone, and there is no fish on his hook, or if there does happen to be a portion of bait left, he finds about half of the original pill bitten fairly off. Now this sort of thing, when repeated time after time, is apt to become a trifle monotonous, and tries the temper of the angler sadly. There may be scores of my young readers who can remember not only one, but several experiences of a similar character when roach fishing in deep and quiet waters, and wondered why it was so. I will try to explain. I have called attention to a gentle being blown by the roach up the gut of the angler's tackle, and inferred that as the fish was capable of doing this with a tough and well-hooked bait, what must it be when a soft and easily-got-rid-of bait like a pill of paste is used? This can be blown by the fish from his mouth with considerable force, and it is, in my opinion, the very act of blowing from his mouth that causes the second and more decided bob of the float as just noticed. The proper time to strike when the roach are coming shy and biting in this peculiar manner, is when you notice the first and smallest bob or quiver of the float. The cunning old fish was then quietly sucking in the bait, perhaps only just getting it between his lips and causing the tell-tale at the surface of the water to indicate a faint nibble below. In almost the twinkling of an eye Mr. Roach discovers that there is something wrong, and that that tempting looking bait is attached to something, and may prove a delusion and a snare, so he promptly blows it from his mouth; and it is this forcible ejection that causes the second and more decided bob of the float, which looks to our angler to be a much better looking bite than the first tiny one was. He should have responded at the first indication, instead of waiting for the second. More roach are lost by waiting for the second bob than are captured by so waiting. As I said before, sometimes the roach mean business, and make no bones of it, but the artist in the craft who pays attention to all these little details can make a bag when the novice, or even a more experienced man is entirely at fault. Try the well-fed aldermanic roach in the month of September, when the water is gin-clear, and the river is still and sluggish in the extreme, and then see if it is not a fine art to make a bag of them. I trow it is, but a bag can be made if the weather is anything like favourable, and our fisherman understands his business.

I think I have made it sufficiently clear as to what a roach bite in still water is like on certain occasions. This being so, the veriest novice will see at a glance that a float is a very important article, and must be selected with a great deal of care. A heavy, clumsy, ill-balanced, water-logged wooden affair should not be had at any price, it must be suited to the water and the surroundings of his swim; it must not be larger than is absolutely necessary, and above all it must be

C

weighted and balanced when in use to a nicety. I mentioned a little while ago that a good porcupine quill was as good as anything that could be used in these deep still waters, and I still stick to that opinion. If the water is infested with huge quantities of small bleak that swim in shoals near the surface, it will be necessary to use a float somewhat larger than can be used where the water is not so infested. There are swims in the river Ouse and kindred sluggish waters, that get full of bleak within an hour of throwing in the groundbait, and if the float is very light and the bait sinks very slowly the bleak attack it and spoil its attractiveness long before it reaches the roach at the bottom. Under these circumstances, in any very still water that contains a lot of those small fish, it is as well to adopt two rules: one is, use gentles as a hook bait as little as possible, rather pin your faith on boiled wheat; paste is nearly as bad as gentles; and, secondly, use a float some sizes bigger than the first sight of the swim warrants. I find a fairly stout porcupine quill, nine or ten inches long, and capable of carrying some half-dozen medium-sized split shots to be about the thing for this purpose. This weight on the gut line causes the bait to sink rapidly in bleak-infested swims, and gives you a much better chance with the roach below. Small red worms on a hook are worse in this respect than gentles and paste. The hungry little fish will bite and pull them all to rags, and torment you to no end. Some anglers may say: "Oh, you can easily get rid of the bleak by throwing some dry bran on the water; they follow it down stream and out of reach." But supposing there is no stream, then the remedy will be worse than the complaint; besides, where you keep throwing ground bait in the bleak will come, and I find that a fair-sized float, if properly weighted, and the sinkers or shots put at the proper distance from the hook and from each other, is not detrimental to good sport. Of course if the water operated on contains no bleak, or, at least, very few, then the float may be a size or two smaller, say one carrying about four split shots of a medium size. I must again impress upon the young angler that the remarks contained in this chapter relate to deep still water fishing for roach, and must not be confounded with stream, or even drain fishing, which will be dealt with in another chapter.

A young friend was talking to me the other day on this question of roach fishing, and he propounded a theory which fairly astonished me. He said: "Now, you know, the reason you get such lots of fish is because you dress your bait and hook with some stuff from the chemist's shop; or, if not, how is it that other fishermen do not meet with like sport? You get them when we cannot." Now, if any reader has got a similar idea into his head, that certain successful roachers get their sport by similar means, he may at once reject the idea. Ordinary means and baits, such as can be procured by anybody, will be found all that is required.

CHAPTER III.

THE ROACH (*continued*).

ROACH FISHING IN STILL WATERS.
(ON GROUND BAITS AND HOOK BAITS).

Still water Roachers—Ground Baits—How to ground bait, and how not to do it—Mixing the ground bait—Roving for Roach—Creed wheat as a Roach bait—Ringing the changes—How to cree wheat—Plumbing the swim—Feeding in mid-water—Stale v. fresh wheat—The postman's knock — Malt — Gentles or maggots — How to breed, and how to prepare them—Gentles in the winter—Paste, plain and coloured—King's bait—the Cockspur worm—The weather and its deceptions.

There are two classes of roach fishermen who ply their craft in the deep still waters of this country. One class we may call fixed fishermen, that is, those who live close to the banks and can always keep a few swims baited up; the other class is the wandering angler, who can only get down for an occasional day. This latter class is by far the most numerous; they dearly love a day's roaching, and, after being cooped up from Monday morning till Saturday noon in some stuffy factory, or nearly red-hot forge, the change does them a world of good. To meet the requirements of these two classes of anglers two distinct methods of ground-baiting is necessary. The roacher who lives on the banks can afford to wait for his sport; he selects his swims, ground-baits them, and fishes at his leisure. He is not frightened at over-baiting them. If he does not get the fish one day he probably will the next, whereas the man who comes down for the day only must ground-bait his swim so that he is likely to have immediate sport, or, at least, within an hour or two of selecting it and throwing in his ground bait. As just hinted, the latter class of roacher is by far the most numerous, so I will commence with him. A proper ground bait and a proper method of using it is more important than some anglers imagine. As a matter of fact, success or non-success depends in a great measure on a judicious use of it. We will suppose our angler has made arrangements for a day's roach fishing, and the place he has in his mind's eye is somewhat similar to a swim or two that I described in a previous chapter. He has some little distance to travel in order to get there; every extra pound he has in the bag or basket at his back is a consideration. He wants to take with him just enough bait and no more than the day needs. This bait must also be just good enough in quality, and no better, than the swim requires. It is the main business of the fisherman to attract the fish, and not to feed them over much. I have seen anglers throw into a roach swim at one time at least a quartern measure full of boiled wheat, and nearly every corn of it as good in quality as the one used on the hook, and then wonder why they don't get the fish. Do they suppose the roach are going to be so very accommodating as to select that individual kernel of boiled wheat that has the hook inside it, when there are some hundreds exactly similar lying all round them? What would have been many good days' roach fishing have been utterly spoiled by an injudicious use of ground bait; and then the angler has blamed the weather or the water, or in fact blamed anything rather than the right cause. When I lived in Nottinghamshire there were a couple of roach swims in the river Witham that I was particularly fond of; they lay in nearly opposite directions from my house, one at Doddington, and the other at Norton Disney, and as either of them entailed a six miles' walk, it was not above two or three times during the season that I cared to visit them. August and September I found to be the best time, and a dozen or more years ago I used to get some very good catches from them; in fact, I think some of the very best samples of roach I ever took came from those swims. With such a long walk before me it must be manifest to the novice that my basket should contain no more weight than was absolutely necessary, and I found, after various trials and experiments, that a ground bait made as follows was the very best that could be used in a roach swim when the fisherman had only one day to fish it. At any rate, I always got the best and most immediate results from a judicious use of it. I must now give one bit of advice, and that is: never mix your ground bait up on the day previous to using it. If the weather is very hot this rule must be more particularly observed, as it has a tendency to quickly turn sour; also bear in mind that the bread used is not very mouldy. Some people have an idea that anything will do for ground bait—bread that is mouldy and bran that is fusty, but a greater mistake cannot be made; it must be sweet and fresh, or instead of attracting the roach into the swim it will drive them further from it. Instead of mixing his ground bait the previous night, it will pay the angler to get up half an hour earlier on the same morning to do this job. There are two things, however, that he must do on the night before, and they are: put his bread in soak and boil his rice. The exact quantities of each article required will be:—Put a pound, or not more than a pound and a quarter, of baker's bread that is not less than three or four days' old, into a pail or tin the night previous to the outing, and cover it with clean cold water and let it stand till the morning, so that the bread shall be thoroughly soaked. While this operation is in progress the angler can have half a pound of common rice—costing a penny—tied up loosely in a linen rag, and boiling in a saucepan over the fire; care should be taken that this rice is well and thoroughly cooked. When quite done, it should be taken out and laid on one side to cool; in fact, let it stop in the bag, or linen rag, till you are ready to mix it next morning; then drain most of the water away from the bread, put the rice in the tin with it, and squeeze both up together till it is a pulp, with no lumps bigger than a pea anywhere in it. Now take not more than three parts of a peck of dry sweet bran and mix the whole well together, adding a little water if it is likely to be too dry. It should, however, be mixed as stiff as possible, and don't be afraid of kneading it well together; work it well in with your hands, for the more you knead it and the more you turn it about and mix it, the stiffer and better it is, and it will sink in the swim much more quickly than if it is mixed up loosely and too damp. This ground bait is improved by the addition of a penny packet of Thorley's cattle food; it seems to give a little scent to it, and I fancy improves its attractiveness. The quantities just quoted will make from two dozen to thirty balls of ground bait the size of oranges, and will be quite sufficient for any swim in these quiet waters. It is a mistake to dump in the huge puddings of grains, bread, bran, wheat, clay and all other sorts of mixtures that I have seen some anglers do, even up to a good-sized sack full. In quiet or semi-quiet waters this ground bait will sink without any addition to it, but if there is a stream, and the angler fancies his bait will be carried out of his reach, then the addition of a little clean yellow clay will improve it. Clay can generally be found close at hand on the banks of these quiet waters, but failing to find any, then a few pebbles the size of walnuts will come in handy. A ball of ground bait tightly kneaded round one will carry the said ball of bait quickly to the bottom of the swim, but, speaking generally, eight swims out of every ten can be managed nicely without any addition to the ground bait. As soon as the angler has satisfied himself that he has selected a likely swim, and found out by a judicious use of his plummet that the bottom is clean and tolerably level, he puts in, say, from six to ten of his balls of bait. He can, if he likes, divide each ball into three portions, squeeze each portion tightly together, and cast it at the head of his swim the exact distance he intends to fish from the bank. Before he throws in this bait he should carefully plumb the depth; take a preliminary swim or two, to see that all is clear, and get everything in proper going order, so that after his swim is baited he will make no more disturbance than he can help. If he has conducted his operations properly the roach should, if all is favourable, come on the feed in about an hour, or an hour and a half, from the time of baiting. If the fish are biting moderately well, use your remaining ground bait very sparingly. I believe in giving the swim nearly half the bait to start with, and after waiting, say, a couple of hours give the remainder little and often. A small handful every ten minutes or so will keep the fish in the swim, and give them confidence; but whatever you do, don't throw a lot of bait in of the same quality that you use on the hook. I might add that the total cost of this ground bait will not exceed sixpence. Another good plan in these deep and quiet waters is roving for roach, instead of putting the whole of the ground bait in one swim and sticking to that place all day, try a dozen places, drop a ball or two in, and fish an hour; then try another, finally going back to the first, expending his ground bait in morsels in any and every likely looking shop he comes across, and fishing none of them very long together, shifting to another after getting a couple of roach out of one, and so on all day long. I have known some capital bags of roach to be made by this method of ground-baiting. When the angler is using wheat as a hook bait, and the ground bait as just described, he can, if he likes, have a little inferior wheat about half cooked, not more than half a pint at the outside, and sprinkle in his swim a few corns from time to time, but not more than a score at once; but whatever he does in this matter, he must mind and have his hook bait of very much better quality than the corns or baits thrown in the swim. Ground baits for roach are very nearly as varied in their character as the hook baits themselves. I have seen some curious mixtures used, and occasionally with very fair success. A ground bait that is very much affected by certain roachers who live on the banks is grains; that is, brewer's grains, and clay. They procure a couple of bushels and put them in a tub and cover them with water; this keeps them sweet and fresh for several days. They then take a pailful at once, and mix them with clay and dump in the swim a dozen huge balls every night for a week. Some odd times they get very large bags of roach and bream after a baiting of that description, but personally I am not in favour of the plan. This ground bait, when put in in such tremendous quantities, is very apt to spoil the swim altogether for two or three weeks afterwards, as I fancy it turns sour and sickens the fish. The ground bait as first described is more to be relied on; in fact, for quiet or semi-quiet waters I know by personal experience that it cannot be beaten, especially in those waters where wheat and paste are the staple and most important hook baits. I have looked at these ground baits at rather a great length, because the subject is one of the most important that can be brought to the notice of the novice.

We will now turn our attention to the hook baits and how to prepare them. A favourite bait with the roach fishermen of these quiet waters is creed or boiled wheat, and I know of no other bait that is cleaner and more pleasant to use. It is very cheap, easy to prepare, and during the summer and early autumn months is first and foremost as a killer. On the Ouse, the Nene, the Welland, the Witham, and the huge network of smaller rivers and drains that intersect that country-side it is used with considerable success; and I make no doubt it would be equally successful if tried in the canals and reservoirs of the north country. It is a standing dish on the rivers and broads of Norfolk and Suffolk, scores of stones of roach being killed every season in those waters by its agency; in fact, I have an idea that no matter where in England roach are to be found the fisherman might do worse than give this bait a fair trial. I once saw it gravely asserted in print that the reason roach took creed wheat in certain waters was because of the flour mills on the banks; the fish got a taste of it by the grain escaping from the mill into the water; but the probability is that had there been any record of the fact the ancestors of those same roach in the dim and distant past would have been as equally fond of the bait, even long before any flour mills were built beside the stream. I know of certain streams and pools where the roach in them are very partial to that bait, and yet there was no possibility of the fish having acquired the taste by grain escaping from mills into the water, for the simple reason that none exist within miles of the spot. When I fished the Trent and the Witham I had an idea that was founded upon actual experience that white wheat was the best for the hook. In the waters of the Ouse district I seem to fancy that honours are about equally divided between the white and the red, sometimes white being the most attractive, and then again red being the greatest favourite; as a matter of fact, I found that a judicious changing about was conducive to sport. I have been using a kernel of white wheat on the hook and had no response for several minutes, and then changed it for a kernel of red, and got a good fish directly; and the same thing has frequently happened when changing a red one for a white. But speaking in a general way, I find that one is as good as the other, and the roach fisherman would find it to be to his advantage to have a little of both mixed together, so that he could ring the changes should occasion require. A good handful of each will be quite sufficient to cook at once, and they need not be boiled separate, as they can easily be distinguished one from the other, even when mixed together. The best plan to adopt in preparing wheat for the hook is to put as much as you require into a basin and cover it with cold water, letting it stand to steep for several hours, eight or ten, or even more would be none the worse. Then put the corn so steeped into a linen rag or any old piece of white calico, and tie a string round it in such a manner that the wheat has plenty of room to swell during the process of boiling. This is a most important point, as it is absolutely necessary that the wheat should swell out to its utmost capacity, and if the rag containing it is tied too closely the main object will be defeated. Now put it in a saucepan with sufficient cold water to well cover it, and set it on the fire, or at least near the fire, in such a position that the water slowly boils. It is not a good plan to let it boil too fast. The more slowly the water boils the bigger the wheat swells out. The water in the saucepan should be emptied out at intervals, and fresh clean cold water put in, and again reboiled for another hour or so, changing it again at the end of that time. It takes four hours, sometimes longer, according to the fire, to properly cree or cook wheat, and during this time the water it is boiled in should be changed and fresh substituted five or six times. When the wheat is swelled out to nearly the size of a pea—which very good quality corn will sometimes do—and it cracks open half-way round the kernel and shows the white inside, it is cooked sufficient and is ready for use. Some tryos may wonder why I recommend the water wheat is cooked in to be changed so often. The reason is because one small quantity of water in use all the time it is cooking is apt to get very much discoloured and turn the wheat dark in colour, instead of being white and clean, as it will be, or should be, if properly cooked. If the angler has a good-sized kitchen boiler to his fireplace it will save trouble. These articles generally hold several gallons of water, and are mostly slowly boiling; he can drop his bag of wheat into that and let it stop in a few hours without any further thought, as the small quantity of wheat would not turn such a large quantity of water as that dark and disagreeable. Some anglers recommend wheat to be slowly stewed in a jar in a hot oven, and not tied up in a rag at all. In my opinion this is only a very fair plan; I pronounce most decidedly in favour of the tied-up rag and the boiling saucepan. The kitchen boiler would not be available to six out of every ten roachers, so I only casually mention it. In using this bait on the hook a single kernel will be found quite sufficient, and for hooks I find a No. 11 crystal bend, or a No. 10 sneck bend, to be the very best; perhaps the former has a slight call for favouritism, and I must again impress upon the angler the necessity of the gut tackle being of the very finest. For this still water fishing the best colour for the drawn gut will be a smoky blue, the shots should be put on the gut line about four or five inches from each other, the bottom one no nearer the hook than fifteen inches (see my remarks on the subject in the previous chapter). I have tried this bait in all depths, and occasionally I have taken good roach when using it in mid-water, but generally speaking I find it the most effective when used as near the bottom as possible. My advice is, the angler should plumb his swim just as far as he can reach with his rod out at arms' length; and when his plummet rests on the bottom of the river, about three inches of his porcupine float should stand above the surface of the water. This I find to be the best plan to adopt. In plumbing the depth of his swim, he should stand as near the edge of the water as possible and reach with his fourteen-foot roach rod as far as he possibly can. This will be about the distance from the bank his float will travel, when sitting on his basket or stool, because he will naturally throw the bait and float so that it settles in the water three feet or so in front of his rod point. He must also take care to throw his ground bait in, directly in the track of his float, and if there is a little stream or current, so that the float creeps down the swim, say about a yard in a minute, the chances of catching roach are more favourable than if it stood still and did not move at all.

Sometimes in fishing these very quiet rivers the bait is taken before it has had anything like time to reach the bottom of the river. This will show the angler that for once in a way the roach are feeding in mid-water. He might now for a change alter his depth to half what it was before and throw out well in every direction, until he covers all the water within immediate reach; a few good roach may be the result of this experiment, but to take things on the whole I find the roach generally go down to where the ground bait is. Fishing in mid-water when the ground bait is on the bottom is a good deal like spreading a good dinner out in the cellar and then going into the top attic to enjoy it. But whatever the angler does, he must bear in mind what I said in the chapter on bites, and must, when fishing with wheat in still water, strike gently on the very first indication of a bite.

I have been asked the question several times as to whether I prefer to use this bait fresh or wait till it gets rather stale; and here I find a difficulty staring me in the face. Personally I prefer to use it when fresh cooked, or at least when no longer than three days' old. Some other anglers say it is the best when a week old, and certainly I have known on odd occasions good bags of roach to have been made, when the boiled wheat has been in the last stages of consumption; but a careful consideration of the subject has led me to come to the conclusion that the fresher it is the better. At any rate it is the best to use it within three days of cooking it, and what is left after that time can be safely thrown away and a fresh lot prepared. One little incident that bears upon this subject I must now give. In this locality we had a rural postman who was a rare good roach fisherman, and one morning he found the river steadily rising, and just a tint of colour coming down with it. It was a roach water and roach weather, but, alas! he had no boiled wheat and no time to prepare any. However, a search on the bank round some well-known swims resulted in the discovery of a dozen or two stale corns of boiled wheat that had been discarded by some other fisherman at least a week previous. These were joyfully seized upon, and within the next two hours fifteen pounds of good roach were reposing in the postman's basket and he himself driven from the banks by the rapidly rising water. This is one instance of the efficacy of stale wheat, but on the other hand I can call to mind several cases where fresh-boiled wheat has succeeded in luring roach when another angler, using stale, got nothing. The best bag of roach I ever got in my life was taken one afternoon from the Ouse with wheat that was cooked the same morning. This bag numbered 136 fish, and many of them were from 1lb. to nearly 2lb. each. I might multiply these cases considerably, but I have said enough to illustrate my point. In certain waters boiled malt is superior to wheat as a roach bait; but in deep and quiet waters wheat has the preference. Malt seems to be more effective than wheat in shallower streams where there is a gentle current, and more particularly in the broken water at the foot of a weir, or the tail of a mill, where the froth of the overfall curls round and round in a shallow eddy, seems to be the places for the successful use of malt, although it occasionally meets with success in slow running streams. Malt is prepared for the hook by boiling or stewing the same as recommended for wheat, only it takes double the time to cook malt as it does wheat. Some anglers stew it in a jar in the oven, and add a spoonful of sugar to every handful of malt, but I prefer it cooked exactly as recommended for wheat.

As soon as October gets well in boiled wheat ceases to be so attractive to the roach of these quiet waters. When the first frosts of the late autumn begin to whiten the grass in the early morning, the dead leaves flutter from the trees in a shower, and the reeds and rushes on the river bank change their colour from green to brown, then it is time for our Fen roacher to turn his attention to something else in the shape of a bait if he desires to make a bag of those fish, which now will be less in number but very much larger in individual size. Sometimes roach will take boiled wheat all through the winter—at least while the weather remains open and the waters are not ice-bound—but, speaking generally, I find that as soon as the middle of October gets over it is not a safe and certain bait. Gentles, paste, and worms are now the principal lures according to the state of the water and weather.

Gentles are now an extremely useful bait for roach, more

particularly if the water is fairly clear and the weather cold. Happy is that angler who has a good supply of those baits at the latter end of October. Opinions are divided as to what makes the best maggots; some will swear by gentles bred from bullock's liver, as being more yellow in colour and more attractive than any other; while others favour maggots bred from fish, because they are whiter and larger. The maggots generally sold to the angler are for the most part bred from refuse fat, but the thoughtful fisherman, if he has any facilities at all in the shape of outbuildings, will breed and feed his own for winter use. I find the best plan to adopt to keep a constant supply of gentles all through the winter is to procure a few small roach or bream—or failing those, any refuse fish from the dealer's will do—about the middle of October, and put them in an old tin or any other convenient vessel. Set them out of the way of cats or rats, but in a place where the blow-flies are likely to find them. If there is a burst or two of sunshine during the days immediately following, the fish will be well struck or blown within a week, and the little maggots start to feed. The angler should now keep his eye on them, and if he finds that the fish already there is not sufficient to fully feed them up, he must from time to time procure a little more. This is one of the secrets of successful maggot breeding and feeding: they must be fed up to their full size. I have had a tin of feeding gentles and dropped in among them two or three half-pound roach or bream; by the next morning the bones of those fish have been picked clean, and the maggots nearly twice the size that they were twenty hours previously. During the season of the year that I am now referring to, gentles do not feed quite so ravenously, nor grow quite so rapidly as they do during very hot weather, but if you can get your fish successfully fly-blown during the latter part or the middle of October the rest is easy. As soon as the angler perceives that his maggots are fully fed he must at once attend to them, for nature now teaches the gentles to crawl away from their food and seek retirement in any old nook, crack, or crevice, and if our fisherman neglects them at this time he will probably find on again looking into his tin that the whole of them have vanished by some mysterious means or other.

No crack or hole in the vessel containing them is too small for them to work through, and the sides must be attended to, for no matter how steep or smooth they are, the fully-grown maggots will crawl up and escape. While they are feeding they will not attempt to leave their food, but as soon as ever they are fully fed up no open vessel will long contain them. The best plan to adopt after arriving at this stage is to turn the whole lot out into a riddle or seive, having previously put under that riddle a pancheon or other wide-topped earthern vessel. The maggots will speedily crawl through the wires of the seive and drop into the vessel below, leaving the refuse and bones of the fish behind them. The gentles should now be mixed with a quantity of damp sand. On no account should dry bran or sawdust be put with them, and this is particularly to be observed when the maggots are intended for keep during the winter. The very best vessel I ever had as a store for them was an old earthenware pickle or jam jar, about sixteen inches deep and seven wide, with a neck big enough to easily admit the hand. If the angler is lucky enough to get a full pint of good well-fed gentles fit for the hook, I should consider that quantity will tide him over the winter comfortably. About a quart or three pints of damp sand will be ample to keep them in, and it does not particularly matter what sort of sand it is, so long as it is clean, small, and sharp. It is the best to keep this jar of gentles in a very cool damp place, say in the coldest corner of the cellar, if you have one, if not, any other cool position will do. Gentles, as a rule, that are bred and fed during the latter part of October do not change into the chrysalis state to any extent; a few perhaps may, but the bulk of them will lie among the sand in a semi-torpid condition. I have kept them from November right round to March, and never been short of a hook bait for the roach when the water and weather permitted them to be used. A good plan is to put the jar containing the sand and gentles into another vessel containing cold water, the water reaching up the outside of the jar about as far or a little farther than the gentles are inside it; but care must be taken that no water goes inside among them. This contact with cold water helps to keep the gentles chilled and cool, as they naturally have a tendency to heat and sweat themselves. They need not be kept in the cold water very long, nor yet very often; a few hours now and again will be quite sufficient. The gentles bred from fish are, in my opinion, capital baits for roach during the winter months in these deep still waters, especially if the weather is somewhat cold, and the water clear. At this time roach are found in the deepest and quietest holes, and the bait, which need not be more than a couple or three of those maggots, should be as near the bottom of the river as possible. The hook can be a size larger than recommended for the same fish during the summer, say a No. 10, and the gut line itself can be, if the angler likes, a little thicker and stronger than recommended for use during the hot summer months. While I am on with the subject of gentles, I may say that they can be bred and fed from nearly anything besides fish; a sheep's head, a lump of liver, a dead rabbit, or anything of that kind; but one thing is certain, and that is, it does not matter what they are first bred in, nothing beats a few fish to feed them up with quickly and to a great size. For the hot summer months the procedure is the same as just described, except that then the maggots change into chrysalis very quickly, and must be used within a week or ten days after putting them among the sand. It takes about three days among this sharp sand to render them fit for the hook; they clean thmselves during that time, and then look bright, white and clear from that nasty black patch they wore when first taken from their food.

A good change bait for these still waters during the winter will be a bit of bread paste made from the white crumb of a two days' old loaf. I recommend a piece about the size of two of your fingers, dipped in clean cold water, then squeezed so that some of the water is wrung out, and worked up well with clean hands till it is of the consistency of soft putty. A teaspoonful of "King's Natural Bait" (a white sweet-smelling powder this is) should be added, and worked up together till the paste is white, tough and stiff. Particular care must be taken that no dirt or tobacco ashes find their way into this paste; well washed and scrubbed hands are a necessity. I like my paste rolled up in a bit of clean white rag, and put carefully into a corner of the basket where nothing else is likely to get mixed with it. This white paste is rather attractive to the roach of these waters, especially during the late autumn and early winter weeks (the bleak do not bother you now so much as they did during the summer, so paste can be used without much fear of them spoiling it before it reaches the roach at the bottom. See Chapter II.). One or two of my best winter bags of roach have been made by the agency of this paste. I have also noticed a very curious thing when using paste as a bait, and that is, if you forget to wipe your hands after landing a roach, and some of the slime sticks to your fingers and finds its way pretty plentifully on your next pill of paste, you are not long before you get another bite; indeed, I make it a rule to just dab the bait on the last fish caught. I have an idea it is effective; anyhow I know it is worth trying. A very nice paste is made by adding a pinch of vermillion to the one just described; this is a beautiful pink colour when well worked together; a little chrome yellow added also makes a capital yellow paste. These are all good at times; in fact, I believe in changing about, using white for a few minutes, then pink, then yellow, and so on; it is not much more trouble and expense to make these three different coloured pastes, and I know by experience that it pays. I have tried all sorts of things one time or other that have been advertised in the sporting papers, but I never found any of them to come up to their advertised qualities; the three pastes, or rather the one paste coloured and plain, will be found all that the angler requires. I might add that it is best to use paste when the water is clear. A very old friend of mine (the late Tom Bentley), a paste fisherman for roach of more than ordinary skill and experience, always used to chew up his bread a little before kneading it together with his fingers. He would have it that wetting it in the mouth made a far more attractive bread paste than dipping it in the water, and certainly his opinion was worth something, as he was one of the most expert paste fishers I ever knew.

If the water during the winter comes down with a little colour in it then a small red worm can be tried as a hook bait, and the best worms for this purpose are the little red ones found in an old manure heap. The Nottingham men call these worms cockspurs; they are a nice little worm, just big enough for a No. 9 crystal bend hook, and can easily be recognised as they range from an inch to an inch and a half in length, and when scoured for a few days in camp clean moss are of a brilliant red, with a light, drab-coloured ring or knob about half an inch from the head end. One, or sometimes two of them if very small, nicely threaded on the hook is a capital lure, especially at those times during the winter when the water in the river is warmer than the surrounding atmosphere. I fancy myself that the reason roach do not bite at all freely during very cold weather in these deep and sluggish waters is because the temperature of the water is very much lower than in shallower, swifter streams. The latter always show the best results during the winter. At odd times the angler in these waters, if he takes the trouble to notice it, will find a strange thing happening. The weather may be splendid, "quite mild like a spring day," and he may congratulate himself accordingly. He perhaps tries the depth with his plummet, and discovers the fact on withdrawing it that it feels to his hand icy cold, or at least several degrees colder than the air outside. Under this condition his chance of sport is only very limited, and worms will be the very worst bait to try; gentles will now stand the best chance, even if the water is a trifle coloured. On the other hand the weather on the river bank may be very raw and cold, and yet on trying the water with the plummet, our angler this time discovers the fact that the water itself is very much warmer than the surrounding atmosphere. Under these conditions the chances of sport will improve, and worms be as good as any bait he can try. My bait table for the roach of these deep and quiet waters is only very limited—boiled wheat for the summer and early autumn, and pastes, gentles and worms for the late autumn and winter months. For ground bait, the same as recommended for use during the summer will be found all that is required, only now the fisherman must be very sparing in the use of it. About one-third the quantity recommended before will be sufficient, and perhaps he may, by judiciously ringing the changes, that is, trying in turn paste, gentles and worms, succeed in getting a little dish of good roach, even if the weather is not so favourable as he could have wished. My experience with the roach in deep and sluggish waters during very cold weather is that for one success you must expect at least two or three disappointments.

CHAPTER IV.

THE ROACH (continued).

STREAM AND DRAIN FISHING FOR ROACH.

(THE NOTTINGHAM AND SHEFFIELD STYLES).

*Stream v. drain fishing—The **stream** fishing rod—The outfit—Floating the line—Floats and Tackle—Ground baiting the streams—Baiting the hook — Fishing the swim — A strange ground bait — A flooded water — "Stret Pegging"—The Nottingham style—Finding the depth—Casting out the bait—Ledgering for Roach—Undercurrents—A heavy stream—The Sheffield style — Shrimps as bait — A killing style — Experiences on the Avon and Frome.*

The two preceding chapters on this subject have been devoted to a description of roach fishing with a long rod, as generally practised in deep and very quiet waters, such as the Ouse, the Nene, and various other sluggish rivers of a similar character, as well as certain lakes and broads. There are two more classes of waters that I am acquainted with, that require tackle of a somewhat different character in order to successfully operate upon them. One of these classes is a stream where the water flows moderately fast. These streams are perhaps of no great depth, but sparkling and lively; such as the Trent, for instance, and the Witham in some parts of their courses; or indeed, like a score more rivers in various parts of England. The veriest novice will easily recognise the waters that I mean, as they are to be found in almost any district; streams that flow from one to three miles per hour, where it is necessary to keep the bait and float constantly travelling backwards and forwards (of course providing these streams contain roach, which I make no doubt many do). In stream fishing for roach the depth of water is of no great account, as I have killed good roach in two feet of water, and also found them in any depth of swim between that and twelve feet. The other class of water I referred to is canals, drains or cuts of no very great width, water exceeding still and quiet and ranging from four to eight feet deep; such waters, for instance, as are to be found in the Fens of Lincolnshire. For the former waters, or stream fishing, the plan that is known as the Nottingham style is the best; while for the latter, or drain fishing, where there is no stream at all, the plan that is sometimes called the Sheffield style must be adopted. These two styles differ widely in their character; but still, when we come to examine them closely, they have features in common. This may sound somewhat queer, but I will endeavour to explain my meaning. In the first place, the rod, reel and line for both styles can be identical; what is suited for stream fishing will do very well for the drain. It is the float and tackle, and the details of using them, that constitute the difference. For stream fishing, the float must be a moderate-sized one, carrying a fair complement of split-shot on the gut bottom. This is in order to swim down the current, and to keep the bait as near the bottom of the river as possible all the way down the full length of the angler's swim; for it must be remembered that a very small float, and scarcely any shot on the tackle, would result in drowning the float, and in addition the bait would work up nearer the surface of the stream than desirable, and the angler's object would be utterly defeated. In fishing the drain, on the other hand, the float can hardly be too small, a tiny porcupine quill carrying a couple of very small shot being about the biggest weight that is required; indeed, I have seen good roachers in some of the Fen drains using a float made from a crow's wing feather that has been very little, if any, larger than a wax match.

I hinted just now that the rod for both these styles of roach fishing could be identical—what will do for one will do very well for the other; and this rod must have two or three decided characteristics: it must be light, well-balanced, stiff, and above all must have a quick and sharp strike direct from the point. The long roach rod described and recommended for deep, still water fishing will not be a success if used as a Nottingham rod down a stream. What I call a perfect rod for the work now under notice should be built after the style fully described in the chapter on barbel, only, of course, shorter and very much lighter. I like my roach rod to have plenty of material in the lower half of it, and be tapered true and fine from the centre of it up to the tip, so that when in conflict with a big roach it will bend in a beautiful half circle from the point to about half-way down its entire length, the bottom end half remaining nearly straight. I don't like to see a roach rod that will bend right down to the winch fittings. This action may be all right in a fly rod, but in a roach rod, especially for stream fishing, it will be found a mistake. This rod can be from ten to eleven feet long; anything over the latter spoils its balance. I don't care for a rod of this class to weigh much less than a pound, and even a roach rod of this weight, if properly made, will feel lighter in the hand than a ten-ounce bamboo rod, for the simple reason that the latter is very thin and light at the butt end, thus causing it to feel decidedly top-heavy, while the pound rod has a good portion of its weight in the hand, thus feeling lighter than it really is. This rod can be built of the same material as recommended for making a barbel rod. The size of the ferrules need not, however, in this case exceed nine-sixteenths of an inch in diameter on the butt, and five-sixteenths of an inch on the centre joint; the rings can be of the same pattern as then described; "Bell's Life" rings on the butt and centre; snake rings on the top; a plain steel loop at the extreme tip end; plain ferrules; and the winch or reel rings seven inches from the end of the butt. Armed with a rod of this class our roach fisherman who plies his craft in the waters now referred to is prepared for anything that may happen to turn up, and can fish his swim in either the Nottingham or the Sheffield style, whichever suits that particular swim the best; and I might add the cost of this rod should not exceed eight to ten shillings.

If the angler operates on a stream where he finds it necessary to swim his float from ten to twenty yards from where he stands, he will find the three-and-a-half inch centre-pin reel that I described so fully in the chapter on chub fishing the most comfortable to use, that is after he has once mastered its little peculiarities. The remarks I then used can be applied with equal force to roach fishing down a stream; the bait must travel without jerk or catch, so in my opinion this reel stands at the head of all Nottingham reels. Just lately, a new centre pin reel, called the "Coxon," has been invented to fish down the streams in the Nottingham style. It is made on the spider principle, like a bicycle wheel. The revolving barrel of this reel is remarkably light, and runs nearly at a breath of wind. It looks a likely tool for roach and dace fishing with a very fine line and tackle; but whether it will stand the heavier streams, when used in barbel fishing, remains to be seen. But if the angler fishes only in the quiet drains or cuts, where there is no current at all, it does not matter so much about his reel; a cheap three-inch one, provided it runs fairly free, and is light, will meet his requirements; but if he is in the habit of fishing both classes of water he must more particularly select his reel for the stream work, and then with care he can easily operate on both. The novice will see, after reading my foregoing remarks, that I am decidedly in favour of using running tackle for any class of water, and any class of roach fishing.

The running line should consist of forty yards of good plaited silk, of the same quality as recommended for barbel and chub fishing, except that it need not be so stout—the finer it is the better, consistent with strength. A stream especially can be fished much easier with a fine line than it can with a stout one; the float can be cast out much further, and the accuracy of the cast is greatly improved; but don't go to extremes and use a line too extra fine and weak, or you may "strike off," as it is known among fishermen, and lose not only the fish, but the tackle and float. Personally I should not dream of using a line for this work any finer than what will lift three pounds dead weight. In fishing a quiet drain where the water is perfectly still the tyro will sometimes wish the line would float upon the surface; perhaps his float is six or eight feet away from his rod point, and the line between the rod end and the quill sinks deep in the water, thus causing some little annoyance when he has a quick, shy bite. Very often this drowning of the line results in missing the fish, whereas if the line floated on the surface the strike from the rod point would be sharp and effective. All sorts of fancy things have been recommended for this purpose, but after many trials I find nothing to beat a little bit of composite candle, not the old-fashioned tallow candle, bear in mind, but the composite candle of commerce, sold by any grocer at a halfpenny each. An end half an inch in length can be easily carried in a little tin box in the bag or basket; rub this down the line as far as you think it will be wanted, while the said line is dry, and the silk will float for hours. Stream fishermen in the Nottingham style should have a small collection of carefully selected floats always ready for any emergency. For roach fishing in water that ranges from eight to ten feet deep, where the flow is moderately fast, and a curling eddy every few yards, a fair-sized pelican quill that will carry some eight or ten B.B. split shots will be the best and safest to use, and these shots must not be crowded all together about a foot or so from the hook, because this plan will cause the tackle and line between the float and the shots to belly and bag when in use; but they must be distributed at irregular intervals all down the gut tackle, a good deal the same as I recommended for chub fishing. I like these split shot put on the tackle in pairs, each individual shot forming a pair, being about an inch apart; the bottom pair should be no nearer the hook than fifteen inches; six inches above those another pair can be put on, and then nine inches higher up another pair, and so on until the eight or ten are fixed, the last pair being about six inches from the loop of the four foot long tackle; and I strongly recommend a tackle to be at least that length when fishing a deep and strong stream for roach. If the water is no more than from four to five feet deep, and the stream not quite so fast, a smaller float must be used, and in this case it can be a small swan quill, and half a dozen split shot distributed as before will be ample; or if the stream is slow, but still a stream, bear in mind, then a goose quill and four shots will be quite sufficient, but in this case, instead of putting the shot on the tackle in pairs, they must be put on singly.

The three quill floats just described will be found the very best that can possibly be used in roach fishing down a stream, and remember what I say in this respect. The pelican quill for **deep** and strong streams; the swan quill for more moderate streams that are not quite so deep; and the goose quill for **slower** waters still. The gut tackle itself for stream fishing should be made **of** very fine natural or undrawn gut, three or four feet long. I am very fond of undrawn gut for **stream** fishing, the reason for which I explained in the chapter on barbel tackle. This gut can be stained either blue or light brown, and tied together in lengths the same as already fully described elsewhere. Brown-coloured tackle is wonderfully good for streams that have a gravelly bottom. Gut **for** roach fishing is known **among** dealers as "finest refina," and runs from eighteenpence to two shillings per hank of a hundred strips. What I prefer for this work is a fine natural gut bottom fully three feet long, and shotted according to the stream as already indicated, **the hook itself** being on a separate length of gut; and this should be 3X drawn gut. I explained in the chapter on barbel tackle why I liked my tackle in two sections, and those remarks hold good when applied to roach tackle. Hooks for stream fishing can be the same **as** for still water, viz., No. 9 **for worms**, No. 10 for gentles, **grain**, and paste; while a few Nos. 11 and 12 will come in handy if the water is very clear, the roach biting shy, and the angler finds himself compelled to use a very small bait. Bright crystal hooks are in my opinion the best pattern that can be tried. Ground baits I mentioned at length in the preceding chapter, when treating of still water fishing; and the remarks as to those baits hold good in stream fishing, except that the angler has to be more careful in using them down a stream. While fishing he must not dump in a whole bag full at once; he must use it very judiciously, putting it in by littles and often. He **must also** be very careful in throwing it in, and must be sure that it is exactly in the space where the hook bait travels. He must judge to a nicety the strength and depth of the current, and throw it in at the proper distance above where he stands, or it may be swept out of his reach below his selected swim. A good plan to try the set of the stream, as it is called, is to throw on the surface a few little bits of dried stick, and watch which way they float. Sometimes the current works towards the bank on which the fisherman stands, and sometimes away towards the one opposite. By this means the angler will soon find out the exact distance from the bank that his ground bait must be cast. Sometimes, when the current is strong it is necessary to throw it at least ten yards above where he stands, and sometimes not above three or four. By exercising a little care he will soon hit the exact spot to a nicety; but one thing is certain, it requires a good deal more judgment to successfully ground-bait a stream than it does to ground-bait still water.

Hook baits for roach down a stream are nearly as varied as they are for still water fishing; but gentles as an all-round lure can be put an easy first. Well scoured maggots are very attractive for one thing, and another thing they are tough and lasting on the hook, and nothing like so liable to get washed off as paste, or even boiled grain. In using maggots on the hook I recommend them to be as near the bottom of the river as possible, and one, two, or even three can be tried at a time according to water and the appetite of the roach. In baiting the hook the point should be put through the thick end of the gentle sideways, so that it sticks out at right angles from the shank; push No. 1 gentle nearly to the top of the shank, thread another in exactly the same way, through the thick end, and let the thin end of this gentle stick out opposite the first one; finally put a third well on the point and barb of the hook, but always mind and keep the point end of the maggots free. By adopting this plan there are three twirling ends wriggling about in opposite directions, and if it is carefully done without bursting the maggot, a very attractive bait is the result. Two can be put on in the same manner as three, and if the angler likes he can try one only on a very small hook. This is a good plan to adopt if the water is very clear: the hook is put carefully through the thick end of this odd gentle, so that it twirls about crossways on the point of the hook. It is the only plan to deceive big roach. Trying dodges like that, a few swims with three gentles, then a few with two, and then again try a few with only one on. It may put these shy fish off their guard. Any time during the summer and autumn, and even during the winter, gentles can be tried as a bait, especially when the water is fairly clear. The bread, rice, and bran ground bait can be used in conjunction with maggots. It will, however, be a good plan to have some small unscoured gentles as well, put a dozen of these gentles in a bit of that ground bait, the size of a walnut, say, and keep casting one of these little balls in every few minutes, and if the angler can drop his baited hook immediately behind this bit of groundbait and let his tackle go in hot pursuit of it, why, his chance of getting either a bite or a fish that swim is a very good one indeed.

Boiled or creed wheat and malt can also be used in a similar manner down a stream, and with the same ground bait. And here, again, one, two, or three kernels can be used on the hook. Some very good roachers that I know put as many on as ever they can, even to a good mouthful; and certainly they manage to land some very good roach indeed. These baits are used with the most success in clear water and during the summer and autumn months, the best of all being August and September, and sometimes nearly through October.

Another ground bait that is much affected by some Nottingham stream fishers for roach is half a bucketful of what they call "muck hole maggots." These are procured from old ash places and dust bins; all sorts of fish, flesh, and fowl offal are thrown in among the dust and ashes, and during hot weather maggots breed and feed among the corruption. These maggots generally are small, and are not scoured and cleaned in any way, but simply collected just as they are with a good percentage of dust and fine ashes among them, and sprinkled down the swim a handful at a time. The angler that has too fine and genteel a nose must not adopt this plan, as the scent is anything except otto of roses. There was one man that I knew who used to regularly bring down that bait in an old square biscuit tin strapped to his back; and I used to tell him that his scent was worse than a glue factory; but he used well-scoured and clean gentles on the hook, and certainly he secured some splendid bags of roach, and won several good prizes by the help of that strange ground bait. This is one of the curiosities of roach fishing down a sharp stream with a clear, gravelly bottom, a stinking ground bait like that can be used with effect; but in quiet waters a dose of musty bran and mouldy bread would result in driving every roach out of the immediate vicinity. During the early part of the season, say the latter end of June and all July, roach are to be found on the gravelly shallows of a stream very often in less than a yard of water. Cad-baits are now a splendid bait to try; one, if it is a large one, and two if smaller, can be put on the hook and swum down any likely place. For this bait, and this season of the year, I recommend the angler to rove about from swim to swim; for ground bait use a few coarse and unscoured gentles, and just sprinkle a few at a time down the swim. Small red worms are sometimes a great favourite with stream roach, especially during the late autumn, or when the water is slightly clouded or flushed with heavy rains. The ground bait generally used with this hook bait is a few hundred large lob-worms clipped up small and scattered down the swim a few at a time. I recommend this hook bait to trip along just clear of the bottom, and while fishing use the ground bait very sparingly indeed, not more than six or eight large worms at the outside at once, and they must be cut up into the smallest fragments and thrown well above the swim, exactly in the track of the float; and always remember to act the dodge recommended in gentle fishing: let the well-scoured worm on the hook go down the stream in hot pursuit of the fragments of ground bait immediately they are thrown in. If you use fifty large worms in an hour it will be quite enough for nearly any roach swim, and put them in as already recommended in small doses at intervals of ten minutes or so. Even when a big summer flood comes tearing down these streams our roach fisherman is not wholly deprived of his sport, as good fish can very often be picked up fishing the grass slopes. If the angler is well acquainted with the water he probably knows of some quiet dyke end, or a corner away from the main current that at ordinary low water time is dry, and which has a level grassy bottom. During a flood the water may get several feet deep in such a place, and no current to speak of, and the angler will find that in several cases the water is nothing like so thick as it is down the main river. The roach, driven by stress of heavy water, and in search of flood, seek refuge in such places as those, and if a few worms are clipped up small and thrown in, a well-scoured cockspur on the hook may result in getting a bag of big roach that will astonish the operator. The grass slopes behind a bush, or the gravels by the side of an old fence, even if no more than eighteen inches deep, are very often rattling good places to try during a summer flood, as the water there is generally quiet; but one thing must be remembered: while the water is coming on is the time to try; when the water is going down again the fish retire into the main stream. Another favourite method of roaching is by what is known among the Trent men as "stret-pegging." This is a quiet, deadly sort of style, and deserves more than just a passing notice. This style is generally practised in swims where the current is not very strong (but still, remember, a stream is absolutely necessary), and in places that can be reached comfortably with the rod point. We will suppose that four or five feet from the bank a long row of weeds and flags are growing, immediately in front of these weeds the water is from four to six feet deep, the bottom of the river clean and level, and just a little stream crawling along, and our novice finds on seating himself on his stool that his rod point will project a couple of feet over those weeds, he has without doubt found a place that is exactly suited for "stret-pegging." A swan quill carrying some five or six medium sized shot will be the thing for this purpose, and this float must be put on the line a foot deeper than the stream; that is, if the water is four feet deep the float must be five feet from the baited hook, and so on according to the varying depths of the streams tried. Sit on the basket or stool as low down and as close as possible, and if you can keep out of sight behind the weeds all the better; but in any case, have all your traps close at hand so that you can pick anything up you require without having to get up from your seat. Sit quiet, don't keep jumping up and down; these are golden rules, and must be observed. Drop a few small bits of groundbait in, and then let the tackle travel down stream until it is some four or five yards below you. Hold it there stationary, the rod being straight in front of where you sit; the float and tackle are now, of course, in a slanting direction, and this is why I recommended the float to be put deeper than the swim. A bite can very easily be seen, as even the smallest nibble when tackle is held back like this will result in the float being drawn under the water, when an instant strike is imperative. Sometimes the float can be held two yards only away from the rod point, and then again it may be five or six yards; and try every foot between those two distances, sometimes holding it for a few minutes in one place, then in another, until the whole of that place is carefully fished over, when the angler can shift his position a few yards lower down stream, and resume operations in a fresh swim. Almost any bait will do for this style—worms, gentles, wasp-grubs, wheat, malt, and plain and coloured pastes; and for groundbait, a few handsful of the bread and bran, or a hundred or two coarse lobworms clipped up small, or a tin of rough gentles, according to the hook bait used. Some men when using paste for this style of fishing, which, I may say, is about as good as anything that can be tried, especially in clear water and a very moderate current, have a few pieces of dry bread as groundbait; this they keep constantly chewing, and throwing in in small bits.

And now, having looked at most of the methods of stream fishing for roach, we will turn to the question of how the rod and line should be manipulated in casting out the bait in the Nottingham style. To fish a stream properly requires, as before hinted, running tackle and some little practice before it can be easily accomplished; but when once mastered, it is as easy as getting your lunch. We will suppose the angler has got his tackle ready, and the depth carefully found, which latter is done, not by throwing in a lump of lead or a plummet, the same as is necessary in very still waters, but by having a few preliminary swims with his shotted tackle. If the float during its passage down the stream keeps bobbing under the surface, you may know that the hook and some of the shots are trailing along the bottom, and that you are too deep; if, on the other hand, the float travels all the way down the swim in a perfectly natural manner without stoppage or bobbing under, you may know that you are not deep enough; and so the float can be altered a few times either way until you get the right depth, which can easily be come at. Suppose the first time you swim the float down the stream you find you are not deep enough, alter it a little higher up the line; after a few trials you find, by the float catching and bobbing under, that you have found the bottom. Now be careful, and alter the float a couple of inches at a time only, and as soon as ever it swims comfortably down you have got the exact depth. The tackle for stream fishing should be shotted so that three-quarters of an inch of the float stands above the surface of the water. Say the angler wishes his baited hook to travel down the swim some few yards further out than he can reach with his rod point. To accomplish this, in either trying the depth or in actual fishing, he takes the rod in his right hand close against the top of the reel with one finger reaching down to the edge of the revolving barrel, on purpose to stop its revolutions, if necessary (this finger, I may say, is the bottom edge of the last or little one); and with his left hand he takes hold of the line between the two first rings on his rod, and draws down and off the reel, as it were, a double length of line. He has now some two or three yards of line in his left hand, and three or four more hang from the point of the rod. To make the cast, he brings the rod point away from the river and partly behind him, and it does not matter in which direction it is done; the rod can either be swung to the right hand or to the left, whichever way suits the locality of the swim best. For instance, there may be a hedge or a bush immediately to the right or to the left of the angler, and the rod must of necessity be put in the opposite direction. Now swing it sharply forward over towards the river again, at the same time easing the pressure of the little finger on the edge of the reel, and also leaving go of the loop of line in his left hand; these two operations should be done nearly together, the loop of line being released as soon as the float and tackle swings forward in front of the rod point, and the pressure on the reel taken off immediately afterwards. After a little practice the baited tackle will go fair and square to its destination. After this cast has been successfully accomplished, and the float rights itself, the angler changes the rod into his left hand, still keeping hold of it close to the reel, and with the finger and thumb of his right hand pays out the line gently and continuously as fast, or nearly so, as the stream will carry it. It will be as well to hold the float a little back, however; that is, don't let it go quite so fast as it wants to do; by this means there will be no slack or drowned line between the float and the rod top; at any rate, this is the way to prevent too much slack line being out. After the float and tackle has travelled down the entire length of the swim as far as he thinks the groundbait is distributed, the line is wound back again on the reel, and the cast repeated. A little practice, and above all proper tackle, as described, will soon enable the novice to successfully follow this deadly method of stream fishing in the Nottingham style.

The tail-end of a well-scoured lobworm is at times a very good stream bait for roach, particularly during the late autumn and early winter, and more so when the water is slightly tinged with colour. Ledgering for roach is also another plan; no float is required for this. The ledger is a small bullet with a fair-sized hole through the centre of it, this hole being large enough to allow the knots of the tackle to pass through. This bullet can be about two feet from the hook; a shot on each side of the tackle allowing it a play of eight or nine inches; the hook for this can be a No. 8 Carlisle round bend, tied on 2x drawn gut, the bait being generally about an inch from the tail-end of a lob. This plan of ledgering is adopted if the angler finds a difficulty in keeping his bait well on the bottom. Speaking about keeping the bait well on the bottom, I am reminded of a curious experience that came under my own observation. One day down the lower Trent, in the neighbourhood of the Sutton Holmes, I came across a couple of anglers trying to fish a capital swim for roach. Subsequent conversation told me that the men were strangers, and used to waters of a far different character. They told me that they liked the look of the place so much that during the two or three days past they had put a nice lot of groundbait in. The current in many places down the

Trent is rather treacherous; sometimes a strong undercurrent that cannot well be perceived by the casual visitor sweeps down and round. This place happened to be somewhat similar. To look at the surface of the water one would think a very small float was all that would be required. In fact, one man was fishing with only a one-shot float, and every now and again he got a bite, and when he struck and hooked his fish, I could see that the bait was taken by bleak, and the undercurrent had swept it to within a foot of the surface. On my suggestion, a fair-sized pelican quill was substituted for the tiny porcupine, and ten shots put on the tackle. This weight enabled the bait to reach the quiet waters at the bottom, where it curled round in the eddy, and under a shelf that projected from a corner in the bank. The first swim down resulted in a half-pound roach, the second in a fair-sized dace, and the third or fourth in a two-pound chub; while ten minutes later a good roach, at least a pounder, came to bank. Those anglers were literally astonished, and said they never dreamed of fishing for roach with a heavily-shotted tackle like that; but the swim needed it. The one shot used before could not by any means carry the bait through the heavy curl of water down to where the roach lay in the quiet water at the bottom under the shelf. A little observation will soon tell the stream fishermen what plan to adopt under almost any circumstances.

What some anglers call the Sheffield style of roach fishing in the narrow drains and cuts, is performed with a rod, reel and line something similar to those used in stream fishing; but in this case the water is very quiet, so the tackle used must be of the very finest 4x drawn gut, and at most only a couple of split shot on it; and for float, a small porcupine from four to six inches long will be quite big enough, for ground baits and hook baits, those already described in the chapters on "Roach fishing in still water," will be about all that is required, so a repetition is not necessary. It is in the method of casting out this very light tackle that constitutes its difference. These anglers generally sit on a stool or basket with the rod in one hand, and draw down a little line in the other hand from between the reel and the first ring on the rod, in the same manner as described for stream fishing. The tackle and rod is then swung over their heads behind them, and then brought forward again with a downward cast straight in front of them, a good deal similar to throwing a fly with a fly-rod; at the same time as the forward movement is made, the line held in the left hand is let go. This sharp, fly-fishing like casting is necessary to throw out the very light weight used in this style. The gentle swing adopted with heavier tackle would not get this light tackle out to its proper destination. To make a fresh cast, the float is picked off the water with the rod, like a fly is picked off, and thrown behind the angler, and then projected forward again with a sharp cast in a similar manner, as I said before, to a fly being thrown. I might mention that in this drain style of fishing for roach where groundbait is used I prefer the hook bait to be as near the bottom as possible.

Shrimps are sometimes a good bait for roach in certain of those still waters. The shrimps that I mean are those that can be purchased at the fishmonger's shop. To bait with them the head, tail and hard shell or skin are removed, the hook point run in at the thick end and brought out at the bend close to the tail; the smallest shrimps are used for the hook. The heads, tails, shells, and also the very large ones being smashed up into pulp in the hollow of the hand and mixed thoroughly with a little of the bread and bran groundbait, and popped in in little balls all round your float. This is rather an uncertain bait for roach, the waters wherein it is a success being very few; that is as far as I can learn, but perhaps this is for want of trying them elsewhere. However, in those corners where they are used, very large roach fall victims. I may as well confess that personally my experiences with that bait have only been very limited indeed; but still, I have an idea that they might succeed in other waters where the fisherman never dreams of using them. I have been told that in certain still waters, and during very hot weather, they are the grandest lure that can be put on a roach hook.

There is another very deadly style of roach fishing that I saw practised in very quiet Lincolnshire waters. The chief peculiarity of this style was the float, and the manner of shotting the tackle. Instead of using two or more shots some distance from the hook, one small one only was employed, and this was fixed on the gut tackle about an inch only from the baited hook. The float itself is a very small one, either a tiny porcupine quill three inches in length and very thin, or else two inches of a peacock's feather, the one shot on the tackle being sufficient to cause about an inch of this float to stand above the surface of the water. Great care is taken in plumbing the depth, so that the shot is just clear of the bottom. When a roach takes the bait in his mouth, he instantly lifts the shot, and the float is at once thrown upwards, and lies flat on the water. This bite is promptly responded to on the first indication, and hooking the fish is nearly a certainty at every attempt. The bait used is generally a small pill of paste, or else a cube of raw potato; this latter bait is procured from a slice about a quarter of an inch thick, cut from the centre of a large potato. A quill or the socket of a penholder is used to cut the cubes; this makes the bait a nice shape and size. This plan of fishing can only be practised in very quiet drains and canals. I have been told that some of the most expert Yorkshire and Lancashire roach fishermen adopt this plan with great success in the quiet canals of those two counties.

As anglers in various districts like to know how experts catch their fish in other waters, I wrote to Mr. S. Hayward, of Trowbridge, who is one of the very best roach fishermen on the rivers Avon and Frome, for his experience in the matter. He very kindly replied to my query in a long and interesting letter, from which I take the following: Says Mr. Hayward—" First, I will take the early part of the sea-
" son, say, the end of June and the beginning of July, when
" the roach are on the shallows. I have been very success-
" ful with the gentle on a No. 9 Crystal roach hook, fishing
" about one inch from the bottom in the streamy parts
" where there is a sandy bottom and about four feet of
" water. I really think that I have killed more roach on
" these two rivers with the gentle than I have with all the
" other baits put together. I cannot say much about paste

"fishing, as I could at any time do better with the gentle.
"In the summer, I use a float that will carry about five or
"six middling-sized shot; and I may as well say that the
"Nottingham style, with reel and fine-running tackle, is far
"away the best plan to adopt. In August and September
"boiled malt is a very good bait, especially in the running
"streams. For this last bait I use the same small float as
"before, but the hook is a smaller one, No. 12 being the
"best, and the tackle must always in the summer time be
"of the very finest drawn gut, as the water is then very
"clear. I personally prefer winter fishing for roach, as I
"consider these fish are not in condition before November;
"in August, and even in September, they are very slimy,
"and bad to handle; but about Christmas time they are as
"bright as a bar of silver; I don't care how cold it is, I
"have fished all through the winter, and have had some
"good bags still using my favourite bait, the gentle. I now
"increase the size of my float, and use one that will carry
"eight or nine shots, with a line, and tackle and a No. 9
"hook, threading four or five gentles on it. For ground-
"bait I use the same that is generally adopted, viz., bread,
"bran, and barley meal, mixed together rather stiff, and
"pitched into the top end of the swim in little lumps about
"as big as walnuts. Sometimes I fish on the bottom;
"sometimes from one to four inches above it. I don't lay
"down a hard and fast rule, but suit my fishing as to how
"the roach are feeding, trying all sorts of dodges to make
"a good bag. I do not agree with a good many anglers,
"who write to the sporting papers and say that roach will
"never bite in snow broth. I have found it just the other
"way. I remember well a friend and myself going out
"roaching one Christmas Bank Holiday. A foot of snow
"was on the ground, and it was melting fast. The river
"when we got there was nearly bank full, and coming down
"thick as soup, and yet we got 24lb. of good roach, fishing in
"an eddy with gentles, a good few of them over a pound
"each. I can call to mind several occasions when I have
"met with good sport in a high and heavy snow water.
[This is rather a curious experience, Mr. Hayward.] "The
"river Frome here contains some splendid roach. I con-

"sider it nothing unusual to pick a dozen fish out of one
"catch, that would weigh as many pounds. In the winter
"and in coloured water our roach prefer the gentle to the
"worm. During the early autumn I use wasp grubs when
"I can get them, but I found Mr. Roach could get these
"grubs off the hook without moving the float, so I used to
"put a grub on the bend of the hook and a long gentle on
"the point to keep it on, and got them then (a very good tip
"this, Sam). I like to fish for roach with the very finest of
"tackle, but on the other hand I have taken them with the
"coarsest; it all depends on how they are on the feed, when
"'well on' I don't think that it makes a lot of difference about
"the gut, if the bait is all right, and you strike at the right
"time; which is just when the float is going down, you must
"not wait till it comes up again or you will be a lot to late,
"stream fishing in the Nottingham style is my favourite
"plan. I find it answers well on our waters, especially on
"the river Frome." This is a very interesting and useful
letter. Mr. Hayward's remarks about taking roach on the
very thickest tackle, will perhaps come as a revelation to
many roach anglers. I have only one experience of the
kind myself, that I can just now remember. A lad and I
were one afternoon roaching from a punt in a baited swim
on the Ouse; I used the very finest 4x drawn gut, he used
very coarse tackle, and yet managed to take two fish to my
one all the afternoon. I could not help thinking then that
the fishermen are sometimes a lot more particular than the
fish. That afternoon's experience was however, utterly at
varience with my usual practice, because I generally could
well hold my own at roach fishing, no matter who I had for
a companion, and in nine cases out of ten I found the very
finest tackle to be the most successful.

I think I have, in the foregoing four chapters, given
instructions for roach fishing in most of the styles known to
bottom fishermen in the various districts where this fish is
found, except the special style adopted by the Lea roacher;
and as this style seems to me to be confined exclusively to that
river a very few words will suffice. The rod most generally
used is a white cane one 18 feet in length, without either rings
or reel fittings. It is built remarkably thick at the butt end;

indeed, I have seen some Lea rods that were as much in diameter as the angler could nicely clasp. The taper, however, to the fine point has to be true and accurate to a remarkable degree, with no suspicion of whippiness about it. A good Lea roach pole is a work of art, the initial cost of which is rather a serious item to a working man angler. The plan adopted is mostly tight-line fishing, with the float about eighteen inches from the tip of the rod. Three or four yards of very fine gut or horsehair is employed as a line, and the hook is the usual crystal pattern and size. A peculiar plan of baiting is to use a pill of white paste on the point of the hook, not much larger than a No. 4 shot, and put round it a bit of bread and bran ground bait, the size of a hazel nut. The stream washes off this ground bait, and soon exposes the white morsel on the point. It is a very deadly plan, and some of the very largest roach have fallen victims to it.

I had intended in this chapter giving a few hints as to fishing for roach on the surface; but the next chapter on rudd and rudd fishing goes so fully into the subject that it would be a waste of space to repeat it, the flies and the method of using them for the rudd being the same as for roach.

THE RUDD.

CHAPTER V.

RUDD AND RUDD FISHING.

Rudd and Rudd fishing—A little known fish—Characteristics of the Rudd—Weight of Rudd—Habits and haunts of the Rudd—Luring them out—Food of Rudd—Baits for Rudd fishing—" Fine and far off"—The outfit—Floats—Gut lines and gut hooks—A slowly-sinking bait—Fishing the runs—Playing the fish—Dr. Norman's experiences—The Norfolk style—Fly fishing for Rudd.

"The Rudd, a kind of roach, all tinged with gold,
Strong, broad, and thick, most lovely to behold."

At the outset of this chapter I must confess that I had been a fisherman something like a quarter of a century before I got what I could honestly call a real practical insight into the subject of rudd and rudd fishing. 'Tis true I got an occasional small one out of the Trent when fishing for roach, and knew them well enough to know that they were a fish separate and distinct from the roach; but beyond that I knew nothing. They were a sealed book to me as far as their nature and habits were concerned, for it did not matter what book on fish and fishing I was lucky enough to get hold of, the information on rudd was of the scantiest possible description; even the great Francis Francis, Esq., dismissed him in about a dozen lines in his work on "Angling," and says: "For all angling purposes the directions given for roach answer for the rudd equally." Now, as a matter of fact, the directions given for roach will not do for the rudd. The Bedfordshire Ouse is supposed to be the very best rudd river in England, and it is also very much noted for its roach. Now, in roach fishing we generally fish on the bottom, use plenty of ground bait, and stick to one swim most of the day. In rudd fishing it is necessary to fish nearer the surface of the water than the bottom, ground bait is not a necessity, whilst roving about to all likely looking swims, as in chub fishing, must be carefully attended to; in fact, to put it plainly, you must proceed exactly opposite as for roach fishing, if you mean to make a bag of very heavy rudd. The author of the "Modern Angler" also treats the rudd with scant respect, telling us "that as a sporting fish he is one of the worst, very seldom exceeding a pound in weight, and hardly worth the trouble of catching." Whereas, he is a sporting fish of a very high order, and in weight reaching a very respectable size. It seems a very peculiar thing that our great authorities on fish and fishing should know so little about the rudd and the method of its capture, because he is one of the, if not the, most handsome coarse fish that inhabits our inland waters. The Nottingham style of bottom fishing, too, is exactly suited for this sport. Fine and far off must be the rudd fisherman's motto; he must use the handiest of chub rods, the easiest of running reels, and the finest and best of silk lines and tackle in order to successfully operate on the fish now under notice.

The rudd, like the roach, is a member of the carp family, and his specific name is Leuciscus, or Cyprinus Erythrophthalmus, and as I have hinted just now is a very handsome fish. He has several local names, such as "red-eye," "roud," and "shallow," and is found in the waters of several English counties in more or less abundance, but perhaps they reach the greatest weight and the finest condition in the Bedfordshire Ouse and the streams and broads of Norfolk and Suffolk. At one time there was a deep-rooted belief among naturalists and anglers that this fish was a hybrid between the bream and the roach; even Walton himself advanced that opinion as being held by some learned in the matter; but now it is generally acknowledged to be a distinct species.

A two-pound rudd in good condition, fresh from the stream in the month of August, presents a sight which once seen is not easily forgotten. The deep and brilliant scarlet of the fins, the golden bronze of the sides, the light golden yellow of the belly, the beautiful brown, green, and blue of the back, varying in shade when viewed from different positions, the golden yellow of his cheeks and gill covers, his colours seem to change when looked at from different lights and shades, like the wings of the " Purple Emperor " butterfly. All these form a picture of fish colouring that an artist might envy; but, alas! these colours soon fade and disappear finally after death. He is probably called "rudd" because of the ruddy coppery tint of the fish, and "red-eye" evidently from the bright red of the irides, and "shallow" most likely from its bream-like shallowness of body when on its side.

There are certain similarities between the rudd and the roach that anglers who are not intimately acquainted with both kinds would have a difficulty in telling at a glance the difference between the two. He might fancy a rudd, if he happened to take an odd one when roach fishing, was a particularly bright and handsome specimen of the latter fish; but in spite of this similarity there is a great difference between the anatomy of the two fishes. We will suppose the angler has a pound rudd and a roach of similar weight lying before him, he will at once notice that the former is the shorter one, that it is a trifle flatter on the sides, and that it is also a full half inch or three-quarter inch deeper than the roach. Two other points of marked difference will be found in the dorsal or back fin, and the nose and mouth. The dorsal fin of the roach is exactly opposite the ventral fins, while in a rudd this fin is nearer the tail; in fact, the dorsal is placed very far back, between the ventral fins and the anal fin. As I have noticed in a previous chapter, the peculiar shape of the top lip of a roach, which is capable of elongation, and is overhung; in the rudd this peculiarity is exactly opposite, the fish looks pug-nosed, its bottom lip projects, turns upward over the top one, and is underhung, and when we also notice the difference in colour between the two fish, as already hinted, it will not be a difficult matter to recognise the rudd, if the angler is lucky enough to meet with it during his outings.

I have been rather particular in describing this fish, as it is not generally known among anglers, and also taking into consideration the fact that fish culturists are now beginning to turn their attention to it, and are stocking waters with rudd that hitherto have had very few, if any, in them, so I am hoping that in the near future it may become better known and more sought after than is the case at present. When cooked and served at the table it is a very palatable dish, but has the same objection that is raised against all coarse fish, it is rather woolly in its flesh, and the quantity of small bones are troublesome; but still, if very fresh, nicely cleaned, scaled, and fried crisp, then served smoking hot with egg and bread crumb, it is by no means to be despised. A rudd that scales up to two and a half pounds or over should not suffer the indignity of the frying pan, but ought to be treated to a glass case, even if the lucky captor should be compelled, as an old friend of mine rather rudely put it, " to pawn his shirt to pay for it." I have seen several good rudd set up and cased, but somehow or other the taxidermist does not do justice to this grand coloured fish. As I have said, the colours soon fade and disappear after death, and as our stuffer is, or ought to be, somewhat of an artist, he should see a specimen fresh from its native element, and if possible reproduce those colours in all their natural beauty. Until this is done an ordinary stuffed specimen only gives the beholder a faint idea as to what the fish is like naturally.

In my opinion, which is based on careful observation of the haunts and habits of these fish, I should say that the rudd spawns a little earlier in the season than roach, perhaps even as much as three or four weeks; at any rate, I have found them during the latter part of June and the beginning of July to be a lot cleaner and brighter than the roach are at the same date; but this forwardness depends in a great measure on the mildness or otherwise of the spring. In a particularly mild spring rudd may spawn as early as the latter part of April and the beginning of May, the extreme brightness of these fish at the time when the roach are very rough and slimy confirming this opinion.

In suitable localities and under favourable conditions the rudd reaches a very respectable weight. A two-pound roach is a fine specimen very seldom caught, whereas a two-pound rudd is not considered even a fair specimen. I should say the very top weight would be four pounds; but I may as well at once confess that I have no grounds for supposing that four-pound rudd exist in any great quantity, as I have never seen one of that weight caught. I, however, firmly believe that odd ones approaching that weight are in existence to-day in the Bedfordshire Ouse, as I have seen in the clear water among the weeds fish that have been veritable giants of the race of rudd. Among the collections of preserved fish shown at the Piscatorial Exhibition of 1892 was a specimen that claimed to have once weighed 3½lb. I made a long examination of that fish, as well as the glass in front of it would allow, and I could not help thinking that it had not been taken with rod and line in the full vigour of its strength and power, but rather that it had been picked up from the water in either a dead or a dying condition. I may be wrong, but appearances were most decidedly in favour of that supposition. It might have scaled, when alive, the weight stated; in fact, I am rather inclined to the opinion that it once weighed several ounces more than it did when finally taken from the water.

In the great Fisheries Exhibition of 1883 a rudd from the Ouse was shown and took the specimen prize; its weight was put down at 2lb. 12oz.; a good fish, although I must admit that I know of several in existence that reached a greater weight. Still, the fact remains the same, the fish from the Ouse beat those shown by exhibitors from other waters. My own top weight with rod and line for rudd was one that went half an ounce over three pounds. I asked Mr. C. A. Bryant, the chairman of the Huntingdon Anglers, who is and has been for many years one of the very best rudd fishermen in the county, if he would give me his experience on this point, and he very kindly does so as follows: "A gentleman, of whose veracity I have not the slightest doubt, informs me that when netting for tench (for stocking purposes) a part of the Ouse of which he has the right of fishing, four rudd were caught in the net, which, when weighed, were found to scale 3½lb. each, and were then returned to the water. The largest rudd that I have ever taken weighed 3lb. 1oz., and the very best bit of sport I ever remember having was in 1882. In three hours I took eighteen, weighing exactly 36lb., the most remarkable thing being that I hooked no other fish of any kind or size. In 1883, one afternoon, out of the same swim, I got twelve which just turned the scale at 24lb. In 1884 the four best specimens which fell to my rod, and which I had set up, averaged a trifle over 2lb. 8oz. each, the largest going 2lb. 15oz.; and since then, up to the present, I generally manage to get a few every season running from 2lb. to 2lb. 8oz., and a few odd ones over the latter weight." This experience of Mr. Bryant's, I should say, is a record, and perhaps stands alone in the annals of big rudd capture.

The rudd feeds somewhat similar to the chub, that is in a general way, either on the surface or in midwater; it is very seldom found on the bottom in very deep water. When the angler does meet with it when bottom fishing for roach, it is mostly in the shallow streams, by the side of a considerable bank or run of weeds during the early part of the summer. I don't wish it to be understood for a moment that rudd are found in exactly similar places to the chub. When I say they feed somewhat similar I meant in taking a bait on the surface or in midwater. The chub delights in smart streams with a clear gravelly bottom, while the rudd particularly likes a very gentle stream with a regular jungle-like under growth of weeds, especially if that same undergrowth is from a foot to eighteen inches below the surface of the water, and where flags and rush beds do abound, with here and there the huge leaf of the water-lily dotted around. In some parts of the river the growth of weeds is so thick as to cover the whole surface, the flow of the stream is checked, and the water rendered, comparatively speaking, stagnant. Such a place as that is not a safe find for big rudd, where they do most abound is where a gentle stream meanders in and out among a scattered growth of weeds, where the water-lily leaf affords shelter to them, for they lurk beneath the shadow of those big leaves. Corners and bends of the river seem to be very favourite haunts of these fish, especially if there are bunches of weeds a yard or so apart, with a little clear unobstructed stream flowing gently between these said bunches. It seems to be difficult to tell on paper their favourite haunts, but a little observation will soon render the angler conversant with this; but what I would most particularly impress on him is this—Don't expect to find rudd in very deep water on the bottom, but rather look for him on the shallows, in the little runs among the weeds, and where the undergrowth is the most dense, providing this growth is in places some little distance under the surface, with all sorts of bunches of weeds, flags, rushes, and water-lilies scattered around. If our angler is, as he ought to be, of an observant nature, he will probably notice a sudden and huge swirl in the water, perhaps where the weeds are thickest; this is a rudd. A bream generally rises in a deliberate manner, puts his back fin out of the water, and rolls over with a lazy flop; a roach mostly rises from the bottom in a slanting direction, and shows himself with scarcely a break; but a rudd seems to give himself up to the full enjoyment of his rise, and swirls over in the water with a decided splash, sending the tiny waves across the stream in ever-widening circles, till finally lost among the flags and rushes on either side. A little practice and observation will soon enable the angler to tell with tolerable precision if it was a rudd that broke the surface, and also if it was a large one, and practice alone can teach him the best method of speedily adding that particular rudd to his basket. We have now found that the fish are at home, and this home appears to be deep among the fastnesses of the flags and weeds; the next idea is to get them out into the little open spaces and runs between the bunches of weeds, so that a bait can be presented to them with some chance of successfully landing them when hooked; for this purpose, if I may be allowed to use an expression that looks at first sight very like an Irish bull, it is a good plan to ground bait on the surface. Little bits of bread about two inches long and an inch wide and them when hooked; for this purpose, if I may be allowed these bits must be thrown carefully and accurately on the stream, so that it floats gently down that run that looks the most handy for getting your hook bait in, if the fish are in a biting humour, out they come into the clear water, showing their fins and bodies, rolling over the bread, poking at it with their noses, and smacking their lips at it in keen enjoyment; now is your time. Out goes the bait with a clean cast that must be long and accurate, and if this is done properly, in three seconds you are most probably fighting it out to the bitter end with a good two-pounder.

During the early part of the summer, immediately after they have concluded spawning operations, the rudd are for the most part vegetarians; they feed upon the weeds and the insects, caddis worms, and minute crustaceans upon those weeds. In fact, I may say that their principal food during the summer months are weeds and insects, for I have opened and examined them at various times from June to October, and found the contents of the stomach confirm this opinion. At the same time, they are on the lookout for any little dainty that may fall or be blown into the stream by the wind, such as flies, caterpillars, small beetles, grubs or worms; while the water-flies, as they are hatched out of the caddis-grubs, are eagerly snapped up. These fish are a summer fish, pure and simple; they delight in hot weather. During the middle of the day when other fish are lying quiet, and refuse to be tempted owing to the heat, then do the rudd show good sport, especially if a warm breeze disturbs and ripples the surface of the water. July, August and September are the best months; August the very best of all. If the weather is very mild during the early part of October, you will stand a chance of getting a few; but it must be warm and mild, for as soon as cold weather sets in, the rudd disappear from their usual haunts and you see them no more till another summer; where they go to, and how they hide themselves during the winter, are questions that I cannot positively answer, but it is certain that they are hardly ever caught during very cold weather. I have watched carefully when roach fishing during the winter, and no matter how freely those fish have been feeding, not a single rudd have I landed, and other anglers have assured me that their experiences have been similar in this respect. With regard to hook-baits, I may say that the rudd will take many baits if they are only properly presented to them, but for all angling purposes my list will only be a very short one, worms, cadbaits, paste and two or three artificial flies being ample. Gentles are a deadly bait, but in a stream like the Ouse they have their objections. Bleak will persist in taking them, and the angler is so often disappointed—time after time pulling up those small and greedy marauders when he expects a lot bigger quarry; and then look at the waste of time in taking these small fish off the hook, and rebaiting. Paste, too, even when flavoured with King's Natural bait, as recommended in the chapter on roach, good as it undoubtedly is, has an exactly similar objection, small fish being very troublesome. It is not advisable to pin one's faith too much on the two very excellent baits just named; they are good, I know, but the objections noted are fatal to a strong recommendation of them. The bait that I have found most effective under all conditions and circumstances is a nice, well-scoured, lively cockspur or brandling worm; it must be red, bright and lively, and well scoured in clean moss. It is not advisable to use too large a worm, one about two inches in length being quite big enough; or better still, two smaller ones about an inch and a half long, put on the hook so that three or four ends twirl and wriggle about, forms a very attractive and deadly bait.

It will now be necessary to look at the tackle most suitable for rudd fishing, and I may as well say at the outset that the Nottingham style is far away before any other method. I have already given the angler some idea as to the swims and places where rudd are most likely to be found, and as these fish are principally surface-feeding, it will be seen at once that the finer and neater the tackle, the greater the chance of success. You must keep as far away from their haunts as you possibly can. Avoid all splashing or unnecessary noise; they are keen of eye, and amazingly shy, and will probably dart headlong into their fastnesses of weeds and rushes if you make your presence, as it were, too much felt. The Nottingham fisherman's motto: "Fine and far off" must in this case be reduced to a science, everything being light, neat, and so arranged that the longest cast, with the least weight, can be easily, promptly and accurately made. This is all the more necessary when the water is clear and the surface like glass. It does not matter so much when a nice ripple disturbs the water—this latter condition being the most conducive to sport—but we cannot always have the wind and weather exactly suitable when we go fishing, so we must prepare for any contingency. It is not advisable even under any circumstance to use a long heavy rod for rudd fishing; this weapon must be light, strong, handy, and, above all, prompt in its actions. Twelve feet in length will be found ample; in fact, the chub rod described in Chapter II., Page 79, Vol. I is the very thing. The same remark also applies to the reel, the centre-pin, three and a half inches in diameter, being so free and easy running is to be recommended above any other (see Chap. II, page 80, vol. I). The silk running line can hardly be too fine, provided it is fairly strong, forty or fifty yards of the plaited silk chub line described on page 82 being the best size and quality that can be procured for this purpose. For floats, almost any good roach or chub float will do. Still, if I have a preference for any it is for those cork and porcupine floats, one about four to six inches in length and painted green, with a white tip being the best; these floats do not show so conspicuously in the water as a long white quill. Another float that I am very fond of for rudd fishing is a small disc of cork painted green, with a hole through the centre, which said hole contains a removeable plug of wood. This float is shaped somewhat similar to a small "pilot" that is used in jack fishing; only it is very much smaller, and perfectly round, the exact size being five-eighths of an inch in diameter. There is a little advatnage in using this float, because you are fishing where weeds are very plentiful, and a long float is liable to be pulled by the fish into the weeds; the point that sticks up beyond the cap and line will catch among them, and cause you very much annoyance. But in this round float with the line threaded through the centre, and secured in its place by the little plug of wood, presents no inequalities or points that can catch under or over the weeds.

It is not advisable to use the finest gossamer four X drawn gut for bottom tackle, as recommended for roach, in rudd fishing, as the latter fish is a strong fighter, and will try his very utmost time after time to reach his hover of weeds, which, if he succeeds in doing, will most certainly break you. I have seen it stated somewhere or other that the rudd is a very cowardly fish, and gives up directly he is hooked, but in actual practice, with good ones, I find the very opposite to be the case, and not until the landing-net is fairly under him can you say he is thoroughly mastered. I recommend fine tackle, of course; the finer you dare use it, the greater your chance of success, but it will be found a mistake to try it too fine. A gut line a yard in length, slightly tapered towards the hook end, of good, round, finest undrawn gut, of the quality known in the trade as "finest refina No. 1," stained a dark blue colour, will be found the best, and this gut line should have a small and carefully knotted loop tied at each end of it, one of these loops being to fasten the silk line in, and the other to loop in the length of gut on which the hook itself is whipped. I recommend for various reasons the bottom tackle to be in two sections, the hook length of gut to be separate and distinct from the main gut line, and yet capable of being joined together in an instant by means of the two loops, the principal reason being that in case of a breakage, which generally happens to the bottom or hook length, as being the finest, a fresh hook can be put on without having to change the properly-shotted main gut line. I have used several different kinds of hooks in rudd fishing, round bends and sneck bends; long shanks and short shanks; and after a careful trial, I pronounce most decidedly in favour of a Crystal hook, No. 10 size (Redditch scale) with a fairly long shank, the holding power of this hook being very good, in addition to which a worm or worms can be threaded on with the greatest ease. The gut itself on this hook should be a shade finer than the main gut line, what is known as 2x drawn gut stained dark blue, being the very best. It is advisable to have a few spare gut hooks of this quality with you, as breakages may happen, and it is also advisable to have a supply of short-shanked hooks as well, in case you may want to try the paste bait, as noted a short time ago.

Now I come to a point that I wish the angler to carefully con, and that is: a rudd always takes a bait "slowly sinking from the surface," in preference to a stationary one, or even to a bait swimming down stream at one even depth. From this it is obvious that a lot of heavy shot must not be in close proximity to the hook. These split shot, which can be three or four BB's sufficient to cock the float properly (and leave about an inch of it out of the water if that float

F

is the long one, or the top of it visbile if it is the round one recommended), must be placed directly under, and touching, the float and each other, so that there is no shot between those touching the float and the hook. This gives the angler weight enough to cast the proper distance, and yet the bait sinks very slowly. The self-cocking float, as recommended in the chapter on roach, might perhaps be used in certain localities with considerable success, but I find, as a general rule, that this float is not bulky enough nor weighty enough to cast clean and easily the long distance required in rudd fishing. The distance between the float and the hook need not be more than from eighteen inches to two feet under any circumstances, while in very weedy, shallow places, a foot will be found ample. It will be a good plan to have two or three main gut lines shotted at various distances from the bottom loop, so that a change can be easily effected should the nature of the swim warrant such a change. A boat is almost a necessity in rudd fishing, as it is imperative to fish over the weeds, and at the back of the rush-beds and flags. A bait can be easily thrown over them, but in recovering the line for a fresh cast the hook is liable to catch in the weeds. Besides, if a good fish is hooked, you cannot keep him from darting towards you, and once under the weeds it will be impossible to land him; your chance is all the better if you have some open water between the fish and yourself. Hence, a boat is best, and, if possible, fish down stream. An iron two-stone weight, attached to a stout cord, will do by way of an anchor. Drop the boat carefully down stream till you see a place that looks suitable, keep as far away from the fish, towards the opposite side, as you can throw nicely, then slip the weight quietly overboard, and when it reaches the bottom fasten the cord tightly to the side or the seat; pull down the line between the rings of the rod, and make the cast as described in Chapter IV.

It is not advisable to try long in one place if you don't very soon get a response. Pull up the weight and shift a few yards lower down, till you do find them at home, and if you do succeed in getting a good one, you may reasonably expect more, as these fish generally swim in small shoals. There is no mistaking the bite of a large rudd. We will suppose the angler is fixed in midstream, fifteen to twenty yards from the edge of the weeds, and he aims his bait so accurately that it drops into one of the clear spaces among those weeds, and then slowly sinks. The float has hardly time to steady itself upright before it disappears sideways with a rush, as Mr. Rudd makes off for his favourite weed-bed. As soon as the float goes under, strike very gently, and put on as much strain as you feel the tackle will stand, and get him into the clear water in front of the boat as speedily as possible. Don't let him rush headlong among the weeds if you can anyhow prevent it, or you will certainly lose both fish and tackle, besides scaring away the remainder of the shoal. And don't forget the little dodge I gave awhile ago—to find the fish by means of the bits of dry bread floating among the weeds.

The main points for the rudd fisherman to observe are: choose a warm, breezy day in preference to a hot, calm one, always remembering that the less wind there is, and the brighter water, the more necessity is there to fish "far off" and fine; always fish as near the surface as you can, and where the jungle of weeds is the thickest; don't trouble with groundbait, except a good supply of dry bread; throw the bait lightly and accurately towards the rising fish if you succeed in enticing them to the top by the surface-baiting of bread; a well-scoured, red worm is the best bait; keep the rod point well up; let no more loose line than can possibly be helped rest on the water, so that an instant strike as soon as the float disappears is practicable; and, lastly, when you have hooked a large fish, be ever on the alert, and prevent him from rushing among the weeds at all hazards.

Dr. Norman, writing to "Land and Water," some years ago, gives the following as his experiences of rudd fishing in Norfolk:—" The best bait is a nice red worm, but the finest fish are taken with a salmon gut foot line and three hooks, a large float, and at least forty yards of strong light line. I have had a brace weighing nearly five pounds several times on my paternoster, and many years ago caught twenty-nine in a few hours, scaling over four stone. The ground should be very carefully baited for two days at least, and a long willow wand stuck in the mud in the middle of it. Anchor the boat very quietly twenty-five or thirty yards off, throw your float near the willow, and you will have such sport as few will imagine. It is really a case of no sooner in than under; and, as an old piscatorial friend said, after an hour's hard work, 'Even in my wildest dreams, doctor, I never had such splendid fishing.' I once took three at a single cast of the line that weighed over five pounds, and a very pretty commotion they made in the water. Another evening, after a very early tea, we landed no less than 194. Sunrise and sunset suit these fish best, but I have had capital sport on a hot autumn day, although that is rather rare." After reading the above experiences of rudd fishing in Norfolk and Suffolk, and knowing that Dr. Norman was an authority on all matters connected with fishing in those counties, and as this experience was somewhat at variance with mine, I wrote to a friend since penning the above, for his experience in rudd fishing in Norfolk and Suffolk. This friend, Mr. J. Deplidge, has had a wide and long experience in this branch of angling, and he very kindly replies as follows (this letter is so very instructive and interesting that I give it in full, and make no apology for doing so):—

"With respect to rudd fishing in the Norfolk Broads, the only successful modus operandi is to fish Nottingham style— 'fine and far off'—and as near the surface as possible. The plan is to use a cork float, say about seven inches in length, which will carry three or four heavy shots, and still show well about the water at eighteen or twenty yards; a No. 1 plaited silk line, casting for your fish from a moored boat; the shots are placed close to the bottom tip of the float, the loop to attach the hook length being immediately below the bottom shot; a No. 8 or 9 crystal hook is just the thing, and you fill it with eight or nine gentles. If the point of hook protrudes it does not matter, the fish bolt it ravenously; indeed, a good fish always takes the float under with an unmistakeable run. You strike just as the float disappears in a slanting direction towards the reeds. A fish that does not take the float under with a bang is not worth striking. When you get to the right spot you will be little troubled by 'scripers,' every fish almost going 14oz. to 2lb., that is on Potter Heigham Sounds and Horsey Mere. Moor the boat, say, twenty yards from the reed beds, always selecting a little bay or short break in the reeds; fish with the wind so that you can cast your line well and accurate to where you see a feeding fish. You draw the fish out of the reeds by throwing pieces of bread, say, half the size of your hand and an inch thick, towards the reeds, and as the bread draws near to the reeds, the fish, if in a biting humour, come out in shoals, flop over the bread, showing their fins and bodies, and suck at the bread. You could hear them smack their lips half way across the broad. As a fish shows himself you cast for him at once. As my fisherman observed: 'It is like shooting your fish.' It is most exciting sport, what with the expectancy of seeing the fish come out of the reeds and rolling over the bread, then trying your skill as a marksman, and finally of bringing and playing your golden-hued game fish to the net. The Norfolk Broad rudd, especially the larger ones, are in my opinion the handsomest fish—bar trout—that swims in freshwater. What a pity it is that their glorious orange golden sheen cannot be revived by the preserver. After being out of water a few hours the colours fade to a pale yellow."

I consider this letter gives a very good description of rudd fishing, and agrees with my own and Mr. Bryant's experiences so accurately (with the exception that I find red worms far better baits than gentles) that the reader may rest assured, if he has a chance at the rudd, the instructions here given are thoroughly sound and trustworthy.

This fish is also a capital one for the fly fisherman, although he is not what we can call a brilliant riser. Still, feeding on, or just under, the surface, at times he takes the fly well. The dry-fly fisherman in this case would not stand so much chance as one using a wet sunk fly. You throw out from the boat towards the haunts of the fish and allow the fly to sink an inch or two under the surface; only use one fly at a time, and let your gut cast be fine but strong, one three yards in length, tapered from strong to finest undrawn being better than the extra fine drawn gut. Eyed flies are the best, and they should be of a medium size, a No. 8 or 9 hook (Redditch scale) being about right. A Red Palmer is a good fly; so is an Alder; while for casting in the evening nothing beats a Coachman with the white wings. The fly that I have found most effective during the daytime is a No. 8 hook Zulu. This is a black hackle fly, ribbed with gold twist, and a scarlet tag; but whichever fly you do use, always tip the point of the hook with a couple of gentles, or failing those a little bit of white kid. You don't get such large rudd with the fly as you do with the worm. I have, however, seen them landed over 1½lb. in weight, and sometimes as many as a score have been taken in an hour, running from that size down to half a pound; but always remember that it is the best for fly fishing when a nice breeze ripples and disturbs the water; and also remember to throw the fly where the weeds and undergrowth are the thickest. The fly rod, reel, and line recommended and described in the chapter on chub, page 114, vol. 1, is also right for rudd, and the angler can please himself whether he uses this rod as a double-handed or as a single-handed one; but, of course, he will have to be guided by circumstances as to this. The above remarks on surface fishing for rudd, apply with equal force to the roach also, except that in weedy rivers and lakes, where the water is quiet, roach prefer very small flies, a tiny Red Palmer tipped with a gentle being as good as anything.

In closing this chapter I must apologise for its length, but seeing that it is a little-known fish, and also that it is, as I firmly believe, on the increase in English waters. I must let the importance of the subject be my excuse. I have said nothing but what the angler ought to know, as personal experience in this matter has taught me that there are scores of fishermen living close to the haunts of splendid rudd that were ignorant of their nature and habits, and even of their presence in those waters.

THE BREAM.

CHAPTER VI.

BREAM AND BREAM FISHING.

Bream fishing — White Bream — Carp Bream — Weight of Bream — Distribution of Bream — Peculiarities of Bream — " On the flit" — Antiquity of Bream — Bream in the frying-pan — The Trent style — The Ouse style — A rustic breamer — A Picture drawn from life — Night fishing — The outfit — Ground-baiting for Bream — A Bream bite — The hook and crutch — The weather in connection with Bream fishing — Special precautions — Lake Bream — An extraordinary ground bait — Hook baits — Ledgering for Bream — "Au revoir."

"The trembling quill in this slow stream,
Betrays the hunger of a Bream."

This distinguished member of the carp tribe is also a fish much sought after by working men anglers. In some waters of England they swarm in countless shoals; and given a favourable day, or more frequently night, the catch of a couple of rods can be counted by the stone, or even at odd times the hundredweight. And when the fact is added that they run up to a good size; also that a ready sale for any captured bream can be effected, and the capture itself made with tackle of the cheapest and simplest kind, to say nothing of the hook baits and ground baits costing next to nothing, or at most not more than a shilling or two for a whole month's supply, it is not to be wondered at that these fish play an important part in the sport of those riverside anglers whose lines happen to be cast in the immediate neighbourhood of a good bream water.

There are three kinds of bream in English waters, but one of them, known as the Pomeranian bream, is so very seldom seen or caught by the ordinary angler that we will at once dismiss him. The second kind, too, hardly deserves a passing reference, as it is only the white or small silver bream, a fish of no reputation whatever, being seldom above a pound in weight, more generally from four to eight ounces; slimy and disagreeable as to his jacket, and no use whatever as an eatable. In some waters they are a positive nuisance, insisting on pulling down the float every minute, taking the large bait intended for their bigger brethren, and when pulled up they perhaps go a couple of ounces in weight, looking for all the world like a bit of tin; indeed, they are known as "tin plates" to the fen fishermen. Worms and gentles are the best hook baits for them; and for ground bait a few handfuls of brewer's grains mixed with clay is all that is required. The colour of the white bream is silver; the fins are light brown, and the eye large and prominent. So with these few remarks I dismiss him with my blessing.

The third kind, which I must notice at greater length, is the common or carp-bream, known to naturalists as Cyprinus Brama, or Abramis Vulgaris. This fish cannot lay claim to great personal beauty, although it is not without certain attractions, especially when in good condition, and an inhabitant of a first-class bream river. Some people call him the "golden bream," but I cannot imagine where this name comes in, unless the bronzy sheen that glitters on the upper part of a freshly-caught specimen deserves to be called "gold." He is also known to other anglers as the "bellows fish." This, I make no doubt, is owing to his extraordinary shape, being wonderfully broad, considering his length and thickness; indeed, I have seen specimens when prepared for the table that, when the head and tail have been removed, the breadth has been greater than the length. He has a small head and mouth, the fins are very dark in colour, and the tail is very much forked. When freshly caught and in good condition, say during August and September, the scales on the sides, especially towards the upper part, glistens with a sort of metallic lustre that gives the fish a very pleasing appearance; but this sheen soon fades, and after being out of the water for a few hours he changes to a much paler colour. I have heard him also referred to as the "black bream." This, I should suppose, is owing to the extreme darkness of his fins. In suitable waters he attains to a pretty good size. I have heard it said that in a certain European water, the name of which I cannot now remember, he not unfrequently reaches the weight of 20lb.; but in England we have nothing like that, although I once saw a statement in an angling paper that a bream of 17lb. had been taken from the Trent. Again quoting from the "Fishing Gazette," I note the following lines:—"Two splendid carp-bream were taken from the Trent by Mr. Beck in his eel nets, scaling respectively twelve and a quarter, and twelve and three-quarter pounds." I must, however, confess that I have handled some hundreds of bream, both by netting and rod fishing, and never yet saw one approaching those weights. I did once see a brace that scaled together a trifle over 13lb., and thought them wonderful fish. A six-pounder is a triumph, while as for a seven or eight pound one, it could be put down as a veritable giant. The general run of bream that fall to the lot of the average angler, even in good waters, would go from two to four pounds apiece, while if the angler succeeded in making a bag of twenty fish that went on the average two and a half pounds per fish, he could set it down as being very good indeed. There is, however, one place on the river Nene, some few miles from Peterborough, where an extraordinary average is frequently made. I once saw a bag of eight fish taken ledgering, the smallest one of which went four pounds, and the largest six; and I was assured that this was nothing out of the way. There is also another place on the river Ouse, in Buckinghamshire, where bream reach a very large size, one in particular, that was taken in the eel traps, tipped the beam at nine pounds, and is now exhibited in the natural history department of a small country museum; and I also know of another case of three Ouse bream, the united weight of which went 20lb.

This fish does not appear to be very widely distributed in the rivers of England, being by far the most plentiful in the eastern and south-eastern counties (of course, lakes, ponds, and reservoirs that contain bream are to be found almost anywhere; but I am now alluding to bream rivers). The Bedfordshire Ouse stands an easy first, if not for quantity, at least for quality of bream. The Norfolk and Suffolk rivers and broads have been noted for them nearly time out of mind. The Nene is also a good bream river; so is the Witham and some of the drains that intersect the county of Lincoln; while last, but not least, the Trent has some good ones in many of its deep, quiet holes. Coming further south, the Medway, the Arun, the Mole, and the Thames, can be set down as bream rivers, and the Warwickshire Avon must not be forgotten, although this latter stream is in the West Midlands. They are generally found in the deepest, quietest parts of the river, and are often packed together in very large numbers. Bream spawn in June, and generally about the time that the dog weed is in flower. This weed grows in large patches on the surface of some waters, and bears a profusion of small white flowers. Riverside men call this weed the "bream weed," and certainly it is a most appropriate name, for as soon as the flower appears then the bream may be looked for on the shallows, scouring themselves among the weeds. It is an extraordinary sight at this time to see a shoal of Trent bream, probably some thousands in number, extending in unbroken ranks for hundreds of yards, rolling, twisting, diving, splashing, and threading these weeds in every direction for sometimes two or three days together; so reckless are they at this time that they can be scooped out with a landing net.

In the deep, sluggish waters of the Ouse, immediately after spawning and scouring, they come to the surface in huge shoals and swim close above the water, and so close together that they nearly touch each other, and perambulate backwards and forwards up and down the centre of the river. After two or three days of this performance they vanish into deep holes.

About the beginning of July I have noticed another peculiarity of the bream: shoals of them would migrate to fresh swims. I noticed this more particularly about three weeks or so after they had done scouring themselves. I have observed shoals on the "flit" even so late as the middle of August; but as a general rule this migration occurs during July. At these times they swim in crowds close to the surface, even showing their back fins above the water. An old friend and I were once lucky enough to see a huge shoal that must have numbered many hundreds, cross a long shallow stream, working their way against a heavy Trent current. We supposed them to be going to a deep, quiet swim some two or three hundred yards higher up the river. We sat perfectly quiet in the boat, and had a good view within a very few yards; but being anxious to see the extent of this shoal, I stood upon the boat seat, and in an instant, as if by magic, every fish sank down and vanished. My old friend used to advance the opinion that these fish were like a hive of bees: when a swim got overcrowded, a " swarm " would leave it and seek a fresh home. There may be something in this; at any rate, I can call to mind several instances where friends and myself have met with such a shoal when roach fishing on the shallows in a stream less than a yard in depth; in fact, in a place where no sane fisherman would dream of bream fishing in; and yet, on their journey these fish were attracted by the ground bait, and came at worms and gentles in gallant style, heavy bags being had in the course of two or three hours. Only a short time ago, I remember a case in point, a youth dropped across a " flitting " shoal of bream; he was roach fishing from an old punt in about a couple of feet of water; a fair stream was running, and he must have had some rare fun. He had no landing net, and time after time two and three pound fish were played up to the boat's side, and then dropped off the hook (a small one by the way) in trying to land them with his hand and hat, and yet he came staggering home with fifty pounds of fish. Next morning an expert armed with every necessary, tried the place; but, never fear, during the night every bream had gone, and a blank, so far as that fish was concerned, was the result.

Another friend once assured me that he had a very singular experience of this kind. He got a rare good bag of bream out of a shallow dyke or stream barely two yards wide, and some quarter mile above its outlet into the river. I have also before me now a very interesting letter that was written by one of the best and most observant anglers on the Trent— Mr. W. Ball, the famous " Trentsider," of Newark. A correspondent had asked him his opinion on this question, and in the course of his reply Mr. Ball says: "From their well-known propensities for roaming about, my correspondent need never despair if, after baiting a swim known to hold bream, they fail to come on in a reasonable time. An authentic instance of bream shifting their quarters was given me a short time ago by a friend: "Some few years ago a gentleman of Newark invited a Sheffield angler for a day or two's fishing in the Newark district, and accordingly baited a well-known bream swim called "Foottits Hole," a few miles below the town. Commencing at daybreak one August morning, they fished more than half the day without the slightest sign of a bream in the swim, and the Sheffielder was getting disgusted with the proceedings, but patience and observation were two of the Newark man's virtues, and in studying the why and the wherefore of their non-success, he happened to cast his eyes lower down the river to an eddy about three hundred yards away, and there he noticed bream rolling and tumbling about in all directions. 'Ah,' said he, 'they are all down there; never mind, we shall have them presently.' And sure enough such was the fact, for gradually they worked their way up-stream, disporting on their journey, until, arriving at their feeding ground, they gradually disappeared; and my friend, taking a longer swim, secured one at the first attempt. 'Now we shall soon be among them,' said he, a remark which was fully justified, for the remainder of the day the bream were fairly 'mad on,' and one of the heaviest takes ever made in the locality was the result of their perseverance." These experiences go to prove that bream at certain seasons are very roving in their habits, and the bream fisherman should keep a good look out for any signs of a "flitting" shoal.

Bream appear to me to be a fish that was highly esteemed in the Middle Ages, and rigorously preserved, the old monks who lived in some of the religious houses being great lovers of them. Indeed, some of the old sheets of water that are to be found in the neighbourhood of the old ruined abbeys contain to this day quantities of fine bream. I cannot help thinking, however, that the tastes of the reverend fathers must have been primitive indeed, and easily satisfied, because pond bream is about the worst dish that could possibly be conceived in the fish line. That they were highly esteemed seems to be a well attested fact; for three hundred years ago, and even less, a proverb was often quoted to the effect that "He that hath bream in his pond hath always a welcome for his guest." Just fancy nowadays a man welcoming his guest with a dish of pond bream. I reckon he would not have a chance of welcoming them a second time, for most assuredly they would keep out of his reach for the future. I know of a sheet of water in Nottinghamshire that contains a lot of large bream, but so filthy and slimy are they that if caught in the early morning and kept in the bag or basket till night they become nothing more nor less than a mass of corruption, more particularly if the weather is hot. Far different, however, is a good Ouse bream; nicely fried and browned crisp with bread crumbs it is anything but bad eating. They should be scaled, beheaded, the fins and insides carefully removed, and scraped well all along the inside of the backbone; a little salt should then be rubbed well in, both outside and inside; and after standing for an hour or two to drain, carefully washed again, and thoroughly dried with a cloth. A lump of good lard should be melted in the frying-pan first, and the bream dropped in among the boiling fat, turning it over when sufficiently cooked on the under side. It should be served and eaten as hot as possible. I might add that bream are all the better if cleaned as soon after capture as possible. I must confess that after my experiences with the Trent bream I was most agreeably surprised at the flavour of a good sample from the Ouse; indeed, many of the people who live on the banks of that river would sooner have a good bream than the best beefsteak that could be purchased; a three-pounder will easily fetch sixpence.

Bream are captured in several ways. On the Trent the angler uses the same rod, reel, line, and tackle as recommended for barbel, except the float is a shade less and the hook a trifle smaller. The haunts of bream in the Trent are deep holes, where the stream is very sluggish. The hook bait, which is generally a worm—and any of the worms recommended in the chapter on barbel will do—is allowed to trip along the bottom. Stret-pegging is also another good method of bream fishing. For ground bait worms are sometimes used, and these are clipped up and thrown down the swim in exactly the same manner as described for barbel. Some Trent fishermen use a ground bait for bream consisting of boiled scratchings, brewer's grains, barley meal, and bullock's blood, mixed up and kneaded together in hard lumps. With this ground bait worms are generally used on the hook, although cadbaits, wasp grubs, and scented pastes can also be tried as a change. Trent bream are cunning customers, and just about as uncertain in their feeding as barbel, very often refusing to come on even after the most careful baiting. Every item of the tackle should be as neat as possible, the float itself being not one shot heavier than the swim actually requires. The bait should also be threaded on the hook as neatly as can be, and no long ends of worms dangling from the point. A good bream bait in a stream is about an inch of the tail end of a well-scoured lob-worm, threaded well on the shank of the hook, and a little brilliant brandling or red-worm twisting and twirling crossways on the point. I used to find that the Trent bream were very roving in their habits, sometimes forsaking a swim without any apparent reason, and then after an absence of a week or more returning to it as suddenly as they left. This stream fishing for bream in the Trent style is a good deal like barbel fishing, with the exception of the two or three little differences noted above; so I will say no more on that subject, but turn to a far different method, viz., bream fishing in quiet waters.

Many of the riverside anglers who live on the banks of the Bedfordshire Ouse, have an idea that it is very little, if any, good fishing for bream in those waters during the day time, and that it is not one time in a score that bream are to be caught, say, between the hours of nine in the morning and four in the afternoon. Personally I don't wonder at it when the extraordinary tackle used by some of these men is taken into account; but I must say that the very best bag of bream I ever got with rod and line in my life was taken between the hours named. They came on the feed at nine in the morning, and did not cease biting until four in the afternoon, by which time fifty, weighing exactly nine stones, had been safely landed; the water was clear, and the sun very hot all through the day. I can also call to mind scores of other occasions when very fair bags indeed of those fish have been made during the middle of the day. Fine tackle and proper appliances were, however, in those cases an absolute necessity. A night breamer's tackle, I have no hesitation in saying, would have failed under the same conditions of weather and water. If you proceed in a workmanlike manner you are bound to get them sometimes, that is, if you stick to them long enough; but I may as well again confess that in bream fishing the blanks have been more numerous than the prizes, but still I always consider that one slice of luck, and, say, 50lb. of fish, makes up for several disappointments. Personally, I don't like fishing during the "silent midnight hours," but there are times when, do as you will, the bream won't bite unless you are on the job with lamp and lantern. I know of no fishing more uncertain than Ouse breaming: you never know at what hour of the day or night they will come on; you can only fish and wait, hoping for the good time coming. I once remember an angler baiting and fishing a swim day after day in the hope that he would soon get them, when at last, on the afternoon of the third day, he got a bite and landed a three-pounder. He now fished away in earnest and landed a dozen good fish in an hour, when they left off feeding as suddenly as they began; and although he stuck to it for two more days, he never got another bream, or even any signs of a bream bite. On the other hand I have known them to keep on the feed for three or four days at a stretch, but, as I said before, it is awfully uncertain.

I will try to give a picture of a rustic bream fisherman and his modus operandi. His tackle is of the most primitive kind, the rod in many cases being simply a long ash sapling cut from the nearest plantation. Reel and running tackle are absent altogether, the line being nothing more than a few yards of stout watercord, tied firmly at the end of the "pole." The float is about the size and shape of a schoolboy's peg-top; quite large enough for pike fishing. A yard of the strongest and coarsest gut, mounted with a large and strong Carlisle hook does duty for tackle. A dozen or more large split shots are pinched on this gut line, and crowded close together within a foot of this hook; this completes the outfit, the total value of which would not exceed sixpence. I have frequently seen these anglers hang the hook into the top of a gatepost and test the strength of the line, by a series of strong pulls. About an hour before sunset, our rustic village angler, with pole on his shoulder, a large pail of brewers grains, and an old sack and stable lantern, proceeds down to the swim, which is generally the deepest and quietest hole he can find. With the help of a rail or an hedge-stake, in the absence of a spade, a few lumps of clay or old pollard are grubbed up from the banks, and mixed with the grains, until he has from twenty to thirty balls, as big as cocoa-nuts. These are dropped in one by one, falling into the water with a sounding splash. A hook and crutch are next looked up, and stuck in the bank about a couple of feet from each other; these articles are to rest the rod on, the crutch being a forked stick, while the hook is another stout stick with a hook at the end, these articles are usually cut from the nearest willow tree. The crutch is stuck in the ground as near the edge of the water as possible, the hook being eighteen inches to two feet behind it; the extreme butt end of the pole is put under the hook, and then dropped on the fork of the crutch, in such a manner that the rod projects straight above the surface. This contrivance does away with the necessity of holding the rod in the hand; the depth is next taken by hanging a heavy plummet on the hook; allowing some six inches or so, so that the bait lies well on the bottom. After fixing the float firmly on the line at its proper place, an old tin containing a supply of worms (brandlings generally), freshly dug out of the manure heap, is produced from the side pocket of his old jacket. Two or three of these worms, according to size are threaded on the hook, and flop, the heavily weighted tackle, and big float drops on the water with a splash. After fixing the pole on the hook and crutch, the old pail in which he carried the grains is turned bottom upwards, and an old sack doubled up on the top, forms a seat; this seat being fixed so that the rod is near to his right hand, ready for immediate action if he gets a bite. Our rustic angler now in all probability, smokes the pipe of peace, and contemplates that motionless float, until it gets too dark to see it. The lantern now plays a prominent part in the proceedings, this is fixed close to the water's edge, and in such a position that the rays from the lighted candle inside, shines directly on the float; (I might say that this float is generally painted white, the light reflecting nicely on it). After a bit this float in a ghost like manner, rises a little, lays on its side, and then moves off, instantly the pole is grabbed, lifted from its support, and with a jerk that makes the water fly, bream No. 1 is fixed. No grace is given a hooked fish, but he is at once hauled to the surface, and run to shore, if our angler has a landing net it is quickly slipped under it, if not he stoops down, seizes it firmly by the back of the head beyond the gills and hurls it up the bank. And so the game continues until the flickering candle tells him it is time to give over. Sometimes he stays till one or two o'clock in the morning, and catches two or three stones of bream, sometimes he goes night after night, and fails to catch a single one. During July when the nights are very short, this man alters his proceeding somewhat, he throws in his ground-bait the previous evening, goes to bed early, and rises before the first streak of daylight is visible on the eastern horizon, arriving at the scene of operations at two a.m., finishing up about five; sometimes with as many bream as he can conveniently carry, more often with only one or two, and still more times with none at all. But still, success or failure he keeps going, and this continues for some six weeks during the early summer, for as soon as harvest sets in our village rustic angler has other fish to fry. This is a picture drawn from life, and can be set down as a thoroughly representative Ouse breamer. There are other men who go to work as far as tackle and groundbaiting are concerned in a far different manner, so I will now explain the method that I have found by practical experience to be the best to adopt in slow running bream rivers like the Ouse. The outfit itself need not be of a very elaborate character, a light but strong cane rod fourteen or fifteen feet long will do very well; a three inch wooden reel, and twenty yards of plaited silk line of medium thickness, all that is required. For floats I like a good stout porcupine quill, one carrying eight medium sized shots, the bottom tackle should consist of two yards of medium fine gut, stained a

G

dark blue, and as for hooks, nothing can beat a No. 8 Crystal bend, on a length of 2x drawn gut. The shots can be put on the tackle the same way as described in the chapter on roach fishing in still water, in fact, the modus operandi for both fish is somewhat similar. For groundbait I prefer a pail full of brewer's grains, a peck of bran, and a bowl full of old bread crusts that have been soaked in cold water for a few hours. This mixture requires kneading together in stiff lumps, the same as described in roach fishing, and dropping in the swim if possible the night before it is fished. A half-peck of ordinary farm-yard barley costing about sixpence, should also be procured, and this should be boiled for several hours in a furnace or copper, until the barley swells out to its fullest extent, and increases in bulk three or four fold. This is for use during fishing, a handful or two being sprinkled all over the swim from time to time as occasion requires. If the angler is unable to procure any barley, he will make shift with a few balls of the ground-bait already described. Brandling worms nicely scoured is as good a bait as can possibly be tried for bream. If there is a very slight stream, I prefer to fish stret pegging; arrange the float about six inches deeper than the water, so that the bait lays well on the bottom. A bream bite in these still waters is very often of rather a peculiar character; all at once you will notice your porcupine quill rising upwards in the water, as if something was pushing it from underneath, and then lay flat upon the surface, immediately afterwards it would glide underneath again, this is a bream bite and should be responded to on the instant, or at least as soon as this gliding away process begins. I suppose it is the extraordinary shape of the bream, when he picks the bait from the bottom, and then rises in his natural position, that causes this movement of the float. In bream fishing the hook and crutch mentioned some time ago are very useful; this fish being rather a slow biter there is plenty of time to pick up the rod after the bite is first perceived. Some odd times when a little stream goes crawling down the river, the bream prefer a moving bait, that is, fix the float at the exact depth, and swim down stream, from one end to the other of the swim, and at these times, particularly if the water is very clear, use only a very small bait, just enough to cover the hook. In addition to worms, sweet paste made of white bread crumb, King's natural bait, a little honey or sugar, and a few drops of gin, all mixed together makes a capital change bait. Two or three kernels of white wheat on the hook is also sometimes very attractive to the big bream of those waters.

July, August, and September are the best months for bream, and if fine tackle is used it is possible to make a bag during the middle of the day, although I must confess that early morning and during the evening are more likely to be the most successful. Three or four lively gentles are also a source of attraction to this fish, while a wasp grub and a cad-bait will not be despised.

And now I must say a few words on the vexed question of the weather, and what effect it has on the bream of these waters. A very old bream fisherman once told me that years ago he has taken bream nearly all the year round—winter as well as summer and autumn—but even in those days it was by no means a certainty catching them as soon as November got well in. Personally I find winter fishing for bream of no great account; now and then I have taken a few odd ones when roach fishing during the depth of winter; but it is in my opinion hardly worth while going specially for them, say, during the Christmas holidays, unless the weather is very mild indeed. I also think there is no fish that swims that is so susceptible to sudden changes of the weather as bream, and I have even fancied that they could tell what was coming; for I have been out on what I considered at the time to be a perfect bream day, and met with no sport at all, and a few hours later a storm of cold wind and rain has swept across the district. I have heard very old fishermen say that the bream knew better than the anglers what weather was coming, and would not bite in face of a pending storm. I have proved the truth of this over and over again. In the chapter on roach fishing I noticed the peculiarities of water temperature: when sometimes the water was very much colder than the surrounding atmosphere, and at other times the water was warmer than the air around. The remarks I then penned as to the effects of this on roach feeding, can be applied with even more force to bream, particularly during the late autumn or early winter months. I remember one morning in early October, getting up at daybreak to join a friend at a bream swim. The rime frost hung heavy on the grass; the weather felt nearly like chilling us to the very bone, and to tell the truth I felt very much inclined to go back to bed; but we found on starting operations that the temperature of the water was in startling contrast to the outside air. By breakfast-time we finished off with 60lb. of fine bream. The would-be breamer should pay particular attention to these little matters, as his success or non-success may depend on a very simple thing; and I find that the temperature of the water plays a very important part in bream fishing. This is more particularly to be noticed in lakes, or deep quiet rivers. The best sport is obtained when a warm breeze ripples and disturbs the surface.

My directions for bream fishing in still waters can be summed up in a few brief sentences: use tackle as fine as you dare, fish well on the bottom, and ground-bait well a few days before you start to fish. And also remember that bream are very sensitive to vibration: a reckless stamping up and down the bank must be avoided, and when fishing from a boat or punt extra caution must be exercised. It will be as well to have some old worn-out sacks, or even door-mats on the bottom of the boat to deaden the vibration of the angler's feet. And, lastly, have an old coarse apron to wear when bream fishing; one that reaches from the chin down to the feet, or the birdlime-like slime that will stick to your clothes after a successful day will make you wish that you had never gone breaming, so awful is it. A friend of mine, who fishes in a small weedy lake that contains a very great number of large and slimy bream, has a special suit for the purpose; this is made of some washing material (drabbett, or jean), and is worn as overalls on the top of his ordinary clothes, and most certainly the advantage is very great. This friend has a special method of ground-baiting his bream swim. As soon as the season gets well in, he takes a large punt and moors it in the deepest and clearest part of the lake, leaving it there as a fixture the whole of the season, going backwards and forwards to it by means of a smaller punt.

After this punt has been fixed in its position for a week or so, to allow the fish to get used to it, he gives the bream a preliminary dose of most extraordinary ground bait, consisting of half a stone of scratchings, pounded up small and boiled, a couple of bushels of brewer's grains, a stone of bran, two stale loaves of bread soaked, half a peck of boiled wheat, and the contents of a bullock's stomach begged from the nearest slaughterhouse, a shovelful or two of good yellow clay completes the ingredients. These are all mixed well together and dropped in a semi-circle in front of the moored punt in balls about the size of oranges, taking care that they are distributed in a pretty considerable space; in fact, as far about as it is possible to reach in every direction with his baited tackle. Twice a week afterwards he renews the baiting, but never again in such enormous quantities as at first. A score balls of bread, bran, clay, and grains are, in his opinion, quite sufficient at once. Worms, tail-end of lob, and brandlings were his favourite baits. At times he varied this somewhat by using wasp grubs and sweet paste. Sometimes his catches bordered on the marvellous, odd times it was an utter impossibility to carry the fish home, that is by himself; and he assured me the last time I heard from him that last season the bream in the water appeared more numerous than ever, judging from the quantities seen on the surface during the early summer.

Before I close this chapter I might say that carp-bream are very often taken with the ledger; indeed, I know two or three very good anglers who always fish for them so. In quiet waters they use a bored lead not much bigger than a pistol bullet, while in heavier streams the size of the lead is increased. The gut line should be fine, and not more than a yard in length; and the lead should be put on a very fine length of gimp. See the instructions in Vol. 1 for ledgering for barbel, only in the case of bream the leads and tackle are finer, and the hook and bait smaller. Sometimes during a summer or autumn flood some good bream are picked up by light ledgering in the slacks and eddies along the grass slopes, back of bushes or trees, at dyke ends, by the side of a sunken fence; in fact, almost anywhere out of the rush of the main stream. Tail end of lob and red-worms are the best baits to employ under these conditions, and roving about stands the best chance of getting sport. Another little thing I should just like to mention, and that is, that some odd times, when fishing in deep and quiet waters, bream will strip every particle of worm from the hook and their presence be hardly felt or seen by even the most wideawake fisherman. He perhaps sees a tiny quiver or shake maybe of the float: our breamer strikes, and finds to his astonishment that his hook is clean and bare, and wonders however the fish managed to do it. Various dodges have been tried to counteract this, such as whipping another and smaller hook on the tackle an inch above the other one, and hanging the top end of the worm on this smaller, or lip hook, as it is known on the Trent. In my opinion this plan is only partly successful when the bream are biting in this fashion. It is the best to use as small a bait as possible, just enough to cover the point and shank of the hook, say about three-quarters of an inch from the tail of a small lob-worm or large brandling, threaded carefully as far as the end of the shank, and a tiny cockspur or brandling wriggling crossways on the point. The angler should strike promptly at anything he supposes to be the slightest indication of a bite; Mr. Bream may be suddenly astonished in his quiet bait-stealing operations. Anyhow, I know it is worth trying; many of my best bream have been hooked when adopting this dodge. I must now bring my remarks to a close, and hope my readers will derive some benefits from the experiences herein roughly described; anyhow, if they get as much pleasure in reading them as I have had in penning them I shall be amply repaid for my trouble, and may all of you enjoy tight lines and a clear conscience when you go a-fishing.

BEING A PRACTICAL TREATISE ON ANGLING WITH FLOAT,
PATERNOSTER, AND LEGER, IN STILL WATER
AND STREAM.

INCLUDING CHAPTERS ON SPINNING WITH NATURAL
AND ARTIFICIAL BAITS, AND ALSO LIVE
AND DEAD GORGING.

BY J. W. MARTIN,
THE "TRENT OTTER."

A Working Man Angler's Experiences; written expressly for the benefit of his brethren of the Craft.

WITH ILLUSTRATIONS.

ALL RIGHTS RESERVED.

PUBLISHED BY
THE ANGLER, LIMITED, AT THE OFFICES, SCARBOROUGH,
1898.

Prefatory Introduction

My Dear Brother Fishermen,—The two small companion volumes that I had the honour and pleasure of introducing to you about a year ago, have been received with considerable success. I am deeply grateful to you all for your kindness, and wish now to still further increase my obligations in that respect. To this end I beg to introduce to your, I hope, favourable consideration, the present little effort of my pen, which is part 4, vol. 3, of the series ; and which I entitle, "Pike and Perch Fishing."

This book is not intended solely for the benefit of well-to-do pike fishermen, who can travel far and wide for their sport, and who have the very best private waters in the kingdom at their disposal; and plenty of money to purchase any and every pike tackle and artificial that takes their fancy. It is rather the working man angler, who has few opportunities to wet his line in well-stocked private lakes and rivers, that I am more particularly addressing in the following pages.

The latter class of angler is extremely anxious to have put before him the simplest and most inexpensive method that can be adopted in well-fished public waters. His pockets have not much of a golden lining, and if he can successfully ply his craft at an expenditure of only a few shillings, he will like it far better than if a whole host of things were set before him and most strongly recommended.

To this end I have brought my own experiences as a working man angler, who has had to toil in factory and farmyard, to bear; and have given what I consider to be the simplest and most effective methods to adopt in all conditions of pike and perch fishing, that the ordinary working man will have placed at his disposal.

This question was once summed up neatly by a journeyman sweep, who one day was spinning a likely-looking stretch of the Trent; his attention had been called to a paragraph in one of the sporting papers, in which it was stated that "Mr. S, fishing Lord B's private lake, had succeeded in landing a splendid bag of large pike." "Ah," said our friend the sweep, at the same time jerking his head in the direction of a woman and two children sitting on the bank, "If Mr. S., the noted pike slayer, was on this, or any other well-fished public water, and had his wife and two kids sitting on the bank, waiting while he caught a jack, which had also to be sold before a bit of bread could be procured for their breakfasts, same as they are waiting for over yonder, I reckon his bags would not be much heavier than the rest of us anglers are." I hope none of my readers will be so hard up as to depend for their breakfasts on the fish they catch, but the little incident is useful in illustrating my meaning.

Personally I don't pretend to have any literary ability. What I have written is only a plain statement of fact, and written as one old worker would write to his mates. Neither do I pretend to be a better fisherman than hundreds more that are found in almost any big town and city in England. I know just enough to amuse myself, but I do claim to be an observant angler; one who notes any strange thing that comes his way, and who does not rest contented until he has reasoned out for himself the why and wherefore of it. Added to this, I have had peculiar advantages that does not come within reach of the generality of my poorer brethren. I have been an angler from my earliest boyhood, and constantly thrown in the society of men who are angling gems of the very first water.

These are a few of the considerations that prompt me to hope for a favourable reception at your hands, of this little volume. I won't promise you an elaborately illustrated, and finely got-up book, but I will promise you a most carefully written, and at the same time plain essay on pike and perch fishing, so that the veriest novice will not stumble during his journey through its pages. For I have taken the liberty of assuming that some of you are novices pure and simple, who know next to nothing on the subject here specially treated.

The principles I lay down are the principles of economy, coupled with the most effective results that a lifetime's experience has suggested and studied from many and various standpoints. I also dedicate this volume to my fellow working men anglers, and ask them to treat it and me as favourably as they can.

1898.

JOHN WM. MARTIN,
"*The Trent Otter.*"

Contents.

PART IV.—PIKE AND PERCH.

     PAGE

CHAPTER I.—THE PIKE AND HIS CHARACTERISTICS.
Ancient writers on the pike—Description of the pike—His habits—His ferocity and voracity—Tench as food, or doctor—The haunts of pike—Jack in a baited swim—Weight and growth of pike—Jack fishing in public waters, a contrast—The first English writer on pike and pike fishing—The gander and the pike—Pike in ancient times—Pike on the table—Different methods of jack fishing -   1

CHAPTER II.—THE PIKE *(continued)*.
PIKE RODS, REELS, AND LINES.
The pike rod—What it has to do—How it should be made—Different woods and canes suitable for pike rods—Rod rings and ferrules—Pike reels—The Malloch casting reel—Slater's cage guard reel—Allcock's pike reels—The plain Nottingham reel—The line—How to dress or waterproof a pike line—The line dryer—Landing nets and gaff hooks—Flight cases and haversacks—Rod and tackle varnish 20

CHAPTER III.—THE PIKE *(continued)*.
CASTING OUT THE BAIT.
Different methods of casting—The Nottingham style—The right-handed cast—The cast from the left hand—How to cast from the reel—Weights and their distribution—The forward swing—Casting with a coiled line—A peculiar cast 43

CHAPTER IV.—THE PIKE *(continued)*.
SPINNING WITH A NATURAL BAIT.
Spinning, what it is—A simple spinning tackle—The Chapman spinner and its contemporaries—Flights and their uses—The spinning trace—Best baits for spinning—"The Trent Otter's" spinning flight—How to bait it—A good season—How to spin to have the best results—Different methods for different waters—Condition of the water—Clouded *v.* clear water spinning—Spinning in deep and sluggish waters—Changing the bait—Striking, playing, and landing a pike—Haunts of pike during the different months—Spinning leads—Preserving dead baits - - - - - - 55

Contents.

CHAPTER V.—THE PIKE *(continued)*
SPINNING WITH AN ARTIFICIAL.
Artificial baits—What shape and colour is likely to have the best results—A seeming contradiction—Three typical Artificials—How to spin an artificial—Best time, water, and places to try artificials—Wind and weather—Ice in the rings of the rod - - - - - - - - - 78

CHAPTER VI.—THE PIKE *(continued).*
TROLLING WITH A DEAD GORGE.
The reel, line, and tackle—How to bait a dead gorge—Working the trolling bait—Different methods of dead-gorging - - 86

CHAPTER VII.—THE PIKE *(continued).*
FISHING WITH A LIVE BAIT.
Different methods of live baiting—Pike floats and pilots—Snap tackles, and the methods of baiting—Traces for live baiting—Stream fishing for pike—The slider float—Striking, and playing a pike on float tackle—The proper depth—A contrast—Live gorging—Paternostering for pike—Legering—Queer live baits—Live bait kettles and store boxes - - 92

CHAPTER VIII.—THE PERCH.
PERCH AND PERCH FISHING.
The veteran and his first perch—Habits and haunts of perch—Perch packing in the winter—A cruel slaughter—Description of the perch—Weight of perch—" His eyes bigger than his belly "—Perch in the frying pan—Rod, reel, line, and tackle for perch fishing—Stream fishing for perch—Paternostering—Float fishing with a minnow—Fly fishing—Artificial baits for perch - - - - - - - 112

PART 4.

THE PIKE.

CHAPTER I.

THE PIKE AND HIS CHARACTERISTICS.

Ancient writers on the pike—Description of the pike—His habits—His ferocity and voracity—Tench as food or doctor—The haunts of pike—Jack in a baited swim—Weight and growth of pike—Jack fishing in public waters, a contrast—The first English writer on pike and pike fishing—The gander and the pike—Pike in ancient times—Pike on the table—Different methods of jack fishing.

> "He loves no streams, but hugs the silent deeps,
> And eats all hours, and yet no house he keeps."

So sang Theophilus Franck a good many years ago, when writing of "that mercenary, the lucit or pike." And all writers, both in prose and poetry, that have taken this fish as a text, are pretty well agreed in the general character they give him. They looked upon his formidable teeth, his wicked eyes, and his villainous aspect as being quite sufficient to inspire any amount of terrible description; even the very look and sound of his name they found to be suggestive of voracity and ferocity. Indeed, the very first writer who mentions the pike—viz., the Latin poet Ausonius, who, writing about the fourth century—says,

> "The wary Luce, 'midst wrack and rushes hid,
> The scourge and terror of the scaly brood."

and Pope, too, sings of him in much the same strains when he says,

> "And pikes, the tyrants of the watery plains."

"The Innocent Epicure," written about the year 1697, contains the following lines:

> "Go on, my muse, next let thy numbers speak
> That mighty Nimrod of the streams, the pike."

These two or three examples go to prove that even old

writers, when trolling for pike was very little known, or at most only in its infancy, regarded the pike as a fish of character preying upon his smaller and weaker kindred; while the very look of his powerful and cruel jaws they held to be sufficient to strike terror into the hearts of the timid and superstitious people of those days.

Years ago, when I only had what I could claim as a very rudimentary knowledge of this fish and his habits, I used to eagerly read everything connected with him that I could possibly get hold of, and, like a true enthusiast, believe it all; and the more wild and improbable the story, the greater was my belief. But viewed nowadays, by the cold light of several years' practical experience, I am sadly afraid that there have been more lies—to put it in very plain English—told about our pike than are exactly good for his character and reputation. For instance, look at that tale that is mentioned, I should suppose, in dozens of books on angling and natural history, about that giant pike, said to have been captured in 1497, out of a lake in the vicinity of Manheim, which legend or tradition said had a medal fastened to one of his gills with an inscription saying it had been turned into the lake by Frederick the Second in the year 1232! It would appear from this that that pike had lived over 250 years, and had survived many social and political changes. But the most astounding part of this fish fable was not exactly its Old Parr-like antiquity, but the giant size it was said to have attained, being no less than 19ft. in length, and reaching a weight of 350 lb.; and then to prove the statement they tell us that his skeleton could be seen by anyone interested, as it is, or was, carefully preserved in the Manheim Museum; but unfortunately on a careful examination of this skeleton by a naturalist, he came to the conclusion that it was a clever deception, and had evidently been built up for the occasion.

Our English pike, or jack, as it is generally called nowadays, when in good condition is a handsome fish, and a fish that is much sought after by anglers of all degrees. I know of no other fish for whose capture such a bewildering quantity of artificial baits, spinning tackles and flights, live-bait tackles, floats, and traces have been invented.

The scientific name of the pike is " Esox Lucius," and on looking up a dictionary I find he is described thus:—" So called from the shape of his head and jaws. **Head depressed, large,** oblong, blunt; jaws, palatine bones and **vomer furnished** with teeth of various sizes; **body, elongated, rounded on the back,** sides **compressed, covered** with scales; dorsal fin placed far back over **the anal fin;** whole body mottled with white, yellow, and **green."** Walton calls the pike " a solitary, melancholy, and bold fish," and certainly this is a very good description, although some odd times they may be found congregated together in **considerable** numbers; but speaking generally they are not **very** often discovered in shoals like roach, dace, and bream; more often than not, especially during **the** winter months, are they solitary tenants of a quiet reedy **corner, away from** the rush **of the main stream, sole** monarchs of that **small** domain, ready to pounce out **at a moment's** notice on any unwary roach or dace that happens to **stray within** striking distance. **One** writer describing the habits and haunts of the pike uses a few **sentences** that are worth repeating, **he** says: " Shrouded from observation in **his** solitary retreat, he follows with his eye the shoals of fish **that wander** heedlessly along; he marks the water-rat swimming **to his burrow,** the ducklings paddling among the water-weeds, **the dabchick** and the moor-hen swimming leisurely on the surface; **he** selects his victim, and like the tiger springing **from the** jungle he rushes forth, seldom missing his aim; **there is a** sudden swirl **and splash,** circle after circle forms on the surface of the water, and all **is** still again in **an** instant." A long catalogue of fables and traditions have been handed down from **one writer to another on** this point of our jack's savage ferocity, and also on his marvellous powers of diges**tion;** and none of these traditions seem to lose anything by being repeated, **and I don't** know that they **need,** for he has well earned **that** name given him by certain writers—the " freshwater shark." What he won't take as a bait would be rather **a more** difficult question to answer than what he will, for there are hundreds of anecdotes told about him, and the astounding things he will seize at a pinch. One writer says " that a swan was once noticed on a lake with its head and neck under the water; the circumstances seemed so peculiar that a boat was procured, and on proceeding to the spot it was discovered that a pike had swallowed the head of the swan, which was firmly fixed in his throat, and being unable to extricate themselves from this extraordinary difficulty the pair of them were dead." I should not suppose the pike opened his ponderous jaws with intent to swallow the swan altogether; perhaps he only saw the head and neck deep down in the water, and had not noticed the body attached. Anyhow, for once in a way he had made a fatal mistake. Another anecdote mentions a pike seizing the lips of a mule that had gone to the edge of the lake to drink; and still another historian puts on record that a pike seized the foot of a Polish woman who had stepped into a stream. But we can hardly take these statements seriously, for, personally, when I have got into close quarters with pike, and peered ever so cautiously through the flags and rushes at them, as soon as ever my eyes met the wicked-looking ones of the fish, like a flash of light he would vanish, and leave scarcely a ripple behind. Once, however, I saw a 4lb. jack maul the hand of a keeper badly, and the strangest part of the story was that the jack had been out of the water nearly two hours. After packing up the rods and tackle, the keeper threw the fish out of the boat on to the grassy bank, and some few minutes afterwards stooped down to pick it up again, when, to our utter astonishment, as soon as his hand neared the jack it made a sudden grab and seized him by the thick part of his thumb, inflicting some nasty cuts, which were weeks before they healed up. The keeper said he was served the same trick once before, only that time he had got the fish home, and was going to remove them from a pump trough after washing, when one collared him in the same way. This was the painful experience of Harry Rout, the then keeper of the Huntingdon Angling Society's water, and the memory of that wounded hand haunts me to this day, and causes me to impress most strongly on the young pike fisher that on no account must he put his hands too near the jaws of a jack, for if he does get operated on with those horrible teeth, he will most likely remember it for the rest of his natural life. Be very careful in disengaging hooks from pike. Always carry a short heavy bludgeon, and as soon as Mr. Jack is safely landed, hit him two or three smart raps fair between the eyes; this will effectually stun him and cause him to widely open his mouth, when the hooks can be poked out with a long disgorger. But I must get back to my text. It has also been put on record that the body of a child was once found in the stomach of a pike. I have never found anything so strange as that in any of the jack I have opened; but rats, chickens, young ducks, moor-hens, and fish of various kinds I have often discovered. Pike have been known to get themselves in strange difficulties, and no possible chance of extricating themselves; but I should question if ever a pair of them were in a queerer fix than the two exhibited in the South Kensington Museum. These two jack, that weighed together about 19lb., and nearly of the same size, are firmly fixed together, the head of one, up to the termination of the gills, being tight in the throat of the other. A boatman saw them struggling together in Loch Tay, locked in each other's jaws, and promptly gaffed them, sending them to Mr. Buckland without being separated, who took a cast of them. We can only wonder what these fish were doing—fighting, perhaps. I should not suppose that one of them opened his mouth with the deliberate intention of swallowing the other, for they are both of a size, unless one of them was suffering from some curious deformity of vision. In Sweden, the land of enormous perch and pike, it is no infrequent occurrence for very large perch to swallow the baited hooks of stationary night-lines, and then for pike in their turn to swallow the hooked perch. In this case, though the pike himself is hardly ever hooked, yet the perch, with the help of his spiked fins and hard scales, sets so fast in the throat of the greedy tyrant that he is unable to get rid of it, and both are taken. Pike when hungry will seize almost anything that is moving in the water which bears the least resemblance to a small fish, a rat, or a young moor-hen; but when he is not on the feed hardly anything will tempt him. Expert pike fishers know very well the difference between the "runs," as they are called, when he is hungry, and when he is not. When not hungry he will often play with a bait; and have no intention of taking it fairly so that he can be hooked. He will often allow himself to be hauled about, and even dragged up to the surface of the water, only, with a flap of his tail, to drop the bait from his jaws, and roll over again into the deep water; and you could almost fancy there was a mocking grin during the process on his villainous looking face. I think it is a good job that the pike are more often off the feed than on, because if they were always hungry there would, in waters were they are plentiful and carefully preserved, be nothing else left with them either alive or dead, for most assuredly everything else that could be eaten would be speedily cleared out; for one authority tells us that a jack when on the feed will eat his own weight in gudgeons and other small fish in the course of a few days. The Rev. Mr. Manley, a gifted writer on the habits and history of our fresh water fishes, says of the pike, "that in reality nothing comes amiss to him. He has no more taste, in the true sense of the word, than he has feeling. All's fish, at least food, that comes into his net. Certainly when left to his natural devices he is a sort of gentleman who would eat the toast on which asparagus is placed to drain, the tinfoil in which Rochefort cheese is enwrapped, the crust of a game pie, or the envelopment of an Oxford brawn. The only wonder is how he can manage to live at all in certain waters. The truth is he is endowed with the power of long fasting, which doubtless he often exercises, either from necessity or choice." But in spite of his great voracity, there are certain things that he does not care much about; he does not like a toad, though he is dearly fond of a frog. It has also been said that he will have nothing to do with a perch; perhaps he may not care about them much, and would pass them by if plenty of other food existed in the water, but I knew one very large pond in the county of Lincoln, that contained nothing else, as far as we could make out, except jack, perch, eels, and a few tench; and yet a small perch about the length of your finger was the only bait, except an occasional frog, that was any use at all to the pike of that water. And then again we hear that he won't have anything to do with a tench; but I knew a gentleman who brought down to a well known pike water a can of small tench, carp, and gold fish, and got half-a-dozen right good jack with the tench as bait; and strange as it may seem, not a single run did he get with the much more brilliant gold fish. Izaak Walton says on this point that "the tench is the physician of fishes, for the pike especially, who forbears to devour him, be he never so hungry." Other old writers have also strongly endorsed this opinion; saying that the slime or touch of tenches, was a certain cure for wounds, cuts, or ailments in the fishy tribe generally; and the pike more particularly. But I am sadly afraid this is only an old legend that has not much solid foundation in fact. If it was true, and our jack could reason for himself like a human being, he might spare him, for no man who is in possession of his senses would want to swallow his doctor. I also read some time ago, that a quantity of tench were turned into a lake that contained a lot of ill-conditioned pike as an experiment, and some time afterwards the pike improved to a remarkable extent! but it did not state positively if this result was due to simply the presence of the tench in the water, or whether the increase of condition was due to the supply of fresh food, that was so generously and plentifully at hand in the shape of that stock of tench. The writer rather hinted that he thought it was entirely due to simply the presence of the tench in the water. I am also afraid that this statement is not worth much, for I knew a sheet of water in Nottinghamshire that contained a large quantity of very fine tench, but the few jack that shared the water with them were the ugliest and most ill-conditioned brutes we ever caught. I fancy that for pike to be in good condition depends more on the water they inhabit, and the abundance of natural food in the water with them, than just turning a few tench in. I don't believe that turning a hundred or two of tench in a real bad jack water will improve the breed and condition of the latter to any permanent extent. As I said a little while ago, the pike, generally speaking, is a solitary fish, though large ones are often found in pairs. After floods and frosts, or owing to some accidental circumstances, they may sometimes be found collected together in numbers in favourable eddies, or in a backwater away from the main stream, or at the tail end of an island where the stream is, as it were, cut in two, with a considerable quiet eddy between those two streams. By the side of reed beds, among flags and rushes, in corners and lay-byes, at e tail ends of old lochs, up deepish backwaters, or a cutting that has an entrance into the river. A deepish corner away from the main stream, particularly if it is fringed along the edge with a dense undergrowth of weeds, and water-lilies, with a scattered crop of flags and rushes here and there, is, generally speaking, a capital spot in which to find pike. Sometimes very good ones are met with in the rough water close under a weir, more particularly if some very large stones stick up above the surface of the water, and a deep eddy is formed at the back, in which the frothing waters keep churning round and round. I have taken some very good jack from similar situations; once in particular I got an eight-pounder with a spoon bait, from close under the foot of a weir, in an eddy barely six feet by three, and not more than two feet deep, that was formed by an old tree root that had been swept over the weirs. In swift running rivers like the Trent it is only occasionally that they are met with in midstream where the current is strong, preferring to hug the shore, particularly if that shore has an overhanging bank, and is thickly fringed with willow boughs, weeds, and flags. If they are found out in the main stream, it is generally at a very deep bend, where the water does not race along at such speed as it does over the shallows; at these places during the early autumn good jack are often picked up by knowing anglers, who sink a spinning bait deep down in midstream, and slowly wind it home. In slow running rivers like the Bedfordshire Ouse, it does not so particularly matter selecting the deepest corners; indeed, during the late summer and early autumn the shallows and weedy places, over which a slight stream wanders along, even if less than a yard in depth, and the spinning bait has to be so manipulated that it must not, for fear of catching the weeds, be allowed to sink even three inches under the surface, are by far the best places to try. During the winter when the weather is cold and frosty, the deeps can be tried with more chance of success; although this is not a hard and fast rule, as I have taken good pike from very shallow water in the Ouse, when the weather has been very severe indeed, but still taking it all round, the deeps show the best results when the weather is very cold. As for good pike lakes; these are generally preserved and protected to such an extent, that the average working-man-angler does not get many chances to wet a line in them. It is not such a difficult matter to find out the haunts of pike in lakes, as it is in rivers; although I am aware that even in the circumscribed space of a small pike lake, those fish have their favourite haunts, some places being tenanted very thickly, while other parts would have next to nothing in them. I remember once going with a gentleman to fish a small lake of some four or five acres, in which he had been given to understand were a lot of good jack; we wandered three parts of the way round that pond trying all likely and even unlikely places, but never saw a pike move, until at last we came to the opposite corner, within fifty yards from where we started, and there we found the home of those fish. I should say that fully nine-tenths of the pike in that lake were in a good deal less than half-an-acre of water. Sometimes when the bottom fisherman has groundbaited a swim in a river some considerable time, and has been enjoying capital sport, the fish suddenly go off the feed. It is quite likely under the circumstances, if the water contains pike, that several of those customers have been attracted into the swim, putting the other fish off the feed, if not exactly scaring them away altogether. Some of the very best bags of jack I can remember, have been taken under these circumstances; some lively dace have been procured, fixed on snap tackle, and run down the whole of the swim, which resulted in the baited bream swim, or whatever it was, being cleared of those pike, and the sport among the other fish recommenced. I heard the late Jim Chatterton once say, that a friend and himself took thirteen in one afternoon ranging from two to ten pounds each, out of a barbel swim in the Corporation Fishery on the Trent, after they had tried for two days without result to catch the fish they baited the place for. It suddenly struck him that the pike had taken possession, because they had been having such good sport among the dace, roach, chub, and bream, a few days before.

A trial proved this theory to be correct. I could select from my own experiences several more instances of the same kind, but I have said enough I think to give our young fisherman a useful hint. Pike spawn between the latter end of February and the end of April, or even under exceptional circumstances right to the middle of May, but it all depends on the state of the weather, as to whether they are early or late. I have noticed them pairing as early as February and in the same season observed them even as late as the second week in May; in fact, I have an idea that it is a long and trying time for them. During this operation they seek all sorts of dykes, ditches, creeks, and backwaters, depositing the ova among the weeds, and so lazy and absorbed are they, that scarcely anything will frighten them. Scores of them have been lifted out with wire snares, or even scooped out with landing nets; to say nothing of snatch hooks on the end of a pole. It is not to be wondered at considering the long and exhausting time they take over spawning, that they should be in the very worst possible condition for several weeks after that operation; they are long, thin, slimy, and even unwholesome as food, and should not on any account be tried for before August, in fact, I don't consider them in condition before the first of October. If my opinion was asked as to what I should consider to be a proper close time for jack, I should most certainly say, between the first day of February, and the first day of September.

Pike, under favourable circumstances, will grow to a very large size, but their well being depends upon the locality and condition of the water they inhabit. Deep holes and weedy shallows should both be in evidence, while if the place is a lake with a gravelly bottom, a stream of some sort should run right through it, so that a constant supply of fresh water could be assured, and last, but not least, the lake should also contain an abundance of natural food; these conditions together with a careful preservation, would be condusive to these fish reaching their very heaviest weight. As to what that weight is likely to be, it is difficult to determine, for so many fables and romances have been written on the subject; that we have to be very careful before accepting all of them. We are told that in some of the large

Irish lakes they have been taken of the extraordinary weight of eighty pounds, **but I** don't suppose anyone ever saw one that weight, it was most probably a tradition handed down from father to son, and most likely grew in the process. If tremendous **pike** like those were got by our fathers in the days that are **past, how** is it **that with our** improved tackle and means of getting at them, we never hear of anything approaching that weight being captured. Pliny, the ancient writer, mentions a fish which he called the Esox, and which attained the weight of a 1,000lbs; but it cannot be identified with the Esox of the present day. I should say the **very** top weight would not exceed forty to forty-five pounds. **We** have authentic instances of late years of odd ones nearly reaching the former weight; but they were like angels' visits, few and far between. Perhaps the heaviest brace of pike that have ever been taken by any one angler, with rod and line, were **the pair taken** by Mr. Jardine, which were weighed in at a Club, and registered no less than thirty-six pounds each **on** the average. We hear of odd ones being taken every season in Ireland, that reach thirty pounds; and sometimes, perhaps once in every two or three seasons, one will reach thirty-four, or thirty-five pounds. An article appeared in the "Angler," last December, 1896, giving an account of an extraordinary female pike, **that had** been taken dead from Dowdeswell reservoir, near Cheltenham, which reached the weight of sixty pounds; at least it was said to have weighed that, but one gentleman who saw the fish, said he should be inclined to knock at least 10lbs off. It appears that the weighing in had been done in a very hasty manner, owing to the fact that decomposition had set in; and the smell was something alarming. So **I am** afraid this pike can only be set down among the list of guess-weights, and cannot be accepted by **any means.** It was also said that the Duke of Newcastle has **a** pike, which he himself or one of his family caught in Clumber Lake (a large sheet of water close **to his** Grace's Nottinghamshire seat), which weighed, when captured, 42½lbs.; but the Duke contradicted this and said, if my memory is correct, that gossip this time had added eight pounds to its original weight. Clumber Lake, I should say, is one of the finest pike preserves in England; and if large pike can be found anywhere, surely that is the place to look for them. I once asked old Charlie Hudson, a Trent professional fisherman, who had fished a celebrated reach of that river for nigh on fifty years, if he or any of his patrons had taken many pike over twenty pounds in weight from those splendid waters. Four only was his answer; and during the long period referred to, he had some hundreds of patrons and customers; the united weight of the four was 87½lbs., largest a trifle over 25lbs., and the strangest part about the capture of the latter, was that it was taken with a worm, when bream fishing in that tremendously deep hole on the Lower Trent known as Dunham Dubs. Taking the Trent all round it is only occasionally that specimens exceeding twenty pounds are taken. The Hampshire Avon, perhaps, is as good as any other river in England for large jack, some odd times we hear of one being taken that scaled up to nearly thirty pounds. The angler can well be satisfied as things go nowadays, if he can get one from any public waters that will go from twenty to twenty-five pounds, and this, perhaps, will only be once in a lifetime, while if he gets a dozen fish during the whole of his angling career, that would go from twelve to eighteen pounds apiece, why he may consider himself fortunate, unless he has access to real good private waters.

I once heard a very old and observant angler naturalist say, that he firmly believed two kinds of pike existed in British waters; externally there was little or nothing to tell the difference, except the size, one sort he believed would reach 20 or 30lb., the other never exceeded four pounds, and in support of this he cited the case of two sheets of water, some miles apart, exactly similar in their size, depth, and general characteristics, both had gravelly bottoms, both were fringed with weeds, flags, and rushes; both were fed by small streams from the higher lands, each contained a good supply of eels, tench, roach, bream, and perch; in fact, the general surroundings of the two were as far as could be ascertained, exactly similar. He had fished in both of them for many years—in one he had taken pike up to 20lb. In the other he never saw, nor yet caught one that exceeded 4lb. There may be something in this; but several other things may also have to be taken into account before a true decision can be arrived at on that point. Shortly then, as this seems to be a question that a lot of interest is evinced in, we may say that a forty pounder is a tip-topper, and one not likely to be caught above once in twenty years, whereas if a lucky fisherman did manage to fairly and squarely land, with rod and line, a brace of pike that exceeds Mr. Jardine's pair in size, why, all I can say is, that not only should the fish be carefully set up, but the angler as well, and he ought to, at the very least, have a niche all to himself in Westminster Abbey, with a brass plate setting forth his achievement. Some anglers seem to think that jack and pike are two separate and distinct fish; that there is a distinction if not much difference between them. Years ago it was an accepted rule to call this fish, if under four or five pounds in weight, a jack, and anything over the latter weight a pike, but gradually this distinctive title has been given up, and all of them, no matter how large or how small, have of late years been more often called jack than pike; so the reader must bear in mind that in using the two names in the following pages, I refer to one and the same fish. We are told by the learned in such matters that a jack will reach eight inches in length during his first year, after hatching from the ova; that during his second year he will go up to fifteen inches; and in his third, total up to twenty, or possibly he might scale as much as four pounds when three years old. After this he increases at the rate of from two or three pounds a year until he is twelve years old; after which he decreases slightly and gets still more thin every year, as old age creeps on him. Naturalists have given him a lease of life extending to forty years, and say that he is the longest lived of any of our fresh water fish; and that when one is captured in the last stages of consumption, long, lanky, and thin, it is a very old fish. I remember a friend of mine once capturing a jack in the Ouse, some three of four miles below Huntingdon, that was the most extraordinary I ever saw; it was no less than 38 inches in length, it had a tremendous head and mouth, and yet it scaled only 6¾lb. I never saw such an eel-like body attached to a pike before; its teeth were wonderfully long, as black as ink, and quite soft. I should say that those calculations as to the weight a jack will put on in a given number of years will depend a good deal on the nature and character of the water he inhabits. I believe it would have to be an extra good water for a jack in a natural way to reach four pounds when three years old, and then increase to seven pounds in his next year. If he is an inhabitant of an indifferent pond, where he only could get an occasional frog, a young moor hen, or a mouthful of tadpoles, it would probably take him ten years to put on four pounds.

As I said at the outset of this chapter, the pike is a fish that is very much sought after by the angler, and good pike fishing, out of public waters at any rate, can hardly now-a-days be expected. When I say good fishing, I mean as it was even during my memory, where a dozen good fish to one rod in a day's spinning was thought nothing extra. Or go back a little further still; but for all that during the memory of an old angler still living, who told me last time I saw him, that he could remember the time when flags and rushes grew in abundance all along the brink of the Trent, and had seen the big jack bolt out of the reeds every few steps; and when employed as puntsman by the late Dr. Waterworth and Mr. Cafferata, he could remember them taking as many as thirty pike during a single afternoon, many of them fish from eight to fifteen pounds apiece. It was also nothing unusual for Tom Beck (an old netter still living), to go down the river to the Meering ferry and Sutton Holme in those days, and take in a net a hundredweight of good jack during a single evening. I can myself remember very well, the late Sam Hibbert, when he rented the Staythorpe fishery on the Trent, getting some splendid bags of pike, nearly every-time he cared to go. But since those days pike fishermen have increased a hundred-fold, and any public water known to contain jack is nearly hunted to death, with the result that they are wofully thinned down; and it is only occasionally that a good bag is made. Suitable pike waters should be constantly re-stocked now-a-days, and a stringent bye-law should be made and enforced, to regulate the size of jack allowed to be taken. All this means money, but still I firmly believe that angling and preservation societies will have to tackle the subject if decent jack fishing in public waters is to be enjoyed much longer. Far different, however, is a day in a real good private water; if everything is favourable the sport to be had would be something to be remembered. There are still, however, a few very fair public pike waters in England, the vast army of fishermen notwithstanding. The rivers and broads of Norfolk and Suffolk being notable examples. The Ouse, as it flows from Buckinghamshire right away down to Denver Sluice, being very fair indeed in many of its reaches; while the County of Lincoln still upholds its reputation for jack. The best season's pike fishing I ever enjoyed, taking it all through, was had less than ten years ago, when I lived on the banks of the Ouse. During that season I took in public water, with rod and line, during my spare time, which was generally two half-days a week—weather and water permitting—109 sizeable jack, not counting the scores put back that were undersized. The most I ever landed from that river in one day was 21, but only seven of them went over 4lbs. The great bulk of my fish have been taken spinning. On two occasions at least, I can remember having had more and far heavier jack than the instance just referred to; but they were from a private water, and a good many years ago. I just mention this as fishermen, in general, like to know how a writer himself has got on; but I may have to refer to this again, when dealing with the various subjects in the chapters that follow. The anxious novice who would like to become a successful pike fisherman, must make up his mind, if he follows this branch of angling in public waters, to two things, viz., he is bound to catch more fish under four pounds than over that weight, and if he gets three or four jack during a day's spinning or live-baiting, he can consider himself extremely lucky. I should say that pike fishing engaged the attention of our forefathers a good many years ago, and trolling with a dead gorge bait, and live baiting, more or less after the fashion that we do it now, were the methods most in vogue. Dame Juliana Berners, who wrote the very first book on angling that was ever penned, gives some very queer and amusing instructions in the art of catching pike. I give one or two examples, as they may prove interesting to those fishermen who never have a chance of seeing the good old lady's book:—

"Take a codlynge hoke, and take a roche or a fresh heeryng, and a wyre with an hole in the ende, and put it in at the mouth, and out at the taylle, down by the ridge of the fresshe herryng; and thenne put the hoke in after, and drawe the hoke into the cheke of the freshe heeryng; then put a plumbe of lead upon your lyne a yarde longe from your hoke, and a flote in mid waye betwene; and caste it in a pytte where the pyke usyth, and this is the best and moost surest crafte of takynge the pyke. Another manere of takynge him there is; take a frosshe (frog) and put it on your hoke, at the necke, betwene the skynne and the body, on the backe half, and put on a flote a yerde therefro, and caste it where the pyke hauntyth, and ye shall have hym. Another manere: take the same bayte, and put it in assafetida, and caste it in the water wyth a corde and a corke, and ye shall not fayl of hym." And then again the good Dame instructeth:—"And if ye lyst to have a good sporte, thenne tye the corde to a gose fote, and ye shall have a gode halyngne, whether the gose or the pyke shall have the better."

This sort of sport, tying a baited hook to the leg of a goose, seems to have been highly popular in former times; for another old writer on fishing matters tells us that:—

"The principle sport to take a pike is to take a goose or gander, or duck; take one of the pike lines, tie the line under the left wing, and over the right wing, about the body, as a man weareth his belt; turn the goose off into the pond where the pikes are; there is no doubt of sport, with great pleasure, betwixt the goose and the pike; it is the greatest sport and pleasure that a noble gentleman in Shropshire doth give his friends entertainment with."

Another account of a struggle between a pike and a gander, was published many years ago, and ran as follows: —"A farmer in the immediate neighbourhood of Lochmaben, Dumfriesshire, kept a gander, who not only had a great trick of wandering himself, but also delighted in piloting forth his cackling harem to weary themselves in circumnavigating their native lake, or in straying amid forbidden fields on the opposite shore. Wishing to check this vagrant habit, he one day seized the gander as he was about to spring into the pure breast of his native element, and, tying a large fish hook to his leg, to which was attached part of a dead frog, he suffered him to proceed upon his voyage of discovery. As had been anticipated, this bait soon caught the eye of a greedy pike, which, swallowing the deadly hook, not only arrested the progress of the astonished gander, but forced him to perform half-a-dozen somersaults on the face of the water! For some time the struggle was most amusing, the fish pulling and the bird screaming with all its might, the one attempting to fly and the other attempting to swim from the invisible enemy; the gander the one moment losing, and the next regaining his centre of gravity, and casting between whiles many a rueful look at his snow white fleet of geese and goslings, who cackled out their sympathy for their afflicted commodore. At length victory declared in favour of the feathered angler, who, bearing away for the nearest shore, landed on the smooth green grass one of the finest pike ever caught in the castle loch. This adventure is said to have cured the gander of his propensity for wandering."

This pike fishing by tying the bait to the leg of a goose smacks very much of trimmer fishing with a moveable trimmer all alive and kicking. I should not suppose that anybody would attempt to entertain their friends with sport of this description, now-a-days, whatever might have been thought about it fifty years ago. As far back as the reign of Henry II., the pike formed part of the coat of arms of the Lucy, or Lucie family, and is one of the earliest recorded instances of fish being used in English heraldry. Old Historians tell us, "that during the reign of Edward I. this fish was so very scarce and dear, that very few could afford to eat it, the price being double that of salmon, and ten times higher than either turbot or cod." A well known authority says that the reason of this is most likely in the fact, that pike had then only just been introduced into this country, and as a natural consequence was very scarce. Coming down a little later to the time of Edward III. we find, "that this fish was most carefully preserved, kept in stews, and fed. In 1446 jack was one of the chief dishes in the High Church festival given in that year by George Neville, Archbishop of York. During the reign of Henry VIII. it fetched as much again as house lamb in February, and a very small pickerel was dearer than a fat capon; and jack figured on all the menus of civic banquets in London and elsewhere for many generations." Personally I look upon pike as being a very fair fish for the table, that is, if the water they were caught in was of first class quality; if he came out of a muddy stagnant pond, I don't suppose he would be up to much; but a good river or lake pike, where the water is fresh, the bottom gravelly, and the food plentiful, is by no means to be despised. I quoted just now some examples from old history, in which this fish was very highly esteemed. An old couplet ran thus:

> " Lo! the rich pike, to entertain your guest,
> Smokes on the board, and decks a royal feast."

While on the other hand some of the ancients did not think much of him, for Ausonius, the Latin poet, writing about the fourth century of the Christian era, says of him as

> " Unknown at friendship's hospitable board,
> Smokes 'midst the smoky tavern's coarsest food."

Small pike, of say three to four pounds, are the best if cleaned as soon after capture as possible, well washed and dried, and then split open like filleting. Remove the backbone, also cut off the head, tail and fins, and then divide each half in two; fry crisp and clean over a clear fire in a frying pan, with a good lump, say five or six ounces of fresh, pure lard; turn each piece over as soon as sufficiently cooked on the under side, sprinkle with a little egg and bread crumbs and serve smoking hot (it is the best for the lard to be at boiling point before dropping in the fish). If the pike runs somewhat larger, say from five to nine pounds, it is the best plan to put a couple of good handfulls of salt into its mouth, and hang it up in a cool place, tail downwards, for five or six hours, or possibly longer if the fish is larger; it can then be cleaned, washed, and prepared in the usual manner, and either steamed or boiled, the same as cod, and served with parsley sauce. Be sure it is well cooked—until the flesh will flake nicely away from the bones, and if the fish was in good condition it will be firm, white, and toothsome. On no account cook a pike from a muddy, stagnant pond, nor yet one from anywhere before the month of September, or you are likely to get a wrong impression as to what one of these fish is like. They are in the very worst possible condition during the summer—thin, flabby, and unwholesome.

Just a word or two now as to the various methods of taking the pike in a legitimate manner. First, by spinning with an arrangement of hooks fixed in a dead bait, in such a manner that when this bait is thrown across the water and drawn back again it looks like a thing of life. Second, by spinning with an artificial, worked exactly the same as just described for a dead bait. Third, by working a dead gorge tackle in places where it is impossible for weeds and obstructions to try either spinning or live-baiting. These three plans are worked with a similar leaded trace for each, and no floats. Fourth, by one or two floats and a live bait fixed on snap tackle, so that the pike can be hooked directly he attacks the bait. Fifth, by float tackle similar to the one just named, except the hook is a live gorge one, which has to be swallowed by the pike before he can be hooked. Sixth, by paternostering with one or more live baits, a lead, and no float. Seventh, by legering with a live bait sunk to the bottom of deep water with the aid of a heavy bored bullet, a live gorge tackle or a semi-snap gorge being used and no float. There are several other methods of taking pike, such as liggering, trimmering, trailing, etc., etc., ; but these are not sportsmanlike methods, and should be carefully avoided, unless the jack are far too numerous in a private water, and the proprietor wants to thin them down. The seven plans given above, of course varying the process to suit certain localities, are about all I dare mention to be within the bounds of legitimate pike fishing. I will try in the following chapters to fully and carefully explain the whole of them.

CHAPTER II.

THE PIKE *(continued)*.

PIKE RODS, REELS, AND LINES.

The pike rod—What it has to do—How it should be made—Different woods and canes suitable for pike rods—Rod rings and ferrules—Pike reels—The Malloch casting reel—Slater's cage guard reel—Allcock's pike reels—The plain Nottingham reel—The line—How to dress or waterproof a pike line—The line dryer—Landing nets and gaff hooks—Flight cases and haversacks—Rod and tackle varnish.

There seems to be a tendency among rod makers in general nowadays to sacrifice strength in a rod for the sake of extra lightness and elegance, and in no rod is this more apparent than in what they are pleased to call pike rods. Even pike fishermen themselves are smitten with the same sort of mania, and will insist in having a rod for jack fishing that is totally inadequate for the work they now and again call on it to do. Personally I am far from being a believer in a heavy, clumsy weapon for the sport now under notice; but I like to draw the line at something like reason, and start with, at any rate, a rod that is not likely to play me false at a critical moment. I have seen jack rods in use that hardly looked stout enough for fly fishing for chub, and as for throwing a bait with any degree of accuracy, why, that seemed out of the question altogether. I once saw an angler using a fourteen-foot grilse rod for spinning for pike, and I think I never saw anything more erratic in my life, the bait very often landing wide on the grassy bank on which he stood, instead of sailing gracefully and gently into midstream. I found, on trying myself, that the fault lay more in the rod than the fisherman, and if he had discarded the top altogether and had an end ring fitted on the second joint, he would have got on a lot better. "But," says one of these believers in extra light and flimsy rods, " I once killed a six-pound barbel and a four-pound trout on that rod ; and if it will kill fish like those, why it surely ought to be good enough to kill any jack I am likely to get hold of." True, my friend, I should have to reply to this argument, because I don't look upon a jack as being anything like such a good fighter as a barbel, while he is also any number of degrees behind a good trout.   But this is not altogether it ; if the rod had nothing else to do except kill the pike when hooked, why, I should have nothing further to say in the matter, because the actual killing of the fish, especially in clear and unobstructed water, is one of the easiest jobs the rod is called upon to perform.

When the angler selects a rod for pike fishing, he must bear in mind the following three things :—First, some considerable strain is required in casting out a heavy bait ; second, when a good jack is hooked and in full sail for his favourite weed bed or old root, it wants a fairly powerful rod to turn him ; third, when you get hung up in some tough old weeds with a strong line and gimp tackle, very considerable force sometimes has to be used to loosen it.   These three points are of frequent occurrence in pike fishing, especially in weedy rivers, lakes, and backwaters, so that a very light, flimsy rod would soon get broken, or else strained beyond recovery.   I don't recommend a hop pole or anything like that, but a rod fairly stiff and powerful, with a nice spring in the top, sufficient to cast out the bait comfortably and accurately.

Pike rods are made nowadays of a variety of materials, and in a variety of patterns ; some of them, I am bound to say, more for ornament than use.   Hickory, greenheart, lancewood, ash, two or three different kinds of cane, and even split and built-up cane, with steel centres, all coming more or less into requisition ; but as the latter are extremely expensive weapons, they are utterly out of the question as far as working men anglers are concerned.   Some men will swear by a rod made entirely of greenheart, and certainly this wood, when of first-class quality, is very good indeed ; but in my opinion, based on many years' experience at the rod-maker's bench, it is not exactly an unqualified success, the chief objection being the very great weight of this wood, coupled with a tendency to snap short off, sometimes without any apparent reason, and no flaw discoverable in the grain of the wood. Of course I am aware that some lovely rods are built from greenheart, that have stood any amount of hard work for years, and to counteract the weight some of them are built up with a cork grip, which certainly does reduce the weight somewhat. A pike rod built with an ash butt and lancewood centre and top is a very fair weapon indeed, but the same objection can be raised against this, as against an all-greenheart one—viz., extra weight in using. Then again there are pike rods made of what some people call whole cane; but this in eight cases out of every ten is not whole cane at all, but simply the very cheapest that a rod maker can buy—viz., " Tonquin." Now, this cane tapers very little, the joints of the rod are nearly as thick at one end as they are at the other, and consequently there is not the power in the lower joints that I like to see in a pike rod. The cane that seems to me to be the very best that can be employed in making a pike rod is what is known as East India cane, and when it is mottled and spotted in an attractive manner, why, I don't know a handsomer or more useful weapon. This material of late years has sprung to the front in an amazing manner, and certainly when we look at it, it is admirably adapted for the purpose, for the rods made from it are light, stiff, and very powerful—three attributes of the very first importance—and when all three are combined in one, why, the value is very much increased. This cane is tapered more than any other I know; a piece four feet long sometimes is as much as one and a half inches in diameter at one end, and only three-quarters of an inch at the other. As good and as cheap a pike rod for all practical purposes that can be used, and one that will be within the reach of any working man angler, should be made of this cane, and in three lengths, or not more than four at the very outside, personally I prefer three—viz., butt and one or two centre joints of East India male cane, and one or two tops, according to fancy, of good tough lancewood or greenheart, the former for choice, as I fancy lancewood has more spring than greenheart; the latter seems to be so very stiff, and does not play as I like to see a rod top play. Greenheart tops have more resistance than lancewood, I am aware, but still I have tried both, and the balance of my opinion goes in favour of lancewood. Twelve feet is a good useful length for a pike rod, particularly for live-baiting or paternostering, while eleven feet would be much nicer and easier for spinning, and as the top of a live-baiting rod should be a trifle more springy than the top of a spinning rod, I recommend two tops for the various purposes, one the full length of the other joints, and tapered nicely to the point for paternostering or live-baiting, and the other nine or ten inches shorter, and a shade stiffer for spinning. The ferrule on the butt of a three-joint rod of this description should not be less on any account than three-quarters of an inch, while it would be all the better if it went nearly seven-eighths of an inch, inside diameter; while the one on the centre joint should not be smaller than from seven-sixteenths to half-an-inch, measuring the diameter inside the ferrule; and I might add that these ferrules should grip the cane properly, and be fixed over the outside; the cane itself should not on any account be cut away to receive the ferrule. Of course it is better to have brazings at each end of the joint, and also a dowel or tenon that fits the hole inside the cane fairly and well, and this tenon that projects beyond the brass counter at bottom of the joints can also be brazed if the angler likes, as it would be less liable to stick tight in when wet. This matter of fitting the joints of a pike rod with properly fitting ferrules and tenons is of more importance than some amateurs would think, because if these joints did not fit tight and close up, the strain of constantly throwing would bend the ferrule out of its proper shape, and the rod look like a dog's hind leg. I should say that the average weight of a weapon of this class would go something like 22 oz. It is difficult to lay down a hard and fast rule, as the cane varies somewhat; some rods might run up to 25 oz., while a similar one, as far as outside measurements were concerned, would only total up to 19 or 20 oz. The rings also should be a matter of consideration, and they should be fixed on the rod in such a manner and be of such a size that the line, no matter in what manner or style the bait is thrown, should run freely through them without the possibility of a catch or tangle; and, for instance, if the angler throws the bait with the line coiled at his feet, and there happens to be a snarl in it, when a pike runs with the bait the rings should be such that the line, kink and all, will easily slip through, instead of being brought up with a jerk by jamming tight in the ring. I don't like the "Bell's Life" rings on a trolling rod; they don't stand the wear and tear of throwing with a stout line and a heavy bait. These rings are splendid for the lighter work of chubbing down a stream; but in pike fishing, especially spinning, I found them to be a mistake. In the first place this ring is of a tolerable length, and the binding that fastens them to the rod is fixed at each end; the centre of the ring is not firmly bound to the rod, and the consequence is that a sudden jerk or strong drag with the line pulls one end of the ring away from its bindings, especially if those bindings are somewhat old and worn, and would be likely to cause unpleasantness; and in the second place these rings are made of rather soft metal, which the line soon cuts and grooves. If these rings could be made in hardened steel they would be a decided improvement on the old-fashioned ones. Taking rings for a pike rod all round, I fancy there are none to beat the snake pattern, made of rust-proof bronzed and hardened steel; and in fixing them on the rod they should be graduated, that is, the largest on the butt and the smallest near the top end; and this small ring should not be any less than will comfortably allow a medium sized lead pencil, say three-eighths or seven-sixteenths of an inch in diameter, to pass through. The ring on the butt can be about five-eighths of an inch in size, and this in a three-piece rod should be fixed immediately under the ferrule. I have seen rings fixed on the butt within a foot or 14 inches from the reel; but this, if we look at it carefully, will be found another mistake, because in using the fair sized reel that is necessary in pike fishing, when the ring is so near it, the line when threaded through forms too acute an angle, and grinds and cuts it more than is good for the lasting qualities of the very best line that ever was plaited. When the ring is higher up the butt, this angle is nothing like so apparent, and the friction on the line a good deal less. If the angler will consider a moment he will find there is more in this than mere theory, for I have seen good pike lines utterly ruined in a very short time by grinding in a butt ring fixed in close proximity to the reel. Shortly, then, we will say there should be one ring on the butt of a pike rod as near the ferrule as possible, three rings on the centre joint, and four without counting the end ring on the top, and the nearer to the tip the closer to each other should these rings be. The end ring of all will be all the better if it has also an inner ring of hardened steel or phosphor bronze fitted in it in such a manner that it will revolve or twist round and round. This will also help to preserve the line, as naturally there is considerable wear and friction going on at the extreme end, of a spinning rod especially.

The winch fittings should be about eight inches from the end of the butt, and these can either be the plain old-fashioned three-ring fittings, or the newer Universal or graduated ones, whichever the fisherman likes, the latter perhaps being slightly the best, as they are so constructed that they will securely hold any size of reel without any of the cane being cut away to form the slot or bed.

The end of the rod can be finished off with either a brass cap, a hard-wood knob, or an indiarubber button, according to fancy. I like my pike rod to play well in the top—that is, dressed down nice and tapering from the ferrule—because I have found by a lengthy experience in casting that the throw is cleaner, easier, and more accurate if the rod feels stiff and powerful in the lower end of it, and a kind of switch at the tip end.

There is just one more point I should like to say a few words on, and that it, some anglers recommend this pike rod to have a hollow butt, on purpose to hold the spare top that is not then in use; but my advice is—don't, decidedly; because if you notice there are knots or joints at intervals down this cane that gives it its strength and rigidity. If these are cut away by being bored out, the butt is likely to splinter up and crack after being in use some little time. And then again a pike rod top, with its fair sized rings and top ring would want a butt of more than ordinary thickness to comfortably carry it.

A good rod, such as I have attempted to describe, would run up to fifteen or sixteen shillings, or possibly a shilling or two more, if everything was of the very best quality. A very fair weapon that would be extremely useful to the working man pike angler who only gets out occasionally could be

FIG. 1. A CHEAP PIKE ROD.

produced from eight to ten shillings. Fig. 1 shows an extremely useful jack rod that is built in four lengths for convenience of carriage if the longer-jointed one would be too awkward to carry about. The material of this is East India cane and lancewood tops. Fig. 2 is an exact reproduction of my own pike rod. This, too, is built of East India cane, and its fittings and rings are similar to what I have described in the foregoing pages. I have touched upon this question of a pike rod in a rather lengthy manner, and some may say gone rather unnecessarily into certain details; but I was anxious to give the would-be pike fisherman a few hints as to what he really required, so as to save him trouble and expense afterwards. When he goes to his rod maker now, he will be in a position to tell him exactly what he wants, and

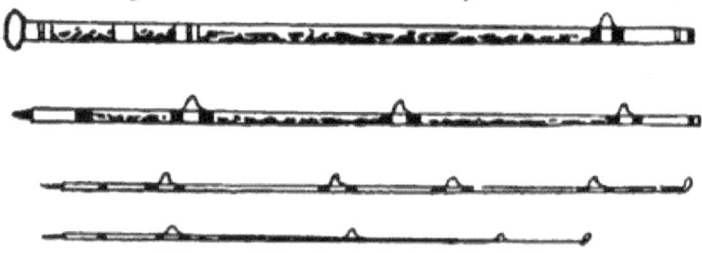

FIG. 2. THE AUTHOR'S PIKE ROD.

the results are likely to be more satisfactory on both sides. I must let this be my excuse, to say nothing of the fact that in the very few pages that I have devoted to this special subject of rods there is the experience of nearly a lifetime at the rod maker's bench and the riverside recorded. One more little thing that I had nearly forgotten in connection with this subject, and it is very nearly the most important of all. Many times I am asked the question as to whether a very stiff top added to a light chub or barbel rod would not make that rod for all practical purposes a good strong pike rod? I am bound to answer all such with a very decided "no." Strange as it may seem, it is nevertheless true that the stronger and stiffer the top is in a light rod, the weaker does that rod become. The old saying that "a chain is no stronger than its weakest link" can be applied with even more force to rods. They are no stronger than their weakest points, and instead of a strong stiff top making the rod stronger in itself, it is very often a source of weakness. More strain would be thrown on the second joint, and eventually, if the rod was kept at this heavy work, that joint, at any rate, would be utterly ruined. I am strongly in favour of having a pike rod made for that special purpose, and use it for pike fishing alone. I am not very much in love with combination rods, although they can be constructed with a very fair amount of success, but they have to be specially built. What I want just now to impress on the mind of the would-be pike fisherman is this: if he has an old favourite roach or chub rod, he must not be deluded into having an extra strong and stiff top fitted to it, under the impression that it is going to make a strong pike rod, or he will probably regret it when too late.

A reel is a necessary article in a pike fisherman's outfit, because he cannot very well fish for jack with a tight line tied halfway down his rod, the same as some roach fishermen do, he must have a pretty fair length of line, and a reel is necessary for one thing to hold it. Pike reels are made at the present time in a variety of patterns, and at nearly all prices; but I consider a good stout Nottingham wood reel as good as anything that can be tried. It is not so absolutely necessary to have an easy-going centre-pin reel for this work, as it is in chub fishing down a stream. A centre-pin is almost too lively for a jack reel. It ought, however, to run fairly free, and as I always in spinning cast my bait directly from the reel, and look upon this method as being the very best to adopt, perhaps I may be excused if my particular fancy turns to these wooden reels. A four-and-a-half-inch one is the best size; it should not be less than four inches, at any rate, and it ought to be made of good dry and hard walnut, of pretty substantial build, and be fitted with a strong brass cross-back. A moveable check action is also a very useful addition to these reels, as it can then be used for all purposes and all styles of pike fishing. A good plain

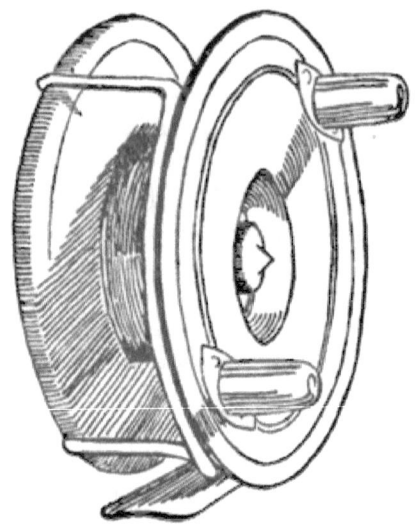

FIG. 3. PLAIN PIKE REEL, WITH LINE GUARD.

spindle reel is my particular fancy. I don't strongly recommend a centre-pin, although scores of good pike fishermen use them. A pike reel such as I have described would run from six to eight shillings. A working man need not spend any more than that, as he would not find one of the most elaborately got-up and expensive reels one little bit better for all practical purposes. Some anglers say that they cannot, try as they will, cast a bait direct from the reel in what we call the Nottingham style. They either have to coil the line at their feet, or else use one or other of the wonderfully constructed reels that are supposed to be helps to this style. It is not a very successful plan to coil the line at the feet, because there are places where the angler has to stand knee-deep among flags, reeds, thistles, thorns, and all sorts of rank undergrowth, where the line would catch and be generally aggravating. One of the best-known of these casting reels was invented by Mr. P. D. Mallock, of Perth, and bears his name. When a bait is cast by this reel the barrel or revolving portion of it does not turn round; it is fitted up with a contrivance, or a sort of a hinge, so that the portion of the reel that holds the line can be turned or twisted half round. When the cast is made the line is pulled from the drum or barrel a good deal like pulling thread from the end of a bobbin or spool, the force of the cast causing the line to unwind itself as the bait travels to its destination. As soon as the bait strikes the water, of course, the line stops, and the revolving or drum part of the reel has to be turned back again into its original position before the line and bait can be worked or spun home again. When the bait is thrown with this reel there are no handles spinning round to rap the incautious novice over the fingers, and no revolving plates into which the line can suddenly catch and jam itself tight. The reel only revolves when the angler wishes to spin his bait and recover the line that he has thrown out, or when a fish bolts off with the bait. There seems to me to be two or three objections to this reel, the greatest of which would be the extreme difficulty an angler would experience in spinning his bait over very shallow and weedy places, which situations, I might add, are very often the best places in which to find pike. Sometimes it is necessary to begin spinning or working the bait home again after a cast the very moment the bait strikes the water. If it is allowed to sink even six inches under the surface the hooks would catch among the weeds, and the cast be spoiled. It seems to me that the time that must elapse between the bait getting to its destination and turning the revolving portion of the reel back into its original position before that bait can be wound back again would be fatal to its success in very shallow and weedy water. In very deep and unobstructed lakes and rivers, of course, this objection does not count, there would be plenty of time to manipulate the reel before the bait reached the bottom or anywhere near it. Another point against this reel is by being made of metal it is rather heavy, and would be tiring to spin with all day; and they are also very expensive, a good one running to something like thirty shillings. There are, however, scores and scores of good pike fishermen in

Ireland and Scotland who swear by them. They say that they cannot for the life of them throw a bait direct from a Nottingham reel, and find the Malloch one of the most useful inventions they ever tried. Personally, I never used one in actual pike fishing; I have seen and examined them. Once I tried my hand at throwing a bait across a grass lawn with one, and consider them wonderfully ingenious, and calculated to assist those pike fishermen who are really baffled in their efforts to master the peculiarities of the ordinary Nottingham reel. Another pike reel that has been a great favourite for many years now was invented by Mr. David Slater, and christened by him "The Combination." In an ordinary Nottingham reel, anglers who are not very expert pike bait throwers find that the line in casting gets outside and hanks itself round the handles, or even sometimes a long loop drops down and catches round the bottom of the butt end of the rod. The revolving barrel of Slater's reel runs in a cage that is fixed firmly to the back, and certainly this is the best invention that I am as yet acquainted with for keeping the line in its proper position. The Bickerdyke line guard is also supposed, when fixed to an ordinary Nottingham reel, to stop the line from overrunning; but this guard, useful as it undoubtedly is, is not, in my opinion, equal to Slater's cage guard. In the Bickerdyke guard there is nothing to prevent loose line from falling out at the under side of the reel. It does, however, keep the line from falling over the top and catching round the handles. I have had one of Slater's cage guard reels in constant use for many years now for pike fishing. I believe my reel was the first, or very nearly the first, that Mr. Slater made; anyhow I have had it since 1882. It is a plain spindle reel without check action, four and a half inches in diameter. Those anglers who really must spin with the line coiled at their feet, and really cannot be persuaded to try any other plan, need not be so particular as to the choice of a reel, a plain wooden or brass one, provided it is large enough to hold the line, will do very well.

Of late years so many reels have been invented for pike fishing that the anxious novice is apt to get bewildered, and be nearly at his wits end in making a selection. There is the "Coxon," that runs round at nearly a breath of wind; but I don't think this really was invented as a pike reel, although I make no doubt it could be used as one on a pinch. It is much more valuable as a stream-fishing reel for roach and chub. Then there is another with an aluminium drum, so carefully and accurately running upon a steel centre that the very lightest minnow can be cast direct with it. This reel is called the "Duplex," and where it differs from the ordinary Nottingham wooden reel is the fact that while the bait is travelling to its destination after being thrown, the handle does not spin round and round; and here it also differs from the "Mallock," mentioned some time ago. The latter has to be twisted half round before the bait can be wound home again. With the "Duplex" the line can be recovered and wound back again in an instant. The "Duplex" reel is manufactured by Messrs. S. Allcock and Co., of Redditch, which fact is generally admitted by expert anglers of the present day to be a sufficient guarantee that the quality is beyond reproach. Of course these reels are rather expensive, and hardly to be thought about by the ordinary working men anglers; but these men need not despair and think that they cannot cast out a pike bait properly unless they have one or the other of them to assist in the operation. I think I shall be able to give such a few instructions in the following pages that, coupled with a little practise, will enable them to cast out a bait clean and neat without tangle or catch with only a plain spindle Nottingham reel, costing at most a few shillings to do it with. I can call to mind some of the very best working men pike fishermen who ever threw a bait across river, lake, or stream, who never used any other reel than a plain, easy-going Nottingham. The whole secret of casting out a spinning bait direct from the reel without overrunning, jerking the bait off the hooks by a sudden stoppage of the line when in mid air, or having a beautiful tangle of line on the barrel of the reel when the bait reaches its destination, or having the fingers rapped by the revolving handles, lies in a judicious selection of the rod, reel, and line, coupled with the easy forward swing that alone is necessary to get the bait out to nearly any distance, and above all to the proper and well-timed pressure of the finger on the revolving edge of the reel. First, the rod should be so constructed that it will play well at the tip end, and be stiff and strong at its lower joints. Some makers and anglers may tell you that it is impossible to cast out a pike bait properly unless you have a very springy rod—one that will bend round, nearly like a fly rod, from the tip down to the handle; but my experience is that the top itself should bend well, the second joint bend a little towards the thin end of it, while the butt and part of the second joint should be stiff and rigid in the hand. The distance and accuracy of the cast is very much improved by having the rod as near to the above requirements as possible. Secondly, the reel itself should run very smoothly; it should not wobble at all, nor yet "chatter," as we call it, while the bait is travelling to its destination. The back, or fixed part, and the barrel or revolving part should fit close together, so that there is no play or looseness between the nut on end of the spindle, and the brass plate under it. There is more in this than meets the eye of the casual observer, because if the reel chatters and does not run smoothly and well, more force is required in the cast to start the bait upon its journey. When the young pike fisherman selects this article of his outfit, he should carefully take stock of it, see that it is strong and well made, that it has a stout brass cross-back, is fitted up with a good moveable check action, and that the handles on the front are fitted to strong oval plates, screwed firmly to the wood by a screw at each end. These oval plates are a great protection to the handles, as without them, in the constant winding that a pike spinning reel is subjected to, they are liable to work loose.

Having satisfied himself on the above points, the novice should then hold the reel firmly by the back in his left hand, and with his right tap the edge of the revolving part smartly downwards. If it will revolve freely and smoothly without wobble or shake, and feels firm and rigid under the brass nut, and its spindle is not loose and shaky, he has without doubt got a reel that is admirably adapted for throwing out and working home a pike bait in this most deadly and easy style; and I might add that he should not on any consideration give more than eight shillings for it.

Thirdly, the spinning line should also be selected with a good deal of care. A strong, heavy, waterproof line is not a success by any means when used as a casting line direct from the reel. It should be an undressed silk, or at most only very slightly and smoothly dressed, and the size need not be too thick, nor must it on the other hand be too thin. I, personally, do not like a line too fine for jack spinning, as in constant use winding in and out through the steel rings of the rod it is liable to be chafed flat, and might play you false when least expected or wanted. What I particularly like and recommend for this work is from 60 to 80 yards of Messrs. Allcock's No. 2 or 3 white plaited undressed silk line. These lines are very strong, the No. 2 being particularly so, and they are also very soft and free from all objectionable kinks and curls, which, I might add, is desirable, especially in a spinning line. A line that kinks and snarls in use is a confounded nuisance. I found Messrs. Allcock's (quality No. 108) lines, size 2, to be the most reliable for spinning that I ever tried. I tested one of them once with a spring balance that would weigh up to 20lb., and as it pulled this down I considered it plenty good enough without extending my experiments further in that direction. The three points noted above, viz., the judicious selection of the rod, reel, and line have more to do with the success or non-success of the angler who essays the Nottingham style of pike fishing, than some people would think; in fact, I consider it a matter of the utmost importance. I have seen men who have been utterly disheartened by repeated failures, and then found out on investigation of their particular cases that three-fourths of the causes of failure lay more in the rods, reels, and lines than in the fishermen who used them.

I hope none of my readers will consider that I have been unnecessarily tedious in treating this part of my subject and gone into details that would have been better left out. So convinced am I that this subject is not studied sufficiently that I have been led to refer to it at length. At one time I should most likely have only just skimmed the surface and glanced at it in a very cursory way, but the hundreds of questions that have been addressed to me by anglers from all parts of the country on the difficulties they encounter, have told me very plainly that the information here given is of more than passing interest to the young pike fisherman. During my wanderings after sport I have seen pike fishermen at work in many and various styles, but none of them I considered to be equal to or more scientific than the Nottingham style. As I have just pointed out, this style requires an undressed or very slightly dressed and softly plaited silk line, and an easy-going and accurately running reel on purpose to successfully practise it. On the other hand, if the angler uses the live bait alone and is not tempted to spin the bait over the shallows, a waterproof line will be best for that purpose, and the easy-going and accurate character of his reel need only be a secondary consideration. Even if he does spin occasionally, preferring to do this with his fingers and with the line laid at his feet or gathered up in coils in his left hand, the waterproof line is still the best to use, and any brass, metal, or common wood reel, provided it is fairly stout—not too heavy—and large enough to hold the line, will do very well. A good waterproof line is rather an expensive item; of course there are cheap dressed lines; but in many cases these cheap lines turn out frauds of the very worst character. You cannot expect a good lasting pike line for, say, a halfpenny a yard. I never knew one yet to be up to much that could be bought for less than a penny a yard, and even some of these were nothing to crack about. I know lots of pike fishermen who prefer to buy the pure silk plaited lines and dress them themselves; but this is a long and tedious job. The cheap dressed lines, I fancy, are waterproofed with some sort of composition that has an acid mixed with it. This, I think, is done for a twofold purpose, that is, to give the line a bright and glossy appearance, and also to dry them very quickly. In some of the cheaper kinds of dressed lines this waterproofing only covers the surface, or outside of them, and rapidly peels or chips off when used for a short time; and then again I have fancied more than once that the acid used in the dressing causes the line to rot after it has been for some little time in contact with the water. If the pike fisherman prefers to buy his dressed line, or has no time on his hands to do it himself, he should see that it is of the very best quality, for this is a case of the cheapest being dearest in the long run; for most assuredly a good one will out-last three or four common ones, and a couple of shillings only at most represents the difference between sixty yards of common dressed line and a similar length of first-class quality. I should say that Messrs. Allcock's "Standard" waterproof line is as reliable as any that can be procured nowadays. That firm makes a speciality of these lines, using only the purest and strongest silk and the very best dressing procurable in their manufacture. I should not like to say that these lines are better than other English makers' best, but I do know from experience as a user and dealer that they are at least equal to any others. The size that I particularly recommend for live-baiting or coiling on the ground is the No. 3, and as this can be procured for a trifle more than a penny a yard, the outlay is not beyond the reach of the generality of working men anglers. Some pike fishermen will have it that for a pike line to be reliable you must dress it yourself. They say that the ordinary dressed line as usually sold in the fishing tackle shops is too stiff and hard to comfortably use, and I am half inclined to agree with this opinion. Anyhow, a good home-dressed line is worth half a dozen common stiffly-dressed shop-bought ones. To dress a line properly is a rather lengthy operation. I don't mean lengthy as far as actual time doing the job is concerned; it is the length of time it takes to dry after being soaked in the solution that makes the job so tedious. I have known lines to be three or four months drying before the stickiness was gone and they were fit to use. Good linseed oil—and remember it must be good, not half of it some foreign fiery fat or other cheap adulterated stuff that is only linseed oil in name—is as good as anything that can be used; and this should be mixed with an equal part of best copal varnish, say a quarter-pint of each. One of my friends used to also add about a couple of tablespoonfuls of best gold size. This is a rare good dressing for a pike line, but takes a considerable time to dry. The undressed silk line that the angler wishes to dress should be taken when new and perfectly dry, and coiled up into as small a ring or compass as possible, say what will easily go into a small basin four or five inches across the top; then pour the mixture as given above, cold, on top of the line and see that every portion of it is well covered. Let it remain in the dressing at least two days, then carefully remove and uncoil it, and with a bit of flannel wipe it gently from one end to the other; that is, hold the flannel between the finger and thumb of the left hand, and with the right draw the line through, taking care that the pressure is sufficient to remove all lumps and superfluous dressing from the line—of course during the process the line can be coiled on a table or round the back of a chair. It should then be hung up in long loose coils in a cool dry position, and where the sun does not shine on it, and remain there until perfectly dry; I should say it will take six or eight weeks at the very least to properly dry. This dressing not only has the merit of being very good, but it also is cheap, any respectable chemist or oilman will supply sufficient of the ingredients to dress a couple of lines for eightpence or tenpence, I make no doubt. After the line has hung until dry it should be stretched out at full length down the garden path, or any other convenient situation, and a sixpenny packet of "King's Ceroleum" procured, this is another very useful line dressing, and is sold at nearly any fishing tackle shop; a bit about the size of a filbert nut should be put inside a bit of flannel and rubbed lightly from end to end of the line, taking care that a very thin coat only covers the whole surface; now take another bit of dry flannel and polish up the line smartly, pinch it well between finger and thumb and rub backwards and forwards, a yard at a time, until the line feels warm between your fingers, this gives the finishing touch to the dressing and smooths the line down with a slight gloss. The dressing will not crack or chip off, nor is it hard and stiff in the slightest, but so soft and pliable that it can be thrown very well from the reel in the Nottingham syle. A great friend of mine, one of the very best pike fishermen I ever knew, always maintained that a line dressed according to the directions just given, had a threefold lease of life given it, it would outlast three ordinary undressed or even cheaped dressed ones and so be a considerable saving in the long run. I think I have made it perfectly clear as to the ingredients required for this dressing, but to make it doubly sure, I might say, that my friend always got a quarter pint each of best linseed oil and copal varnish, and two tablespoonfulls of best gold size, mixing and stirring them well together before pouring over the lines. This quantity being quite sufficient for two eighty yard lengths. If the gold size cannot be procured, it does not matter so much, but still we always fancied it gave the line a more finished appearance; and don't forget the finishing touches with "King's Ceroleum" and flannel. After this it should again be hung up for two or three days before finally wound on the reel. I might add that the long or short life of a pike line depends on more than a careful dressing, it should also be thoroughly dried after using, and by having good steel snake rings and steel end rings on the rod, also contribute to its long life. There are several more ways of dressing a line, such as putting it in a mixture of beeswax, resin, and boiled oil; or melting a lump of solid parrafin and dropping in the line; but the first that I have given at length will be found enough for all practical purposes. Personally, as I generally throw direct from the reel, in either spinning or livebaiting, I don't care much about having a dressed line; but there is no question that the great bulk of pike fishermen find a dressed line of the very greatest convenience, particularly in casting out and working a live bait. Once or twice during a busy season I have rubbed my spinning line with a little bit of "King's Ceroleum," and found it helped to preserve it, besides making it stand the wear and tear of constantly running through the rings of the rod somewhat better, and also preventing it from getting quite so much waterlogged while in use. This is the very outside that I care about, in the shape of a waterproof or dressed line, and as this preparation is so easy in its application, and can be put on so quickly, and does not alter the softness and flexibility of the line, the novice will find it to be to his advantage if he keeps a cake of this dressing by him; the cost is only sixpence, and I think it is kept by most fishing tackle dealers, but if any difficulty is experienced in procuring it, a note to the inventor, Mr. Wm. King, chemist, Ipswich, will, I make no doubt, result in a satisfactory reply. I used to stretch my line at full length in the most convenient situation, and smartly rub a small piece of the ceroleum with the help of a bit of flannel from end to end, taking care that very little was put one, and this rubbed well in till the whole surface was smooth and bright. The line was then hung up for a couple of days, after which interval it was safe to use; I found that this very slight dressing did not hinder the free running of the line when thrown direct from the reel in the Nottingham style. Of course three or four coats of this preparation can be applied in the same manner, at intervals of a couple of days between each one, if the angler wishes to have his line more thickly and thoroughly waterproof. This does not take anything like so long drying as the oil and varnish dressing mentioned some time ago; a week after applying the last coat will be ample. And now having looked at what I consider to be the very beau ideal of a pike rod, reel, line, and its dressing, we will glance briefly at one or two sundries that the pike fisherman should have if he can anyhow afford them. One of the most important is a line dryer, because it is imperative that the pike

FIG. 4. THE LINE DRIER.

line should be dried after you get home from a day's fishing, or if you are foolish enough to neglect it, in all probability you will have a sudden and startling reminder during one of your subsequent outings, sooner or later. The line will rot if allowed to dry on the reel time after time, and the fish of the season may be hooked and lost. There is nothing more annoying than to have a good fish break away owing to the line being rotten by neglect. The accompanying illustration gives a good idea of what a line dryer is like; it has a clamp on one side near the centre, so that it can be screwed to the edge of a table, or the bench, or the chimney piece, and a handle on the other side to wind the line off the reel. I daresay any handy man could soon knock up a similar article, anyhow the expense is not very much, and most decidedly it is not a useless expense. I should unwind the whole of the line from the reel, and put the drier somewhere in a dry, cool position, and let it remain a couple of days if you anyhow can, before winding back again on the reel. Even if you are out in a strange place for two or three days' jack fishing, the line will be all the better for being dried every night and wound again on the reel next morning. On no account should a line be dried in close proximity to a fire, particularly a dressed line, as the heat may blister the waterproofing and cause a weakness.

Another actual necessity in a pike fisherman's kit is a good landing net, or a gaff hook; I prefer the former, and this I recommend to be of pretty substantial build. A strong four jointed folding iron frame, or ring of a circular

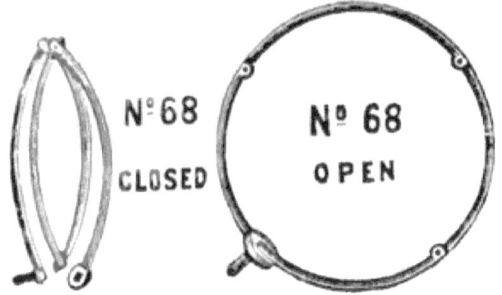

FIG. 5. FOLDING LANDING RING.

shape not less than sixteen inches in diameter, being, in my opinion, the best to employ. This ring should screw firmly and tight into a socket fixed at the end of a staff, the staff or handle can be about four and a half feet long, and made of good East India mottled cane, and if it is made large enough, so that when it is bored out it will hold the rod top that is just then not in use, it will be found a great convenience. The illustration shows a ring I recommend open for use, and also closed for convenience of carriage. With regard to the net itself it should be fairly strong, and the material barked or tanned, and it will be all the better if it is pretty deep, say from twenty-one to twenty-four inches, and roomy at the bottom, so that when a jack gets inside it is likely to stop in; because if you are spinning with a number of hooks on your flight and get a jack into the net, if this net is narrow at the bottom and shallow, he will most likely roll out again; and if the hooks of the flight catch inside the net while the pike is hanging outside, you stand a very good chance of bidding him a good bye within the next two seconds, for most assuredly he will speedily shake himself free. Some good pike fishermen, on account of the extreme likelihood of this accident happening when landing a pike in a net, prefer to use a gaff hook for this purpose, striking it into the fish near the shoulder or under the gills; but I have known a good pike to twist a gaff clean out of the hands of a fisherman, and at least once or twice I have known the gaff hook to snap off at the bend, and the pike escape with the broken portion

FIG. 6. GAFF HOOK, OPEN AND CLOSED.

sticking in him. The illustration shows the usual sort of gaff that is most in use, open for use, and also closed for convenience of carriage; but, taking things all round, I most certainly prefer a good strong landing net, wide at the bottom and pretty deep. Another very useful article is a tackle case, and this should be of japanned tin, black on the outside, enamelled white on the inside, and made with several partitions, so that traces and flights can be kept seperate. A good useful size is about eight inches long by five wide, and about one and a half inches thick, with two closed boxes in the lid for traces. A tin box is better for pike tackle than a leather case, as in the latter the treble hooks are liable to be broken if anything heavy is thrown on the case. The annexed drawing shows one of these tackle cases

FIG. 7. BOX FOR PIKE TACKLE.

open, so that the inside arrangements can be seen. A strong canvas haversack of a pretty fair size is also another useful article, particularly if the pike fisherman goes in for a good deal of spinning, as it can be slung across his shoulders, and so out of the way while at work with his spinning bait, and does not have to be picked up and carried in the hand to every fresh place he wishes to try. A pike fisherman should also always have a bottle of varnish handy at home, as it is very useful for a variety of purposes, the best that I know for pike tackle being two pennyworth of the wood naphtha, in a doctor's medicine bottle, with two ounces of best brown shellac dissolved in it. Wood naphtha is far better than spirits of wine, as the latter evaporates, and after being some time on the bindings or whipping of rod or tackle the gum rubs off like a dry dust. The bindings of all pike tackle should be from time to time painted over thinly and lightly with a little of the before mentioned mixture; a small camels hair brush being the best for this purpose. This small brush should always be kept in a little of the naphtha in a separate bottle or vessel, or if allowed to get dry the bristles would be as hard as a bit of stick. I am certain it will pay the angler to touch up his tackle pretty frequently, as it helps to keep the bindings secure, and doubles the life of it. A little good carriage maker's varnish is the best for his rod, painted lightly and thinly over the surface, but this should only be done at the end of a season, when it could stand on one side for a week or two and get thoroughly hard and dry. Finally, I might say, that the pike fisherman who values his health should always, in bad weather, wear good waterproof boots or shoes, and keep them well dressed with "Dale's dubbin." The various flights and tackles for spinning and livebaiting; how to make and how to use them, will be illustrated as far as practicable, and described in the chapters that follow.

CHAPTER III.

THE PIKE *(continued).*

CASTING OUT THE BAIT.

Different methods of casting—The Nottingham style—The right-handed cast—The cast from the left hand—How to cast from the reel—Weights and their distribution—The forward swing—Casting with a coiled line—A peculiar cast.

In this chapter I propose to leave the beaten track for awhile, saying nothing about the merits or demerits of the various flights and tackles in use for pike fishing, but devote the whole of it to a subject that I think has hardly ever been satisfactorily explained—I allude to the question of properly casting out a bait. There seems to me to be two or three different schools of fishermen, each throwing out the bait in its own particular fashion, each more or less proficient in its own peculiar style, and all of them suited up to a certain point to the requirements of the various waters in which they ply their craft. As I hinted in the previous chapter, there are those who coil the line at their feet, casting the bait from the rod point; but this, in my opinion, is not likely to be an unqualified success when tried in every conceivable situation, and under every condition, and in all the difficulties to be encountered by the side of the river, lake, or stream. Then again there are others who never use the rod when casting out a pike bait, they simply coil a lot of line on the ground, with the rod on rests, hanging the bait in the crutch of a forked stick, and so slinging it out without the aid of the rod at all. Then again there is the ever increasing army of casters who throw directly from the reel in what is known as the Nottingham style. In my opinion this style is far away and above any other, taking all things into consideration; places can be successfully spun over where it would be impossible, owing to stones, bushes, trees, reeds, and rank undergrowth, to cast with line coiled at the feet. Some pike fishermen say that a bait, wound home on the reel in this style, is not so attractive as one worked home by the fingers with line coiled; the long sweeping drags of the bait when travelling through the water, which is the chief characteristic of the latter plan, is absent when the line is simply wound up on the reel to spin the bait home. There is, they say, too much of the jog trot, monotonous sameness about the bait when cast out and wound back again direct from the reel. But I would point out that by simply raising and lowering alternately the tip end of the rod, and varying the pace of the winding in process, sometimes even, if the character of the water permitted it pausing for a second or so, the sink and draw motion and the long sweeping drags of the bait could be imitated as faithfully with the reel, as by the hand. Then again, when spinning from a boat the line when coiled at the feet is apt to be a confounded nuisance, and will insist on catching round everything within reach, now and again

Fig. 8. Snake Rings, The Four Largest Sizes right for a Casting Rod.

hanking round the neck of a bottle, or upsetting a tackle box, perhaps throwing overboard a cherished pocket knife or a favourite bit of tackle. I have heard several pike fishermen say under these circumstances, that they wished they could spin from the reel, as it would prevent much bad language to say the very least. As I have hinted more than once in the foregoing pages, that my favourite plan of spinning is by casting out the bait direct from the reel, I will commence with that and trust I shall be able to make it so clear that even the most inexperienced angler will have no difficulty in understanding exactly what I mean, but be able, after a little practise, to perform in a very creditable manner, without any serious mishaps. Of course he will not be able to do it all at once, he is bound to jerk his bait off the hooks some odd times, and also find after an unsuccessful attempt that his line has managed to get into a beautiful tangle on the barrel of his reel. The greatest difficulty that I have to contend with, is the fact that it is almost impossible to lay down a hard and fast line as to how the rod and reel should be manipulated in casting out a pike bait, in what is known as the "Nottingham style." Even experts are by no means agreed on the subject; and so on looking at it by the light of many years practical experience, and also calling to mind the various plans adopted by some of my personal friends who, in their own way of throwing out a bait in this style, are as good fishermen as ever threw across river, lake, or stream, I say again that no fixed rule can be laid down, as some men check the reel with the right hand, others with the left. All men are not alike, the plan that is free and easy to one may be difficult and even painful to another; he must throw in the fashion that is easiest to himself, and to get into the fashion that is easiest can only be acquired after very careful practice. I have seen anglers whom nobody who knew them, and understood the matter, could by any means call inexperienced fishermen, cast out the bait with the right hand above the reel, and the fingers of the left guarding the revolving barrel at the top edge, and I have also seen as equally good and as long experienced men proceeding exactly opposite, with the left hand above the reel and the right below it, guarding the reel at the bottom edge. Each of these plans is equally as good as the other; that is, so far as throwing out the bait, and checking the speed of the reel at the proper moment is concerned. A man must find out which is the easiest and the most accurate of the two plans, that he, per-

sonally, with the most comfort to himself, can adopt, and
then he will be in a fair way to success, no matter which of
the two he selects. The plan that I found to be the easiest
for myself is what is known as the right-handed cast. This
is a cast that is adopted by many first class men in various
parts of the kingdom; men who, as it were, graduated on
the Trent, and then left their native river to settle on the
banks of other waters, carrying their style to places where it
was practically unknown before. I have heard it said that
the introduction of this style to various well known rivers,
marked a new era in the history of their angling. In the
first place the angler must find out exactly where to hold
his rod so as to have the best command over it. It will not
do for him to hold it in a careless manner, he must be
master of his rod—and not the rod master of him—or in
all probability he will land his bait into the nearest hedge
instead of on the water. The proper right-handed cast is
made by grasping the rod firmly with the right hand, about
eight or nine inches above the narrow stop ring, or band of
the winch-fittings. This small stop ring or band, by the
way, should be firmly fixed on the rod butt, about an inch
above the slot that is cut into the wood to receive the reel.
When this reel is put on the rod in its proper position, the
two handles should be pointing to the right. The right
hand, as I have just said grasps the rod firmly, nine or ten
inches above the reel; the left hand is close over the reel
or winch fittings, in fact, to be exact, the rod is in the hollow between the thumb and forefinger of the left hand, close
to the reel, so that the fingers of the left hand can clasp the
back of the reel, the second finger reaching over the barrel
and just lightly touching the rim of the front or revolving
plate of the barrel on the top edge. By this plan you are
out of the way of the handles, and in no danger of being
smartly rapped over the fingers by them. After seeing that
your bait hangs some four or five feet from the point of
the rod—but this is regulated by the length of the trace—on
no account should any of the gimp or gut, whichever is used,
be wound through the top ring of the rod before making
the cast. The flight of hooks, the leaded trace, and the loop
where the silk line is joined to the trace, should all hang

free below the top ring on rod. After seeing that all is clear, you face exactly the place on the water where you want the bait to drop; keep your eyes fixed on the exact spot where you would like that bait to strike the water, never mind looking at the bait just when the cast has commenced, if all is clear, it will look after itself very well. To make the cast you swing the rod point to your right-hand side and partly behind you; then with another, but this time a much more smarter forward swing, you bring the rod over the water. As soon as ever the bait swings forward you partly release the reel by easing the pressure of your finger on the revolving front rim, taking care, however, that this pressure is not altogether removed, or the reel will overrun, and also minding at the same time that this pressure is not too tight, or the bait will be checked and drop on the bank to your left hand. Your finger should just feel the rim of the reel, and that is all. As soon as the bait strikes the water the finger is pressed tight on the reel edge, so as to effectually stop any further revolutions. Still keeping hold of the rod and reel with the left hand close at the top of the reel, as already described, you press the knob or button of the rod into the hollow of the left thigh, and leave go of the rod with the right hand, which hand is brought down and takes hold of the reel handles on purpose to wind the bait home again. With a little practice these three operations can be performed in a couple of seconds with the ease and regularity of clockwork, viz., stopping the reel by a pressure of the finger as soon as the bait drops into the water, pressing the butt end of the rod into the hollow of the thigh, and leaving go with the right hand (which in making the cast was 9 or 10 inches above the reel) in order to wind in the bait. This is what I call the proper right-handed cast; in fact, by this plan I can cast the bait to the right hand or to the left, or even straight forward, although in the case of a bait being required to be thrown wide to the right hand, I usually bring my rod over the left shoulder instead of the right, as described before; but in any of the three directions I hold rod and reel in the same hand and in the same manner. In this right-handed cast the most natural direction for the bait to travel is wide to the left hand, in a slanting direction across the river. It requires some practice before a given point in any direction can be successfully, time after time, struck. Some very good Nottingham pike fishermen that I know always make what I call a left-handed cast; the rod is grasped with the left hand just above the reel, and the right hand below it, checking the speed of the reel with the end of a finger at the bottom edge. But with all due respect I maintain that this is a very awkward throw, because ere you can wind up your reel to spin the bait home both hands have to be shifted, the left lower down to have command over the rod and the right to wind in the reel line; and if the place spun over happens to be shallow and weedy this extra fraction of time may make all the difference between the bait being clear and the hooks catching hold of the weeds just under the surface. Again, I always imagine that the finger under the reel does not regulate the cast so well as the finger over the top, and you are more liable to get your fingers rapped by the revolving handles. It is more than probable that you may sometimes stand facing the river in a very awkward position, with a lot of boughs or other obstructions immediately at your right hand, and no possible chance of swinging the rod point in that direction. Under these conditions no other cast except the left-handed one is possible. But even here I should hold the rod and check the reel exactly the same as for the right-handed cast, the only difference being that the rod point would be swung towards the left hand instead of towards the right. It is much more difficult to make a clean and accurate cast from the left shoulder than it is from the right. I have known very good pike spinners who threw out the bait in a manner peculiar to themselves. Not one angler in a dozen could, if they tried for a month, imitate it. I don't condemn all these styles, far from it. If a man can throw out his bait well and accurately, and his style of throwing is to my eye very peculiar, I should say nothing in condemnation because that style differed widely from my own. One of the most curious throwers that I ever saw was a Nottinghamshire angler of long and wide experience. He always used to put the reel on his rod with the handles pointing to the left, and wind in his line with the left hand. His style was peculiar in the extreme, but his worst enemy (if he had one) could not say that he was a bad thrower. Personally, in giving practical lessons in this style, I found that the greater number of my pupils could manage the right-handed cast much quicker and easier than any other; but it needs practise, and practice alone, to make a man perfectly master of the style. But there is one comforting thought in the whole business, it is as easy as A B C when you once know how, and it is not at all difficult to learn. The main thing to be observed and impressed most strongly upon the would-be spinner, is to grip the rod firmly with the right hand the proper distance above the reel, and with the fingers of the left regulate the speed of the revolving barrel, and he should also bear in mind most strongly that while the bait is travelling towards its destination, the slight pressure of the finger on the edge of the reel must always be there, regulated according to size of bait and weight of lead. If a heavy natural bait a little more pressure must be applied, and if it is a light artificial bait a little less pressure will be ample, as a light bait takes more force than a heavy one to start it upon its journey. In using a natural bait, say a small dace of from one-and-a-half to two ounces in weight, a gentle throw with an easy swing will be all that is required to get it out a moderate distance, say from 25 to 30 yards, provided the reel is an easy-running one and the line moderately fine. It is not advisable to exercise tremendous force in casting out a natural bait, for various reasons; not much would be gained in the distance cast for one thing, and a sudden jerk, which is always liable to happen when extra force is applied, might buckle up and spoil the shape of the bait. I found on several occasions that the longest cast was made with the easiest swing, that is when bait has been fairly heavy. On the other hand a light lead and small artificial bait of not more than one ounce in weight altogether would have to be started much smarter upon its journey—more force is necessary in this instance. The gentle throw or swing that would be ample in the case of a very heavy bait would not cause the reel to commence running with sufficient speed for the light bait to travel the requisite distance.

But all these points cannot be learned very well from reading about them; a hint or two, of course, that will be useful to the novice can be given. For all the rest, such as holding the rod in the best place, easing or checking the reel with the ends of the fingers in the best manner, the proper distance for the bait to hang below the rod point, and the correct swing to give the rod, in order for each individual spinner to have the best and easiest results, can only be acquired by long and painstaking trials and experiments. But don't be frightened, peg away, and you will soon learn. One man of my acquaintance who knew nothing whatever about this style, but was anxious to learn, made such rapid progress during his first lesson that at the end of an hour he could cast out 30 yards without jerk, tangle, or catch. There is one little thing I should like to say here before I forget it, and that is, when making a cast, and the bait has travelled nearly to its destination, lower the rod point to about a couple of feet from the surface of the water, if the nature of the place makes it anyhow possible to be done. More particularly must this be observed if the place spun over be shallow and weedy and the angler not very proficient in recovering his line to wind home again. As soon as the bait strikes the water, the rod point can be raised, and this will keep the bait on the surface, and the hooks not be so liable to catch hold of the weeds until the winding-in process commences. And now just a few words as to the weight that can comfortably be thrown and the distance that can be cast.

Careful trials with various reels and lines have shown me very clearly that a small feather-weight minnow, without any lead on the trace, cannot be thrown direct from the reel and rod point. The smallest weight that I found possible to cast over 20 yards was a small spoon which, with its lead and gimp trace, weighed three-quarters of an ounce, this weight being distributed as follows:—The spoon at the extreme end of two feet of fine gimp; at this distance from the spoon was a small barrel lead, then two more feet of gimp, the whole of these weighing as just stated; and even this wanted a No. 4 line and a Coxon reel to do it with. The ordinary pike reel and line was not equal to the task. A larger spoon and heavier leaded trace, with weight distributed as before, the whole weighing a little less than one-and-a-quarter ounces, was next tried with the ordinary reel and No. 2 line, and this time by using some considerable force in the cast I managed to get it out about 30 yards. The result of my experiments convinced me that the bait with its necessary swivels, gimp trace, and lead, the whole distributed in a proper manner, and not put altogether at the far end of the gimp, should weigh not less than one and a half ounces to have a comfortable and satisfactory result, that is if distance and accuracy were the objects aimed at. A leger bullet weighing seven-eighths of an ounce, tied firmly at the end of a stout barbel line, was thrown a little over 50 yards from the reel, while a spoon and leaded trace weighing one and a half ounces only reached 40 yards when thrown by the same rod, reel, and line. The bullet, of course, would have far less resistance to contend with in travelling through the air than would the spoon, hence the difference between the distances cast under the same conditions. A small dace weighing from one and a half ounces to two and a quarter ounces can be comfortably thrown without any danger of straining the rod; anything much over the latter weight is not desirable. With regard to the distance that can be cast direct from the reel, I should say that 60 yards would be the very outside, and then the bait would have to be fairly heavy, and of such a torpedo-like shape that it could cut through the air with the least possible resistance, and the conditions of the weather would also have to be very favourable. I have heard some men say that they have cast out the bait from the reel 70, and even 80, yards at a guess; but I must say that I have never seen it done yet. If they had the distance properly measured I am afraid they would find it considerably shorter than that. Shortly then, we may put it that 50 yards is a very long cast, 40 yards is a very good one indeed, while in a day's spinning there would be more casts under 30 yards than over that figure, that is as far as the ordinary run of mankind is concerned. I once saw some Thames professional fishermen competing for prizes by casting out an artificial bait from the reel in a style that they were pleased to call the Nottingham style. Instead of swinging the rod to the right hand or to the left, and propelling the bait forward by a gentle side cast, two or three of them handled the rod a good deal like a country labourer using a frail. They grasped the rod with one hand above the reel, and the other below it, and swung the point and bait over their heads straight behind them, so that the rod was in a direct line with the middle of their backs, and both hands at the back of the head. In making the cast the rod was brought smartly forward with the point high in the air; in fact, the rod described a semi-circle, or very nearly so; and such was the force of this terrific cast that the bait travelled to a great height before dropping on the ground. This cast, if applied to actual pike fishing with a tender natural bait, would result in dire disaster to the bait, at any rate; it would be thrown all to atoms in two casts. The gentle side swing with the finger on the edge of the reel is the correct and proper style, that is if your baits are scarce and you want them to keep attractive as long as possible. Of course it does not matter so much with a strong metal artificial bait how it is thrown, so long as it goes out to the best advantage. Sometimes you may stand in a very awkward position among trees or bushes, where it is impossible to swing the rod point to either side, or even upwards; there is perhaps no more than two or three yards of clear space immediately fronting the spot on which you stand. Under these circumstances a very creditable cast can be made by drawing down a length of line from between the rings of the rod as high up as you can reach, and letting the bait swing backwards and forwards by moving the rod point as far upwards and downwards as the circumstances of the place will allow. When the bait has acquired sufficient momentum and swings sharply forward, release the loop of line that you hold in the left hand, which has been drawn down from between the rings on the rod, and at the same time ease the pressure of the little finger of the right hand on the edge of the reel, and away goes the bait, the weight of which will cause the reel to revolve sufficiently to get out 20 yards, at the very least, if it is wanted. In this cast the rod must be held in the right hand above the reel, with the edge or side of the little finger resting lightly on the top edge of the revolving barrel. When this cast is made and the bait strikes the water, change the rod from the right hand to the left as quickly and promptly as possible, and wind home again, repeating the process as often as required.

One of the very best casters that I ever saw throw out a pike bait had his line hanging in coils from his left hand; his right hand grasped the rod some little distance above a brass winch; his right arm and body acted as a fulcrum in a very peculiar manner, so that he had the most possible leverage and power with his rod at the least expenditure of strength. It was marvellous to see the way those coils of line straightened themselves out one after another and went through the rings of the rod as the bait flew with unerring accuracy to the exact spot required. Nor was it much less marvellous to see the way that line recoiled itself in regular sized folds on his left hand as the bait was spun home. That man's skill could only have been arrived at by long and constant practise, as I never saw him all that afternoon make a false cast or get his line into the least semblance of a tangle.

Before the introduction of the Nottingham style on the Thames and the southern rivers, the great majority of the pike fishermen on those waters used to cast with the line coiled at the feet, and certainly some of the experts in this style can throw out a wonderful distance. There is no question that so far as distance is concerned a first-class Thames-style man will beat the Nottingham-style man by at least a dozen yards, using the same weight; in fact I have seen it demonstrated more than once at those popular bait-casting tournaments held at intervals at the Welsh Harp, Twickenham, and Wimbledon, when the very best exponents of both styles have been competitors. In this style the bait is thrown direct from the rod point, only instead of the line being wound on the reel it is laid in loose coils on the ground. Of course the line as it picks itself off the ground travels through the rings on the rod during the flight of the bait, and when it is spun home again it is drawn in by hand and again laid in coils at the angler's feet. But with all due respect to the many excellent Thames men I don't consider the plan half so neat and clean as casting direct from the reel, for the reasons stated at the commencement of this chapter. The pike fishermen of the Welsh Harp seem to me to have a plan of throwing out a bait peculiar to themselves. In this case the line does not travel through the rings of the rod. Like the Thames style, the line itself lays in coils at the angler's feet; but instead of using the rod as the motive power of the cast, the bait, or at least the line about a yard from the bait, is hung across a steel or brass fork that is screwed firmly into the end of a staff like a landing handle, and it is marvellous the distance an expert can cast the bait, that is if line and all is clear and goes freely. Another plan of casting out a bait that I have sometimes seen is by having the line wound tightly on the left hand, each fold of the line crossing the previous one, the hand itself being moved in a peculiar manner as the line is coiled on and the bait spun home. When the cast is made direct from the rod point, the line unwinds itself off the angler's hand and passes through the rings on the rod. When the bait has reached its destination and is travelling home again, the peculiar motion of the hand that gathers in the line fold over fold causes the bait to travel in a manner that could not be imitated by any other plan. It is a wonderfully killing style, and is adopted by some of the best minnow spinners for trout, as well as certain pike fishermen who delight to spin with a very small bait and fine lines and tackle.

CHAPTER IV.

THE PIKE *(continued)*.

SPINNING WITH A NATURAL BAIT.

*Spinning, **what** it is—A simple spinning tackle—The Chapman spinner and its contemporaries—Flights and their uses—The spinning trace—Best baits for spinning—" The Trent Otter's" spinning flight—**How** to bait it—A good season—How to spin to have the best results—Different methods for different waters—Condition of the water—Clouded v. clear water spinning—Spinning in deep and sluggish waters—Changing the bait—Striking, playing, and landing a pike—Haunts of the pike during the Different months—Spinning leads—Preserving dead baits.*

Spinning for pike with a natural or artificial bait has been a favourite pastime of mine for many years now; in fact I look upon spinning as being the most scientific as well as the most sportsmanlike of all the many plans that are adopted for the capture of our fresh-water shark. Of course, I am aware that there are certain waters containing pike in which it would be utterly impossible to work a spinning bait, or even for the matter of that a live bait. Obstructions and weeds might be so strongly and thickly in evidence that the novice would despair of ever getting a bait in, to say nothing of safely getting it out again. I shall show presently how it is possible to fish a place like that; for the present my object is to give a few plain instructions on spinning over the more open waters with a dead natural bait.

I suppose I need not **tell the amateur** that spinning is done by fixing a small fish on an arrangement of hooks in such a manner that when drawn through **the water it looks** like a wounded or disabled fish trying to **escape from some** imaginary foe, the main object being to have as much of the bait and as little as possible of the **hooks** visible. The spinning bait must also be kept constantly moving, that is, turning over and over more or less slowly or rapidly, as the case may be, during its passage back to the angler after being thrown out. Spinning is hard work if stuck to all day long, for it is absolutely necessary to be on the move throwing out and winding home again time after time. It won't do to let the bait sink to the bottom and stay there for any length of time. Spinning is working the bait all over the place, anyhow and anywhere, wherever there is a bit of clear water into which it can be thrown. A friend who had never done any fishing except a little bit of roaching once or twice with a tight line, had a curious idea about spinning. He was staying with a farmer friend who had a bit of very fair pike water running through his grounds. The farmer rigged him up on the second morning of his stay with a strong rod, reel, line, trace, and a spoon bait, all fitted up and ready, and told him he could amuse himself spinning for an hour or two, till he had time to join him. Some two or three hours later the farmer went down to see how he was getting on, and was considerably astonished to find him with the rod laid across a bed of weeds, the line in the water, and blowing a cloud of tobacco smoke into the air as contentedly as possible. He had actually thrown the spoon bait into the water, allowed it to sink to the bottom, laid the rod across the weeds, and had been waiting all that time for a bite.

A glance through a wholesale manufacturer's illustrated catalogue would be enough to convince the veriest novice that the making of artificial baits and spinning tackles for pike fishing had brought out the ingenuity of the maker to a remarkable degree. The almost endless variety there displayed would be to the tyro, as our old friend Dick Swiveller used to say, "a staggerer." Of the merits and demerits of the various forms of artificial baits, from the old-fashioned spoon to the elaborately gilded and fish-shaped article that spins through the water like one line of glittering silver, I will not just now touch upon, but reserve that subject for another chapter. My business now is to briefly look at those tackles that are used for spinning a natural or dead bait, and see wherein and under what conditions of shape and spinning powers the most sport is likely to be had.

I am old enough to remember one of the old school of

Trent anglers who lived at Newark-on-Trent, who used to spin for pike in a manner that I should suppose to be a survival of the most ancient form of trolling known. This old angler's name was Crosby, and there are fishermen still living at Newark who can very well remember him. He used neither rod nor reel, but simply a coil of very stout cord, about as thick, I should say, as a sea-fishing hand-line, which he carried in his left hand, with one end tied tightly round the same arm above the elbow. His tackle was simply a length of stout gimp with one or two large swivels, and a long heavy pipe or barrel lead. The gimp was mounted with one only very large treble hook, and this gimp was threaded through the bait, the hook being underneath between the vent and the tail. This tackle was thrown by hand, and in spinning the bait home the line was drawn in by the right hand and laid in coils on the left. Of course all fish hooked had to be played by hand. I cannot remember seeing this angler at work myself, but I knew him very well, and have been assured by old fishermen that years ago he used to kill many and heavy fish by that very primitive style and tackle. There are many tackles in use for spinning a dead bait that are a good deal more ingenious than useful, that is some of them, at least are so. The main object of the inventors of these tackles appears to be a desire to save the angler from being at any trouble in the matter, and also to secure a very brilliant and even spin. One of the oldest of these is the Chapman spinner, which I should say is familiar to anglers in every part of the civilized globe where fish that will take a spinning bait are to be found. For the information of those who don't know what it is, I may say that it has a leaded brass wire with a hook some two-thirds of the distance down it, which is thrust in the mouth and down the belly of the bait. At the top of the leaded wire, close to the mouth of the bait, there are soldered on a couple of fans, one being bent one way and the other in an opposite direction, somewhat on the Archimedean screw principle, that gives the bait its rotary movement without having to curl the tail. A swivel is fixed at the top end above these projecting fans, from which depends a couple of short lengths of gimp; two treble hooks are firmly whipped on the longest length of gimp, and one on the shortest length, the two hooks being on one side of the bait, and the odd one on the opposite side, one hook of each treble being stuck in the bait in such a manner that the odd treble is about midway between the other two, only, of course, on opposite sides. I have had my attention drawn to lots of these spinning tackles that are known by various names, and brought out by various makers, but the whole of them seem to take the old-fashioned Chapman as a model, and are only imitations and improvements of that

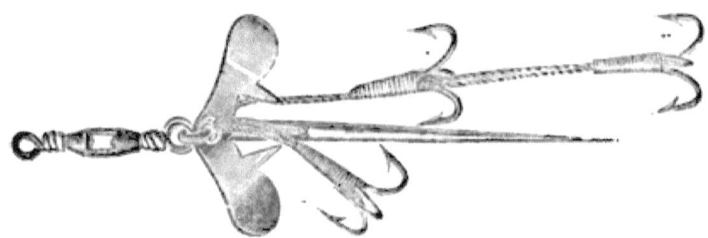

FIG. 9. THE ARCHER SPINNER, STANDARD PATTERN.

good old spinner. There is the Bedford spinner, the Archer spinner, Gregory's Archimedean spinner, the Angler's spinner, and a whole host of others, some differing in the shape of the hook, others differing slightly in the blade that is thrust down the belly; while others again have the contrivance that fastens the bait firmly, slightly different to other makers. But look at them all, you will find the method of mounting to be nearly similar in every respect, and the old-fashioned Chapman to be strongly in evidence in nearly everyone of them. The Coxon spinner is about the simplest of the lot; but it is not an unqualified success in any and all conditions of streams and waters. It is a capital spinner when tried down the heavy waters of the Trent, and kills a fair percentage of the pike it hooks; but when used in very quiet waters, where the jack take a spinning bait in a much more quiet and deliberate manner than they do in a rapid stream, the percentage of losses is very great indeed, and its action as a spinner is not so good as might be desired. I fancy it would be better if instead of having only two trebles both on one side of the bait, it had an extra one high up near the shoulder on the opposite side. Several friends have tried this spinner at my earnest request in various waters of the kingdom, and the majority of them say that the idea is a good one. It wants improving in one or two particulars to make it suitable for still-water spinning, and then it would be about as perfect as it is possible to get a spinning tackle. My own opinion is that the two trebles are fixed too far apart; they should be nearly close together at the tail end of the bait, with a reversed single hook near the shoulder to keep the gimp in its position close to the bait, and an additional treble on the opposite side nearer the head than tail. Anyhow my experience with spinning tackles has shown me very plainly that the best results have been obtained by having the trebles distributed over the bait in this manner. And even now, on looking at the improved Coxon as just suggested we again find that the old-fashioned Chapman-like method of mounting has become strongly in evidence, the only difference being that the unsightly fans that are close to the head of the bait in the Chapman are absent in the Coxon, the blade of the latter that goes down the belly of the bait, being bent by the fingers after baiting to

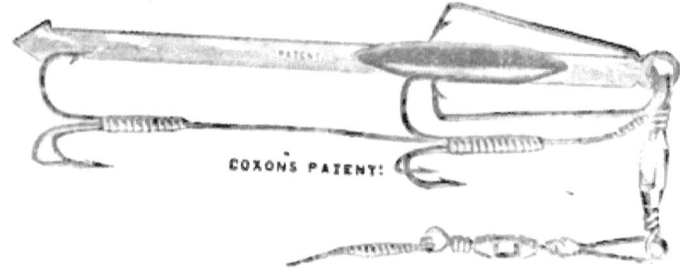

FIG. 10. THE COXON SPINNER.

give the rotary or spinning movement. I personally do not care very much for any of these elaborately-made spinners, preferring to mount my bait on a simple flight of hooks and trusting to these hooks and the shape of the bait to secure the most attractive spin. There is, however, one thing to be said in favour of these spinners, and that is, a bait will last longer on them than it will when mounted on an ordinary flight. I know some very good men of the old-fashioned school of Trent anglers who to this day spin that river with only one large sized treble hook fixed on the end of a length of gimp, which gimp is threaded right through the bait from the vent to the mouth, and kill fish on it, too. Others, again, use two trebles threaded in the same manner. I very seldom saw more than two trebles on a spinning flight used down that river. In nine cases out of ten the pike of those fast streams would grab the bait near the tail, while in a lake or very slow running stream they would seize it in a much more deliberate manner, and generally crossways nearer the head, necessitating a slightly different tackle to what is so effective down the Trent. Some anglers seem to consider that it is also the correct thing for a spinning bait to travel at a very fast rate through the water, and to spin brilliantly and evenly, so that when drawn through the water it appears to travel in one straight and even line; my own experience is not in favour of this theory. A pike, although a greedy fish, does not like too much trouble in capturing his prey. A small fish in difficulties, or one wounded, is far more likely to be the victim than a dace or small chub in the full power of its strength and swiftness. I find that a spinning bait which travels in all sorts of curious ways to be the most attractive; in fact, as just said, the more it looks like a disabled and wounded fish the more likely is the jack to follow it. A dace in full health and strength when startled will shoot through the water like a flash, and Mr. Pike has sense enough to know that it is a lot of trouble to openly pursue that quarry, whereas a wounded one in trying to swim away from danger will turn from side to side and make all sorts of curious curves and twists in its endeavours to reach a place of safety. In my opinion and experience I find that the nearer we can approach this motion the more likely are we to attract the attention of the pike. Some spinning flights are made with three or four treble hooks and fixed in the bait all down one side; and most likely these hooks are three or four sizes too big. In a flight of this description it is very nearly necessary that the bait should turn over rapidly, so that the rank arming of hooks is not presented too glaring to the pike. I have never yet found that large sized hooks and too many of them are an advantage, rather the reverse. I have often wondered why the makers of tackle should recommend these treble hooks for spinning to be so big. The simpler the flight the more chance has the spinner, especially on those days when the pike are not in a very taking humour. Sometimes they will dash at almost anything, and lay hold with such right good will that it is almost impossible to miss them; but these chances do not often occur. Nowadays they are getting so very cautious and cunning, especially where constantly fished for, their education has been complete and thorough, so that any sort of a glaring deception will not work satisfactorily for the angler, at any rate. I have used some brilliant spinners, such as the Francis and the Pennell flights, that will spin a bait in a most attractive-looking manner; but, somewhat or other, results do not point them out as being the best that can be used.

In spinning for pike in a slow-running river like the Bedfordshire Ouse, or the clear water of some of the Norfolk Broads; or again in the generally bright water of some inland lake that is fed from hillside springs, it is necessary first to mount the bait so that no more of the hooks are visible than can possible be helped; second, use no more of those hooks than are really necessary; third, use them as small as you dare; and, fourth, spin slowly if possible, and see that the bait wobbles and comes through the water in all sorts of curious curves and twists. I once saw a couple of anglers spinning on the river just named; one fancied himself as an expert of the first water, the other was a novice pure and simple. "Look at that now, my boy," says the expert as he swung his brilliantly-mounted bait right across the river, and spun it back close to the surface with great rapidity and in one straight and even line. His companion did look, but could not imitate that cast if he tried for a week. In all probability if a good jack had seen that bait he would have wondered at the curious apparition, and known very well that fish are not naturally in the habit of going across the river in that headlong manner. That angler's companion, the novice, had a very simple flight, on which he mounted a bait in a very rough and ready manner. He was constantly getting into difficulties with his reel and line in throwing out, so that the bait would nearly sink to the bottom before he got all straight; the bait itself would sink and draw, wobble and twist, but—and here is where our expert wondered—this novice caught the fish. Why? Because by accident he had without knowing it imitated the actions of a bait in difficulties.

The very best flight that I ever used in slow-running waters was the simple two-treble flight of the Trent men, and the size of hooks No. 5 or 4 Redditch scale, plenty large enough. These two hooks are whipped nearly close together, so that there is not more than a quarter of an inch of gimp between the end of the shank of the bottom hook and the bends of the top treble. When the water is very bright and clear No. 5 hooks will be the best, and they will be all the better by being dressed on, say, five inches only of ooo copper gimp (the finest size); a single strand of strong stained salmon gut can be joined to that little bit of gimp by two neatly, but strongly, whipped loops;

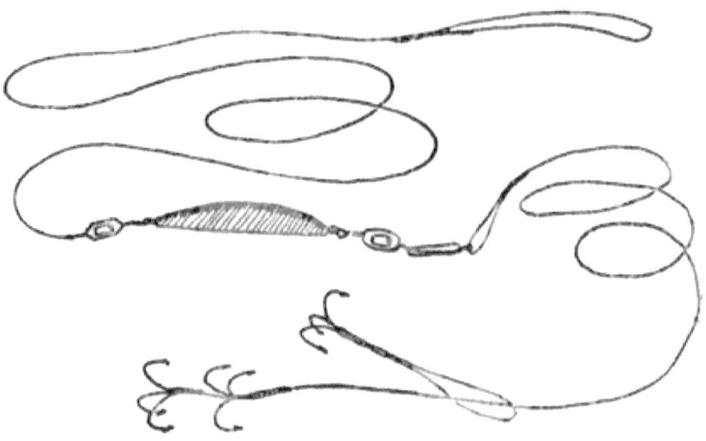

FIG. 11. THE "TRENT OTTER'S" FLIGHT AND TRACE.

one good long single strand will do, so that the flight proper, gimp and gut, is about 16in. in length. For this clear water spinning a trace of one and a half yards in length of strong single salmon gut is best, with a drop-lead and buckle swivel on the end, and also one or two more swivels in it above the lead. When the water is clouded or charged in any way with colour it does not matter so much about using gut, gimp will do then very well.

The best natural baits for spinning are small dace, say of about five inches long; large bleak, or whitlings as they are known on the Trent, and toughened sprats; these last two are rather tender and require mounting on the hooks in a very careful manner; but all three of them are splendid bright and glittering spinning baits to use in a clouded water. Small roach, gudgeon, or the tail-end of an eel are also pretty fair spinning baits, the two latter the most useful perhaps when the water is very clear. In using small dace or roach I suppose I need not say that the fresher they are the better; indeed, I fancy it is the best if possible to carry them down to the riverside in a bait can alive, and knock them on the head before using, and use them fresh and bleeding. In baiting this two-hook flight that I have just described, you detach the hook part of the tackle from the buckle swivel of the trace, and with the aid of the baiting needle pass the loop in at the vent of the bait, and bring it out of the mouth, pulling it through till the shank of the top treble is in the vent of the bait; you then stick one hook of the end treble in the root of the tail about the centre, or perhaps a little nearer the back. This causes the bait, when the hooks are pulled tight, to bend slightly downwards and sideways, giving it that attractive wobbling spin that I have found so deadly. This tackle, threaded through the bait like that, is very neat, and does not show the small hooks anything like so plainly as the ordinary sidehooked flight does. I found after a very long and careful trial of this flight in quiet, or nearly quiet, waters that with the two trebles being close together and near the tail-end of bait, it was possible to miss your fish if the pike seized it by the head end. So to counteract this somewhat I made a small addition in the shape of another very small treble, which is dressed or firmly whipped on a loop of fine gimp one inch in length from the end of the shank. After the bait is put on as already described, this small looped treble is dropped over the gut or gimp of the flight, and brought down to the nose of the bait, and one of the hooks is then stuck in the side towards the back, on the same side of the bait as the tail-end hook is, as far beyond the gill covers as the small loop will allow it to go. This is a valuable addition to that tackle; since I adopted it I have hooked a fair percentage of my pike on that top loose treble. I once saw an illustration of a Nottingham spinning flight, and the method there said to be adopted by the Trent men in mounting a bait on that tackle. The two treble hooks were there, but rather further apart than usual, and instead of the gimp being threaded completely through the bait from the vent to the nose, the two hooks were simply stuck in the side about middle way, and the loop of the gimp passed under the gill covers and out at the mouth. For years I fished the Trent in company with some of the very best men who lived on its banks, and I never once saw a bait mounted in that manner; indeed, I greatly question if one could be used there with any chance of success. Heavy currents are very prevalent in that river, and pretty long casting has also to be the order of the day in a very many places. The bait would soon be thrown loose or wear away from the hooks by the action of the current, and very soon be hanging by only the little bit of gimp under the gill covers. It hardly mattered how many or how few hooks were used on a Trent flight, the main principle of mounting was alike in nearly every case, the gimp being threaded through the centre of the bait and the hook or hooks close to the tail. Of course I saw strangers at times using different kinds of flights, sometimes having one treble, sometimes two, and sometimes three trebles, and a lip hook fixed outside the bait; but the old-experienced anglers, who had had a lifetime's experience, always considered the gimp should go through the centre of the bait to have the best results. An old saw runs, that "the proof of the pudding is in the eating," and my strong recommendation of this tackle is based very much on the same lines. In the first place I have done well with it in all sorts and conditions of waters, down the heavy streams of the Trent, on the deep and sluggish waters of the Ouse, across the weedy shallows of the same river, and among the reedy fastnesses of broads, lakes, and backwaters.

During the season 1889-90 I was out on public waters

twenty different days, and successfully landed on that flight 79 sizeable jack, to say nothing of the scores put back that were undersized. That was my best season as far as pike fishing was concerned, and the result fully confirmed my previous good opinion of the flight. In the second place, the tackle is cheap, and as these pages are written more particularly in the interest of the working man, I don't feel justified in recommending an expensive flight or spinner, when one costing about sixpence is as much or even more effective. In spinning over places when the water is shallow and weedy, and very little, if any, stream at all is running, it will be necessary to spin rather near the surface and a little quicker than in waters deeper and clearer from weeds. It is not the correct thing to spin your bait home like lightning under any circumstances, if it can anyhow be avoided. In a deep and sluggish water which is comparatively speaking free from weeds and obstructions, let it sink deep down until you think it nearly touches the bottom, and keep moving your rod point at intervals during the process of winding the bait home from right to left, and back again; and then again let the rod point drop towards the water, raising it again after a few seconds, all the time winding home slowly. These movements of the rod, and varying the pace of the bait, all have a tendency to cause that bait to come through the water in a series of curious curves, dives, and twists, which in my opinion is the main source of attraction. A wobbling bait with an uneven spin I have proved over and over again to be far more deadly than a bait spun home in one long, straight, and glittering line. Just before the bait reaches the end of its journey, that is, within two or three yards from where you stand, before you lift it out for a fresh cast, it will be as well to lower the rod point to nearly the surface of the water, and fish the place clean out, if you anyhow can; that is, let the bait come as close as possible to the bank on which you stand. Sometimes a good jack will follow the bait from right across the river and take it close under your feet. He probably thought it was trying to escape from him by diving under the bank, whereas if the bait had been lifted out when at full length of the rod, he would have turned tail and retreated back again. I have seen this done more than once. If you see the jack following the bait with his nose nearly against it, as I have done lots of times, and you stop spinning for a moment and let the bait sink a trifle, in six cases out of ten Mr. Pike will dive after it in a hurry and lay fiercely hold. But in all these proceedings you must keep a cool head and a steady eye, and be ready to tighten on him at any moment; don't get flurried like a friend of mine once did when throwing his first spinning bait. A good jack came at the bait in deadly earnest, when it was close to the surface, and within half a dozen yards of the angler. This sudden onslaught so frightened our fisherman that he dropped the rod and sprang backwards in alarm, thus losing his first run. I admit that it is a bit startling to a beginner, the sudden rush of a fair-sized pike, when you are thinking of lifting the bait out for a fresh cast, is enough to unnerve the inexperienced in such matters, but if he takes it deep down out of sight, the first experience is not so startling.

If the place you spin over is choked with weeds, that is, growing in a dense mass everywhere, with only a few spots where there is six inches of clear water above those weeds, and here and there a rather deeper opening, don't miss it. Very often the best jack lie lurking among those weeds, but keep the bait near the surface, above the weeds, and also work it well in the clear runs between the beds. When you first begin to fish a likely-looking stretch of water, it is not the correct thing to throw your bait right out to the furthest extent of your cast; but just toss it into the nearest opening at first, and gradually work further away in every direction, until you cover the entire distance you can comfortably reach; searching the nearest water first should always be strictly attended to. Any sort of water, provided it is fairly clear, can be spun over. I once heard an old angler say that spinning proper could only be done in weir pools and streams, and down the faster currents of a running river; but this is all nonsense. Ponds, lakes, railway cuttings, meres, broads, or anywhere else, provided pike live in it, can be successfully operated on if a clear opening can be found. In casting it is a general thing to throw the bait across and down stream, if there is any stream, and draw it back against the current searching all the possible water well over. I have found after searching the water by that plan to have had a slice of luck by throwing the bait up stream and drawing it down the same direction as the current is running. Many a good fish have I picked up by this plan, after having searched all the water by the orthodox down-stream cast. I have sometimes fancied that it was because the bait looked more natural going down stream.

Another flight that was a particular favourite with one or two of my friends was constructed on the same lines as the flight I described a little while ago, except the tail-end hook, which instead of being a treble was a large single hook some three-quarters of an inch wide in the bend with a shank fully an inch long. Immediately at the end of this shank a small treble, about a No. 6, was firmly whipped to the same gimp, and the loose looped treble completed the tackle. This flight is baited the same as the other, with the gimp run through the body from the vent to the mouth, the single hook at the end being stuck firmly into the solid flesh near the tail in such a manner that the tail itself bent slightly towards the right hand, and a full quarter inch or more of the point and barb of the hook protruding free. One old spinner of long and wide experience would have it that this tackle was a slight improvement on my favourite, one reason being that the large hook at the end buried, or nearly so, in the tail of the bait gave it a more brilliant spin; and another reason was the treble hooks being a shade smaller, and also the tail-end hook being nearly hid gave the tackle a neater appearance, and nothing much except the bait visible to the keen eyes of the jack. I had to admit on looking at the two flights when baited that this was so; but it had one drawback, it was not such a safe-hooking tackle as mine. I very seldom lost one when hooked; he had several mishaps in this direction. I simply laid the difference to be his use of too small trebles. There are several more flights and tackles in use for spinning a dead bait; but I don't propose to look at the merits or demerits of any of them here. I have given a full description of how I consider a bait should be spun, and also the best style of mounting that bait to give the best results. When a whole host of tackles are recommended and described, it makes a book look, in my idea, more like a manufacturer's catalogue than a practical guide to the sport.

And now I must give a few words as to the best condition of the water to expect sport in. Some little time ago I mentioned the very best season's jack spinning I ever had, and turning to my note-book to find out to what cause I attribute the sport there alluded to, I find on a careful perusal that nearly the whole of the time the water was clouded, and the best fish and best days were when it reads: "Water very much clouded." When I say very much clouded, I don't mean a tearing pea-soup flood, nor anything like that, but a fair colour in which the bait is nicely visible when sunk a foot below the surface, and when sunk a couple of feet or so it can still be seen, but looks to be in a decided haze. This was the condition of the water when I got my best bags. Very fair sport indeed was had occasionally when the bait could be seen when sunk three feet below the surface. Anything brighter than this was not conducive to great success. Some time ago I read an article that was published in one of the angling journals, in which the writer boldly declared that the water could not be too clear for spinning, especially spinning with a spoon. My experience is exactly opposite. I have thrown a spinning bait thousands of casts in all sorts and conditions of waters, and even when a natural bait was used success was all the greater when the water was clouded, and this was even more to be noted when spinning with a spoon. In 1892 I find on reference to my note-book that the water in the River Ouse had been for several weeks exceedingly low and clear, and no sport to speak about. Then came some heavy rain, and a flush of water came down the river. On one afternoon when the water rose at least two feet during the time I was fishing, and was "heavily charged with colour," as my note-book has it, I ran no less than 18 pike, some of them very good ones indeed, in not more than one and a half miles of water. The same water, bear in mind, that I had thrown over a dozen times previously during its extreme brightness with scarcely any success; in fact, a careful perusal of my note-book for several seasons confirms this. When the water was very clear and bright—when every hook is plainly visible halfway across the river to both fish and fisherman, it is very little good throwing a bait. I have tried under these conditions all sorts of dodges, using a single gut trace with the very smallest hooks dressed on ooo copper gimp, and only four or five inches of this, just where the pike's teeth are likely to be if he takes hold; and for bait a four-inch glittering bleak. I have stirred the fish certainly—fair sized ones I mean—and seen them follow it, and tried everything I knew to make them take hold, but no, they appeared to me to be a deal too crafty to take a bait when even that fine tackle was so plainly exposed. Small ones of a pound, or even less under these conditions, are apt to be a nuisance; they will persist in taking the bait when their elders consider that bait is to be avoided at any cost. I have been forced to put extra bright water as one of the conditions not very conducive to sport when spinning. A few odd small ones may be got, with here and there at long intervals a fair sized one; but that is about all. Of course, I am now alluding to public rivers that are pretty well spun over nearly every day. A good private water that is not so hunted to death, especially if it is a clear-water lake, is a different thing; it hardly matters what sort of tackle is used, or what sort of baits, the only condition being whether the fish are on the feed or dead off.

In spinning over public well-fished waters, when the streams have run down very sluggish and they are gin-bright, a gudgeon is as good a bait as can be tried, and this should be mounted on very small hooks with a trace of pale blue stained salmon gut. An eel-tail mounted on a large single hook, with a bit of lead round the shank is also another very good clear-water spinning bait. The looped side treble, as recommended for spinning a dace, will also be a valuable addition to the eel-tail bait. In a clouded water the two best baits to use are bleak and sprats, next to these come dace, while roach or any other small fish can be tried if nothing else is forthcoming. In a river or lake where the jack run very large and the water is at all coloured, it is not advisable by any means to use too fine tackle for spinning, No. 0 size copper gimp being plenty fine enough, while if the water is clear perhaps it will be better to have the last two feet of the tackle a size, or even two sizes, finer gimp. In spinning for jack on a large lake or broad, where the water is deep and the fish very sluggish, and moreover where you are as likely to get hold of a twenty-pounder as a three, it is not a bit of good spinning near the surface, those large and lazy jack are not going to be at the trouble or rising all that distance. If the water is free from sunken trees or other large obstructions, you must use a heavier lead and larger bait, and let it sink deep down, spinning it home very slowly, and chance hooking on to a stray weed bed now and again. For this sort of spinning it will be as well to have a stronger and heavier set of tackle, with hooks of a fair good size, say No. 1's, at the very least, so that a 5 or 6 oz. dace or roach can be mounted comfortably on them. It is the only way to get the large ones spinning that live deep down in the sluggish depths of quiet deep water. Of course they can be got at by live-baiting with a paternoster tackle, but just now, remember, I am treating of spinning with a dead bait. On the other hand, in spinning over a canal or small stream, or even a backwater, where a five-pound fish is a rarity not often met with, and the fishermen themselves are nearly as numerous as the fish, the tackle can scarcely be too fine nor the bait too neatly mounted; five inches of the best ooo copper gimp on which the hooks are dressed, then 18in. of strong single barbel gut, then the drop-lead and two swivels, and finally two more feet of very strong single gut. This is about the best arrangement that can be tried under the circumstances just alluded to, and for bait an ounce dace or a four-inch sprat. In spinning over well-fished water when it has run down very clear, sometimes you stir a fish, you see a good jack move, probably only just notice a swirl under the water, Mr. Jack came and went again, refusing the bait. It is a good plan to keep pegging away for ten minutes or more over the same place with the same bait, although you feel that he does not mean to have it; but I believe you are aggravating the fish, and after a time slip the bait off you are using and substitute another totally different in shape and colour, and throw again; the chances are that he will take it with a savage grab the first time. Some people tell us that if a pike stirs to a spinning bait and refuses it, it is best to give him an hour's rest and then try again. My advice is to keep throwing over him, a dozen or even a score of times, until he probably knows every outline of that bait, and then put on something else of a different shape and colour, and very often success will crown this little dodge. I remember once in particular the club I belonged to fishing a pike spinning match one afternoon. One of the competitors, who was fishing a cunning corner of the river, told me that he had stirred a good fish nearly an hour previously, and although he had stuck to it well, not another move did he see. He was spinning with a bright and glittering dace. He told me that as he was off to another place I might have a go at that fish if I liked, and I fancied there was a sort of sarcasm in his tone. However, I took off my natural dace that I had been using, and put on an old dull-coloured wobbling spoon, and got him the first cast; and it turned out to be the first prize fish. This is only one instance out of several in my long experience when a change of bait has resulted in success. When a fish is just slightly hooked, and then after a few seconds' play lost, it is not much use in a general way to keep throwing over him; give him an hour's rest if you anyhow can before trying again. Some odd times he will come again instantly; indeed, I have had one or two fish that have been hooked and lost three times in less than ten minutes, and then got him the very next cast. It is not often, however, that they are so very accommodating as this. If, after losing one, you find he does not come again in two or three casts, you can safely leave him to settle down for an hour or so.

And now just a word or two on a very vexed question, and that is, should a pike be sharply struck when hooked on a spinning tackle? My decided opinion is—no, certainly. I believe that more pike are lost when hooked by striking too heavily, than if you don't strike at all. A pike generally collars the bait when it is revolving through the water. If you strike at once and sharply, the chances are that you will snatch bait and hooks out of his mouth. He may lay hold in such a manner that scarcely any of the hooks are in a position to bury themselves in his jaws, and a sudden stroke may pull the lot away after two or three seconds' play, whereas if you waited for a second, holding tight until the fish turned, the hooks have a better chance to bury themselves below the barb. When I am spinning a bait home and feel a sudden check deep below the surface I keep on winding until a strong pull in the opposite direction tells me that a fish is going off, I never slaken for a moment if anyhow possible, but keep my finger tightly pressed on the edge of reel and let him drag strongly for every foot of line he takes out. There is no necessity to let a pike run away with a lot of line if you can in any way prevent it. Of course if it is a very large one the case is a bit different, but moderate sized jack should be stopped before they have a chance to run you into difficulties among the weeds. I always play a fish heavily from the very first, and find this quite sufficient to hook them securely without striking sharply at all. Of course you know thereabouts what your line and tackle will stand, but it is folly to allow a five or six pounder to run right across the river and all over the place. I have killed, or at least got, eight-pound pike out of the water in three minutes after being hooked; but as an old friend put it, I always did take energetic measures with my pike when hooked. I did not believe in letting them run headlong into a bunch of weeds or round an old post or two if a little persuasion could keep them out; but the extent of this persuasion would have to be governed by the nature of the stream, the size of the fish, and the fineness or otherwise of the tackle.

It is not advisable under any circumstances when using spinning tackle to strike suddenly and heavily. The fish might be a heavy one, and the jerk might result in disaster to the line or tackle. In waters that are nearly choked up with weeds, where it is necessary to spin the bait near to the surface, it is far the best to give a hooked fish no more law than can be helped; keep a tight line on him, and get him to shore as quickly as possible. You might as well lose him one way as another, if he bolts right under the weeds, why he is as good as lost; but if you can keep him near the surface the chances of getting him out are good. If you really cannot do this owing to the fish being a large one, you will have to chance it and let him go and trust to luck to land him. In spinning over deep waters, or indeed any waters, and a hooked jack suddenly, as it were, stands on his tail with his upper part straight above the surface, opens his jaws and gills wide, and shakes his head like a savage dog, you stand a very good chance of losing that fish; but don't be flurried, keep the line tight; if you let the line go very slack he will probably shake the hooks out. A tight line is the only way to save that fish if it can anyhow be saved. A hard and fast line cannot be set down as to how a pike should be played. The angler should consider the circustances attached to each individual place, and lay his plans accordingly. I certainly have found it the best to take prompt measures if the cast was in a dangerous place, and trust to having a broken tackle. And, finally, while I am on with the subject of playing and landing a pike, I may say that if a large landing-net is used don't on any account try to use it until the hooked fish is well within reach. And then use it as promptly and quickly as possible; get it well under him and lift him speedily out before he has time to jump out again. In using a spinning tackle the hooks are liable to catch in the net before you get the fish fairly in as well, and if this happens you will be landed in a sweet little difficulty, and in all probability lose the fish. I found the best plan was to hold the pike's head above the surface, run the net up behind him, and scoop him out at once. In some waters it is a frequent occurrence for hooked pike to leap a couple of feet or even more into the air; when this happens, if you keep putting a heavy drag on the line you are liable to part company at once. The best plan is to instantly, as soon as he jumps, lower the rod point, and very slightly ease the pressure of the finger on the edge of the reel, so that he could have a yard of line if necessary, taking care, however, that the line is by no means slack; the pressure should always be tight enough to prevent the reel from paying out more loose line than is required.

Nothing is more fatal when playing a hooked fish than to have some loose line hanging about the reel handles. Every yard of line that I allowed a pike to take out had to be worked for by the fish.

The best months for spinning are September, October, and November. December is fairly good, but the pike then are getting fat and lazy, seeking the deepest and quietest holes as a general thing. There is nothing in law to prevent spinning for pike in public waters as soon as the season opens in June, unless a fishery board, for the district extends the close time. I most certainly do consider that June and July should be observed as a close time by every pike fisherman; while even in August those fish are by no means in condition. During the early part of the season pike are found on the weedy shallows of a quiet river, being also very partial to a streamy place that flows over a gravelly bottom, runs in the vicinity of flags, reed beds, water lilies, and bunches of weeds are also affected by them, while good ones are often deep in the fastnesses of the reed beds themselves. Quiet corners away from the main current, eddies at the tail of an island, behind some sunken trees and bushes; in fact, in a quiet pikey river there is no telling where the jack are and where they are not. All likely or even unlikely places should be well tried, especially during September and October. Later on, towards Christmas time, especially if the weather has been very cold, deeper holes close under the cover of huge banks of weeds would be more likely to shelter the fish. At this time of the year the spinning bait should be sunk deep down and spun very slowly home. In rapidly flowing rivers like the Trent, pike, during the early part of the season, love the eddies that curl round and round from the tail of a weir, or on the shallows away from the main current in quiet corners and lay-byes, or down those long stretches of the river where the water flows much quieter than it does in the majority of places. It is difficult to tell exactly where pike are to be found and where not found during the early part of the season; but if there is a portion of the river that is quiet, weedy, and free from navigation, that is the very place to expect them in. Later on they retire to the deeper and quieter waters, or else seek the pools and backwaters that have outlets or inlets to or from the river.

In spinning for pike it is necessary to have a drop-lead to the trace. By a drop-lead I mean one that hangs below the line, so that it cannot turn over and over in the water. If the lead turns round and round the line will kink up badly. There are several leads that have been specially made for this purpose, one of the best known having a spiral groove running round it. The great merit of this lead lies in the fact that it can be put on the trace exactly where best required for the particular place spun over; also that it can be bent to form the drop to nearly any degree, and that it can be taken off the trace without undoing any part of the tackle, and a lighter or heavier substituted as the particular case requires. My own lead that I have successfully used for a number of years now, is made and mounted on a thin brass wire with a swivel at each end of it. Traces should have at least two swivels in them, and these swivels should be slightly oiled from time to time, as it won't do for them to stick fast during the process of spinning. I give an illustration here of my own particular flight and trace, showing the extra side treble. This trace can be either gut or gimp, according to fancy; but in either case I find the best results are arrived at by having the trace in that particular shape. Sixteen inches is a good distance to have the lead from the bait, and about 30in. of gimp or gut between the lead and the silk running line. Speaking about the spinning line having a tendency to kink, I may say that it is a mistake to have too many swivels in the trace above the lead. I have seen as many as three, or even four, swivels in the trace, and yet the line kinked up worse than if no swivels at all had been used. I found it the best to have two swivels only in the trace, one of them immediately above the lead, and the other just below it. The very thing that some spinners thought would cure a badly kinking line, viz., putting an extra swivel or two in, only served to make the complaint worse.

Years ago we used to sigh for a good preservative, so that baits for spinning could be had when it was impossible to get them in the ordinary way. It used to generally happen that when we did not want any baits we could catch any amount of them, and when they were wanted badly not one could be procured. We tried salting them, putting them in glycerine, using spirits of wine, and trying a dozen other dodges, but none of them was a howling success. Of course, as I have said elsewhere, I preferred them fresh and bleeding if they could be got, but still a good preservative was a thing badly wanted. Formalin is the latest, and I am bound to say by experience far the best that has yet been tried. This mixture has two great merits, it is cheap and remarkably easy in its application. Experiments have shown that even the very smallest quantity of formalin among a quantity of clean water is sufficient to preserve small fish. A teaspoonful of it to a quart of water is quite ample for any ordinary purpose. The small fish—sprats are as good as anything—should be put in a wide-necked bottle, or a stoppered pickle jar, care being taken that not too many are put in each bottle, and then filled up with the diluted mixture just named, corked or otherwise fastened securely down. Sometimes the baits after being in the mixture for a time turn dirty and look very disagreeable. If this happens the best plan is to remove the cork, pour away the liquid, wash the baits well in cold water, rinse out the bottle, put back the baits, and fill up with a fresh lot of the mixture, only this time made weaker than before, say a proportion of only one teaspoonful of the formalin to three pints of water. One in forty is a strong proposition; one in sixty will do very well; while even one part to a hundred parts of water will preserve sprats if they are for immediate use. I might say that formalin is a poison, but when mixed with water is harmless. It is a liquid itself and colourless. I don't advise anyone to mix up more at once than he requires for the baits he just then wishes to preserve. I trust I have made this perfectly plain. The formalin itself is a poison, and should be kept under lock and key away from children. When mixed with water in its right proportions it is harmless. A teaspoonful to a quart of water is the proportion to use. Sprats especially, treated like this, are considerably toughened, and will keep for a long time. I have some now before me as I write that have been in the bottles eighteen months, and look as fresh and bright as when first put in; but the angler must remember if he wants them to last for a long time that he must cork and seal them down secure and air-tight if he uses an ordinary wide-necked bottle. A lever-stoppered bottle with a band of expanding indiarubber round the stopper is, however, far the best vessel to employ. I might also add that the small fish that are wanted for preservation, such as sprats, bleak, dace, minnows, stone loach, very small roach, and the tail-end of eels should be put in the preservative when perfectly fresh; on no account should stale ones be used; reject all that are tainted in the slightest, they must be perfectly fresh. I might also add that formalin is sold by The Formalin Co., Ltd.," 10, St. Mary's-at-Hill, London, E.C., at 2s. 6d. per bottle; but most of the tackle dealers now sell the preserved baits in lever-stoppered bottles at ninepence to a shilling per bottle.

In closing this chapter on spinning, I find on looking over my notes that I forgot to mention a very cheap and effective spinning lead that some of my friends on the Trent used years ago. It was simply a piece of sheet lead cut in an oval shape, about one and a half inches long, three-quarters of an inch wide, and one-sixteenth or so of an inch thick. This lead is bent lengthways down the centre, lapped across the trace in its proper place, and pinched tight. This lead can very easily be taken off or put on the line anywhere where wanted, and by being cut in an oval shape and bent in the centre hangs below the line and forms a wonderfully effective drop-lead for spinning. For all other spinning tackles and contrivances for working a dead bait, I must refer the reader to tackle dealers' illustrated catalogues. I have given what I consider to be the best general principles to adopt.

CHAPTER V.

THE PIKE *(continued)*.

SPINNING WITH AN ARTIFICIAL.

Artificial baits—What shape and colour is likely to have the best results—A seeming contradiction—Three typical artificials—How to spin an artificial—Best time, water, and places to try artificials—Wind and weather—Ice in the rings of the rod

Artificial baits for spinning for pike are now made in almost an endless and bewildering variety, and all sorts of material are used in their manufacture, brass, copper, nickel, German silver, aluminium, indiarubber, composition of various kinds, silk, natural skins of fishes, and even bunches of peacock's feathers and silver tinsel, so tied together till the lure looks like a huge humming bird when thrown on the water. Some of these artificials, like the famous "Clipper," for instance, are so constructed that a light breeze is quite sufficient to set them spinning round and round with great rapidity, and when drawn through the water looks like one even and glittering line of silver. This is a famous bait to use when the water is slightly clouded with colour. When the streams have run down very low, and the water is so bright that you can see the bottom very plainly, it is very little good throwing a bright silver-like artificial, or, indeed, for the matter of that, an artificial of any kind, unless it is a soft indiarubber bait of a very dull colour, a good deal after the pattern of the "Jubilee," I think it was called, and even this should be mounted on very fine grey-coloured gimp with hooks small and not much exposed. Almost any artificial, no matter what its name or shape will kill pike some odd times when the conditions are favourable; but tastes seem to vary in different waters. Some waters I have fished in the pike must have a bait that is painted a brilliant red inside with a huge tassel of scarlet wool depending from the far end hook. Others, again, in other waters won't look at one like that, but must have a plain dull-coloured article like the wagtail to tempt them. Some places the pike seem to prefer a small and glittering bait with a very even and rapid spin, a good deal like "Geen's Minnow," while others will have none of it, preferring a wobbling spoon. When we take into consideration all these things it is a very difficult task to determine which bait is likely to be the most useful under all conditions, and as a working man angler cannot afford or does not want to be troubled with one-tenth of the artificials that come under his notice, he would like to know which shape out of the whole lot is most likely to do him the best service. Personally I prefer a good plain spoon; this bait is one of the oldest artificials, and in my opinion still equal to anything or everything that has yet been invented. Pike have been killed on a spoon bait in all British waters where pike are to be found—down-streams like the Trent, or on quieter waters like the Bedfordshire Ouse and the Norfolk Broads. I have an old spoon now in my possession that has killed numbers of fine jack. One season, on reference to my note-book, I found I got no less than 40 with it, many of them reaching a very respectable size, and it is only a plain spoon, gold colour on the outside and bright silver within, with a narrow red line running down the centre on the inside. Some lucky angler on a certain occasion, when everything was in his favour, might be using any one of the numerous artificials that are made, and get a catch that his wildest dreams never thought about before, and straightway write to the sporting papers about his wonderful discovery of the finest artificial that ever was made, whereas he might have been using something else at the time totally different in shape and colour, and had the same luck on that. He might use the same bait a dozen times afterwards and not meet with anything like such success again. On one occasion I got 40lb. of jack during a single afternoon on my old spoon bait, but the weather and the water was in an extremely favourable condition, and the fish fairly on the rampage; and once the Clipper accounted for nine good fish in one day; but I should not like to say by any means that just because on those occasions I was lucky enough to get the fish that those baits will kill any time and under any conditions. It is only by a most careful trial during a number of seasons, and a most careful record of fish caught that a decision affecting this point can be arrived at. One season on the Trent there was not another bait that could touch "Bink's Jubilee" spinner as an artificial. This is a soft rubber bait, if my memory is to be trusted, while since that time I cannot hear that it has once met with more than ordinary success. A friend of mine who occasionally fishes in the big Irish loughs tells me that one day the pike of those waters seem to prefer a large Devon minnow of a dull brown or blue colour, while the next a bright silver Clipper with a red tassel at the tail seemed to have the greatest attraction; and still again, the very next day they would not run at either, but would take a huge wobbling spoon. Looking at my own practical experience I am forced to the conclusion that a good plain spoon of some two and a half inches in length, coloured either copper or gold on the outside, bright silver inside, with a red line down the centre (this line, by the way, can be painted on with a drop of the varnish mentioned elsewhere, mixed with a pinch of vermillion, and applied with a small camel-hair brush) is the best artificial that can yet be employed, even if it is somewhat old-fashioned. It must be 35 years since I saw a spoon bait used for the first time down a Lincolnshire canal, and as two or three fair good jack were taken on it on that occasion, I thought it a most wonderful bait. And so it is with most amateur pike spinners; just because a certain artificial on one occasion killed a good bag of fish, they needs must swear by that particular bait for ever afterwards. But some of the most curious pike spinning experiences I have ever had have been made up of contradictions pure and simple. One day the jack down a certain stretch of water would come at a bait of one particular shape and colour only, utterly ignoring anything else I happened to try; while the next day that bait itself was left alone and one of the rejected ones of the previous day would prove successful. In the face of all these difficulties and contradictions, it is a hopeless task, in fact I have had far too long a practical experience in pike fishing on various waters to attempt to recommend any one particular artificial as the very best that can be employed. As I said a little while ago, if I have a preference for any one, that one is an ordinary spoon; but when a pike spinner has killed over two hundred jack during his career on spoon baits in well-fished public waters, he is apt to speak feelingly. Here are three typical baits now before me that represent extremes in artificials. First there is an old wobbling spoon, that twists, curves, dives, and spins with a curious erratic movement, especially in still, or nearly still, **water**; second, there is the Clipper, a most brilliant silvery **fish** shaped bait with a scarlet tassel that spins extremely rapid and in one straight line; third, there is the Wagtail, a most curious bait made out of a thin and narrow, or rather two **narrow strips of** soft indiarubber, of a dull colour, which, when drawn through the water, seems to throb and heave like something alive and breathing. These are totally opposed to one another as far as shape, colour, and spinning powers are concerned, and yet I should say under certain conditions they all would meet with occasional sport. There are also dozens more artificials that come up in some particular way or other to those just named, which might be equally successful. It is no use pinning your faith on any one of them. Sometimes after an unsuccessful day with an artificial you might say, "Now, if I had had such and such a bait I might have got hold of one or two," **when** in all probability, no matter what you used, the result might have been the same. It depends more upon two things than the shape and colour of the artificial. First, the condition of the water, and, second, whether the pike are on the feed or not. Putting it broadly then, I should say that if your tackle case contained three different types of artificials that are opposed **to** each other in shape, colour, **and** spinning powers, I care not under what name they are **known,** nor yet who is the manufacturer of them, the chances **are** that one or the other of them would some time during the day attract the attention, and so arouse the curiosity of a pike that he would throw prudence to the winds and seize

G

hold, although the water might be as clear as gin, and everything unfavourable for the sport. It is only by acting dodges like the one I gave in the previous chapter, that is after throwing some considerable time over a place that you know holds a good jack, without success, or at most which only moves him, with one kind of artificial, slip another one on as much opposed to the one you have been using as you have got, and he may come the very next throw. You can never tell your luck; you can only keep pegging away, chopping and changing about, first one artificial and then another, sometimes spinning quickly then again more slowly; sometimes deep down in the water, and then again nearer the surface. It is only by this that a jack will repose in the bag at close of day, that is, bear in mind, when the water is extremely clear and everything unfavourable, remembering always what a well-known angler once said when writing to one of the angling journals: "That you cannot expect to catch many fish if your rod is all the time reared up against a tree." I cannot hold with the remarks that the writer I previously quoted used in one of his articles, that the water could not be too clear for spinning with an artificial, especially a spoon. It appeared to me to be a necessity that in certain waters, particularly in well-fished public rivers, that a certain amount of colour should be in the water; but see what I say on this subject in the previous chapter on spinning with a dead bait. Those remarks hold good in discussing the use of an artificial.

In rivers like the Trent, that are subject after heavy rains to sudden and thick water floods, that come tearing down with terrific force, it is very little good to throw an artificial of any kind while the water is in that state, rather wait a little until it has somewhat fined down; in fact so much that when your bait is sunk two or three feet down below the surface you can see it gleam, as it were, in a haze. Try then all the quieter corners and lay-byes, letting it sink deep down and spinning home no faster than is really necessary. Taking it all round the Trent fishes very well indeed when it is moderately clear, that is as far as pike spinning is concerned; but I should suppose this is because it is a very wide river with a good volume of water generally running.

In quieter waters like the Ouse, the Witham, and similar streams, I found it the best for spinning when the water was on the rise, and once or twice I have had very good bags when it has been too thick to see the spoon when sunk a couple of feet below the surface. During the late summer and early autumn, when the water is very clear, almost the only chance you have to pick up a fish by spinning an artificial is just after sunset, immediately before the dusk of evening creeps down on you. I have had some of my very best fish under these circumstances. A splendid place to try an artificial is in the rough and broken water at the foot of a weir, particularly if large stones and sunken trees break the force of the stream and form eddies behind. If the frothing waters keep churning round and round, and you hardly think there is room to get a spinning bait in, never mind, have a try, there might be a specimen lurking under the shadow of those big stones. I am very fond of spinning in all those streams and eddies that curl round and round from the foot of a weir. The same trace and droplead that I recommend for spinning a natural bait will do for an artificial, only when water is clouded, weeds and obstructions are plentiful, and fish run large, I should use them rather thicker than ordinary, say No. 1 gimp; but on well-fished rivers like the Lea and Stort, say, when water is clear, gut traces and small hooks must be the order of the day. And now just a word or two on another very vexed question, and that is what wind and weather are likely to be the best for sport with a spinning bait, either dead or an artificial? Some anglers prefer a gale of wind, when the water is rolled up in miniature waves, caused by the wind chopping or blowing up-stream. Certainly I have had some sport under circumstances like that, but then on the other hand I have had far better luck when not even a wind ripple disturbed the surface of the water. Once in particular, I find on reference to my note-book, that I had been spinning all one afternoon when the water was clouded and the wind blowing just sufficient to ripple and disturb the surface; but not a touch did I get. Towards evening the wind suddenly died down, not so much as a move could be seen on the water, and the rain that had been threatening all day came down in earnest. Not caring to go home with a blank, I again tried over a place that I had twice previously thrown over during the afternoon without success, and within the next half-hour five fish going 25lb. lay on the bank. I am forced to admit that several of my best bags have been taken during a dead calm. I don't think it matters in the slightest when the water is clouded a little as to whether there is a good breeze or not. If the water is very clear then the case is different, a little wind being necessary to hide the angler's movements and the deception of his line and tackle. I have taken jack when spinning in all sorts of weather—when a gale nearly blew me into the river, when a light chopping wind only just rippled and disturbed the surface, and also when not a breath of air could be discerned. You cannot lay down a hard and fast line in this respect, but speaking generally and broadly I should say, taking all things into consideration, the whole season through, clear water and clouded, a little breeze stands the best chance of sport. As regards the best quarter for the wind to be in, I don't think it matters very much where it is. A strong east wind with a touch of frost that will clean drive the roach off the feed, will sometimes serve to make the pike ravenous. Wind and weather don't matter very much. One of the most favourable conditions to find the water in is after a few frosts have rotted the weeds, then a heavy rain which causes a rapid rise and sweeps the decayed weeds away and washes the jack from out their fastnesses into the more open water. As soon as this flood-water clears away sufficiently to enable the bait to be seen fairly well, then that most assuredly is the time for getting sport. I have got jack spinning when the weather has been very warm and summerlike, and also have got them when the frost has been so keen that every few minutes I have been obilged to suck the ice from out the rings of the rod; when a nor'-easter has been raging; when the rain has been coming down in dead earnest; and also during a snowstorm. In spinning during very frosty weather the ice will accumulate in the rings of the rod and cause considerable trouble and annoyance. Several things have been recommended to counteract this somewhat, but none of them appear to me to be a permanent success. The spinning line is generally an undressed silk, and holds water to some extent, so naturally freezes. You cannot do better than rub a few drops of castor oil, applied with a flannel, down the line before starting out on a frosty day. This is the best remedy I know of, but grinding the line in and out the rings when the latter are nearly choked up with ice is not one of the best things to subject a line to. If ice forms in the end ring or any of the rings for the matter of that, you must suck it out again and chance the disagreeableness of the task.

CHAPTER VI.

THE PIKE *(continued).*

TROLLING WITH A DEAD GORGE.

The reel, line, and tackle—How to bait a dead gorge—Working the trolling bait—Different methods of dead gorging.

Trolling for pike with a dead gorge bait is a sport that I don't hold with, if the place operated on can anyhow be got at with a spinning bait. All hooked fish, no matter how small, must be killed after swallowing a dead gorge. It is true there is a disgorger made now that will occasionally get up gorge hooks without hurting the fish very much, more particularly live gorge tackle; but the fact that the gimp of a dead gorge is threaded completely through the bait, and also that a lead is cast round the shank of the hooks, prevents the disgorger just named from getting to the points of the hooks on purpose to push them back. But as there are certain waters containing good pike that cannot possibly be got at by any other plan, I must just briefly look at it, but this chapter will be a very short one indeed.

Certain backwaters, pools, railway cuttings, etc., etc., are very often so choked up with weeds that there is scarcely a hole a yard square anywhere all over the surface, and yet good jack are known to be in those waters, the object of a dead gorge being so that when it is moved up and down in a sink and draw movement and a pike swallows it, there are no hooks, no leads, and no float to catch among the weeds and so help him to shake himself free; and if the pike does thread himself in and out among those weeds you stand a chance of getting him out if line and tackle are strong, which they ought to be in dead-gorging, and the weeds somewhat rotten and tender. I remember once seeing a very large jack taken by this method, which, when landed, was so embedded among a huge lump of weeds that it positively could not be seen; weeds and jack together must have weighed close on a hundredweight. In dead-gorging among the weeds the rod should be as stiff and as strong as possible, and the line as strong as you like; in fact, it cannot be too strong. One of those tanned plaited hemp ones, No. 1 or 2 size, that is capable of standing a strain of from thirty to forty pounds, will be plenty good enough for this purpose, and as a forty or fifty yard length only runs from two shillings to half-a-crown the price need not be a serious consideration. I don't recommend a good silk spinning line for this job; if the angler is in the habit of frequently fishing certain waters among the weeds with a dead gorge it will pay him to have a strong, easy-going, cheap, wooden reel, and a length of plaited hemp line, and use them for that purpose only, the price would not exceed five shillings for both, and as this line is rather sharp and harsh in its texture it would be likely to saw through a bunch of dead weeds like a reaping hook when a big jack threaded his way through. The usual gorge hook is simply a double hook of the pattern or shape known as a parrot beak, securely fastened to a short length of stout twisted brass wire, hook and wire being about five inches long over all; a piece of lead reaching from nearly the bends of the hooks to within a couple of inches of the small eye at end of wire, that is about three inches long and three-eighths of an inch thick in the centre, tapering slightly towards each end, is cast on the shank of hook and the brass wire in such a manner that the whole is stiff and rigid. Joined to the small eye at end of wire is a length of strong gimp, say from 18in. to 2ft., and this gimp should be fairly strong and in keeping with the rest of the tackle. A short trace without any lead on, say about a couple of feet long, with a strong buckle swivel on the end, completes the troller's outfit. The lead is inside the bait, so none is required on the trace; besides you want nothing on the line to catch over or under the weeds, more than you can possibly help. It would be all the better if there was not even a swivel; but I consider a swivel a very necessary evil for this work, as without it the line is liable to kink when wet.

In baiting a gorge hook, the loop of the gimp is put in the eye of a baiting needle, and the point of this thrust down the throat of the bait, keeping it as near the backbone as possible, and as near the centre of the fish as you can, so that the leaded wire will have a foundation of solid flesh to rest in, and not be so liable to tear away by contact with the weeds as it would do if threaded through the intestines only. Bring the needle out between the forks of the tail, and carefully draw the gimp through until the lead and wire are completely hidden in the bait, with the bends of the hooks close up to the nose. Some anglers then tie the tail with a bit of fine twine or shoemaker's flax to the gimp, wrapping it round and round, so that there are no inequalities hanging free to catch under the weeds when the bait is withdrawn from the water. Other men clip the tail off altogether with a pair of scissors, but one plan would, I daresay, be as good as the other. Now remove the baiting needle and fasten the loop of the gimp into the buckle swivel of the trace, join the latter neatly with a good fast knot to the running line, and all is ready for action. The best bait for trolling is a good five-inch dace, a small roach will do, so will a large gudgeon; but a dace appears to me to be the best shape for shooting down quickly, besides being tough and lasting on the hooks.

Where trolling with a dead gorge differs in a material manner from spinning with a dead bait, is the fact that almost any preserved or pickled fish will do for the latter, the former must have a bait perfectly fresh. When a pike runs at a spinning bait and lays hold, he has no chance, as a rule, to reject it, whereas if the taste of a dead gorge was not to his liking, he could drop it at once. I found that if a bait was freshly killed, and slipped on the gorge when bleeding, the chances would be much better than if the bait was old and stale. In trolling, the angler selects the clearest place he can find and draws down a length of line from between the rings of the rod, and just tosses the bait towards that opening, at the same time leaving go of the loop or length of line he holds in one hand. As soon as the bait hits the water it will dive down very quickly, the heavy lead inside it causing this. Always keep a tight line; don't have any slack hanging loose if you can possibly help it. As soon as the bait begins to dive downwards lower the point of the rod until you think the bait has gone far enough, and then raise the point slowly until it again comes near the surface, then drop the rod again quickly so as to cause the bait to again shoot downwards towards the bottom, repeating this a few times until the bait works too near the weeds; then withdraw it as well as you can, clear off what stray weeds may be sticking to the hooks, and make a fresh cast. If the water is very much choked up with weeds, you cannot very well work a gorge bait in a small opening beyond the reach of your rod; if you can reach the place with your rod point it will be all the better. I have known before now a long 18-foot bamboo, stiff and strong, with a reel whipped or tied to the butt end, and a few very large rings at long intervals up it, to be used in a foul and awkward place with considerable success, the extra length enabling the angler to reach holes that he possibly could not get at with a short trolling rod. But if there is a considerable clear space over the weeds and just beyond the reach of the rod point, the bait can be thrown to the furthest edge of the hole and worked up and down a few times until it reaches the weeds that are nearest the rod point, when it must be withdrawn in the best manner that the circumstances of the place will allow. It is the best plan to let a dead gorge plump down quickly, being careful all the time that the line is tight, and to lift it back again towards the surface more slowly. The action of the water, in conjunction with the shape of the bait, causes it to gyrate more in its upward journey than it does during its downward plunge. I have always fancied that a dead gorge bait looked more natural in the water than the very best spinning bait I ever mounted, anyhow I know that a dead gorge, worked as it should be among the weeds, is the most deadly plan that can be tried. When a pike collars the bait, you must not get excited and strike at once, or in all probability you will simply jerk it out of his mouth. A dead gorge must be swallowed; and it all depends on the humour of a jack as to how long it will take to perform this operation, he might swallow it within two minutes, or he might be a quarter of an hour. When he runs off with it, ease the line and let him go, don't check him in the slightest, and when he stops allow him five minutes, or maybe eight would be safer, to get it down. If he has swallowed it all right you need not strike, but simply wind him out the best way you can, weeds and all.

I have seen all sorts of hooks and tackle recommended for this job, some of them without the twisted wire, and instead of the stiff and rigid lead they are fitted up with a flexible or jointed lead, so that the bait can move about in any direction. I don't recommend any of these, believing that the stiff wire is a protection to the bait when it is dragged through the weeds. It seems to be the usual plan to mount a gorge hook so that when the bait is worked upwards towards the surface the points of those hooks faces the same way, and are liable to catch the weeds during its upward journey. One man who used to do a lot of deadgorging always used to let his bait plump downwards, tail first, bringing it up again towards the surface, head foremost; that is, exactly reversing the position of the bait from what it would be if worked in the ordinary way. To accomplish this he used to have the twisted wire on his hook very stiff and strong, and exactly long enough to reach from the bottom edge of the gill covers of his bait down to about half an inch from the fork of the tail. In baiting this, instead of running the baiting needle in at the mouth, he used to drive it in close under the gill covers, bringing it out about half an inch or a little less from the root of the tail. After drawing the leaded hook and wire completely through the bait until the points of the hook, or rather the bends of the hook laid on the bottom edge of the gill covers with the points free. He used to again push the needle straight through the root of the tail, and bring it out on the opposite side to where the hooks laid, and again pass it through the bait lengthways, but this time carefully bringing it out of the mouth and drawing the gimp after it. Now, you see by the gimp going in at the gill covers, right down to the tail, and up again to the mouth, the position is reversed, the tail of the bait goes downwards through the water first, and the bends of the hooks faces the weeds, instead of the points, when it is jerked upwards and withdrawn. In this plan it is a necessity to have the wire of the gorge hook pretty long and stiff, and firmly embedded in the solid flesh of the bait, or the wear and tear of dragging it among the weeds would soon rip it all to pieces. I have seen this tackle and plan of baiting used in very deep and open water where no weeds and obstructions exist, instead of a spinning bait, and certainly when the fish laid low and were very sluggish it was more successful than either spinning or live-baiting. It is thrown right across to the opposite side and allowed to sink to the bottom, and then very slowly, inch by inch, wound home again. The bends of the hooks coming first prevented any fouling. This is a deadly plan that I have had proof off more than once; but I say again that I don't like it, because no matter if the fish weighs one pound or twenty pounds, it must be killed when hooked on a dead gorge; but for all that in very deep and open water with a clear bottom it is more deadly than even the paternoster tackle.

CHAPTER VII.

THE PIKE *(continued)*.

FISHING WITH A LIVE BAIT.

Different methods of live baiting—Pike floats and pilots—Snap tackle and the methods of baiting—Traces for live baiting—Stream fishing for pike—The slider float—Striking, and playing a pike on float tackle—The proper depth—A contrast—Live gorging—Paternostering for pike—Legering—Queer live baits—Live bait kettles and store boxes.

Live-baiting for pike can be divided into four heads, or rather sections, two of them practised with one or more floats, and the other two without floats at all; but I don't propose to go at very great length into this part of my subject, describing the dozens of tackles that are recommended for this branch of angling. I shall only briefly look at them from a working man's standpoint, and just see which tackle out of the whole lot is most likely to have the best results when used in any and all circumstances and conditions of live-baiting. The four heads under which live-baiting can be subdivided are as follows:—First, with a snap tackle, and one or more floats so arranged that the bait swims at any depth the angler pleases, mid-water or nearer the bottom or nearer the surface, the snap hooks being such that when the pike seizes the bait he can be struck at once. Second, with similar floats, but with a double side or gorge hook threaded under the skin of the bait, so that a pike must swallow it before he can be hooked. Third, with a paternoster that is used without floats, but has a pear-shaped lead at the extreme end below the baits, and one, two, or sometimes three sets of hooks projecting at right angles from the main trace at fixed distances from each other above the lead. Fourth, with a leger tackle sunk to the bottom of deep holes, with the bait below the lead, and fished as either a gorge tackle or a semi-gorge snap. Snap fishing with float tackle is a plan that is now very much in vogue amongst the anglers who ply their craft on lakes, cuttings, backwaters, and other quiet waters and rivers that are, comparatively speaking, free from weeds. Floats themselves are made in various shapes and sizes, round, long, egg-shaped, and one that has been registered has the body made like a hollow cylinder with different coloured tops fitting in like corks, so that under various aspects of the weather and the lights and shades that play about on the surface of the water and the shadows from flags and bushes, the colour of the top could be altered to suit the eyesight of the angler without having to remove the whole float. Various sorts of material are also used in the manufacture of pike floats, such as wood, cork, celluloid, etc., etc., and some anglers who cannot afford to spend much over their sport use a plain bung from an old barrel with considerable success. Personally I like an egg-shaped one, with a hole lengthways through the centre, into which a plug of wood can be fitted, so that when the line is threaded through this hole the plug holds it tight in its position at the proper depth. The "Fishing Gazette" float is the most useful that can be tried. This float has a slit or nick cut down one side through to the centre plug hole, the object of the slit being so that the float can be taken off the line and a larger or smaller substituted, as the case demanded, without having to undo the knots and take off the tackle. One about two and a half inches long down the longest part will be the most useful general size that can be used, although it will be necessary some odd times, I daresay, to have one much larger, or even smaller, for special occasions. About a couple of feet or so from the larger float, nearer the rod point, there is another float, called a pilot. This is generally a much smaller one, and quite round in shape, one about three-quarters of an inch in diameter being plenty large enough. The object of this small float or pilot is to keep the line on the surface and prevent it from sinking down and getting mixed up with the bait and tackle; indeed, some anglers that I know when fishing in shallow water have two pilots a yard or so apart, in addition to the float proper.

The trace for live-baiting differs slightly from the one recommended for spinning, although the latter will do very well at a pinch. The one most generally in use, however, is a yard length of gimp, or strong salmon gut, with a loop on one end and a No. 4 or 5 buckle swivel on the other. Just above the swivel, threaded on the gimp, is a barrel lead about one and a half or two inches long, and about as thick as a fair sized swan quill. The lead and swivel should be about 14in. from the bait. The main object of the lead is not so much cocking the float, as it is keeping the bait down and preventing it from rising to the surface. In the trace for spinning there are at least two swivels and a drop or hanging lead; in a live-bait trace the buckle swivel fixed at the end is ample, and the lead need only be a plain one, with a hole lengthways down the centre, so that it can be threaded on the gimp or gut.

Snap tackles are now made in almost an endless variety, each one of them claiming to be better than any of the others, the object of the snap tackle being, as its name suggests, snapping or striking the pike directly after he seizes the bait. The best known and the most widely used tackle at the present day is the old-fashioned Jardine snap, which is simply two treble hooks, only one hook that forms each treble is smaller than the other two, fixed a certain distance from each other to suit the size of bait used. Indeed, it is a general plan now to have one of the trebles made with eyes so that it can be shifted closer to the other or further apart to suit the size of bait used. This old tackle holds its

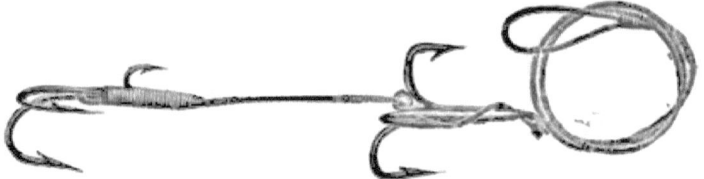

FIG. 12. THE JARDINE SNAP.

own among the many that have since been introduced to supersede it; in fact, in my opinion, none of them are any better, and some of them decidedly not so good. The usual Jardine snap that is generally sold by tackle dealers, has the small hook of the end treble much too small. I prefer it at least half the size of the other two, so as to take a good hold into the root of the shoulder or pectoral fin of the bait. The accompanying illustration of the Jardine most in use nowadays shows the small hook of the end treble, no larger than a roach hook, whereas in my opinion it should be several sizes larger. Some anglers, Mr. Jardine, I believe, among the number, sometimes fixes this tiny hook into the gill cover of the bait itself, in which case a small hook would probably be the best; but I most certainly prefer a larger one and fix it firmly into the root of the shoulder fin. The moveable treble is fixed in such a place on the gimp that it can be run fair under the root of the back fin, taking hold of, at least, a quarter of an inch of solid flesh. I have seen anglers who did not understand the proper use of this tackle, fix a bait on it in strange positions, such as one of the trebles through both lips, and the end one fair into the sides, or one of the trebles under the back fin and the other into the root of the tail. This rough sketch shows the position of the two trebles on the bait, only for the sake of plain illustration they are pictured much too large, with the gimp, the shanks of hooks, and the bindings much too coarse, and the draughtsman has also drawn both hooks in a straight line, whereas the shank of the top treble should be pointing straight upwards about level with the top corner of the dorsal or back fin, instead of so much to the right hand. But, anyhow, it shows what I consider to be about the proper position for the hooks to be fixed in the bait in

FIG. 13. METHOD OF BAITING THE JARDINE SNAP.

order to give the best results. Another Jardine tackle is now made that has a wire fastened to the end treble in such a manner that it can be threaded in at the mouth and out at the gill covers, a spiral twist at the end like a corkscrew enabling it to be fastened to the gimp between the two sets of hooks. This spiral wire was made to supersede the small hook of the end treble, the wire holds the bait firmly in its position without sticking the small hook into the shoulder fin, or, indeed, having the small hook there at all. It was claimed for this so-called improvement of the Jardine tackle that a bait could be held much more secure than with an ordinary one, and that it could be hurled long distances in wide lakes or rivers without throwing off. But unfortunately on a careful trial by practical men this long casting was a source of danger and injury to the bait. If the casting was made ever so careful, sometimes the gill cover of the bait would be torn completely away, and even if the bait was only used at close quarters and no damage done to it by long casting, the wire props open the mouth and gill covers, with the result that the bait soon dies and won't work as it should do from the very first; it seems to be cramped and choked, and does not work about as I like to see a live bait work.

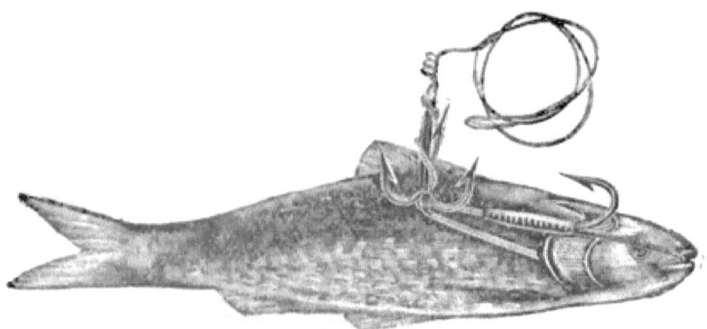

FIG. 14. THE WIRED JARDINE SNAP.

Another tackle that used to be a great favourite with us some years ago was a good deal like a Jardine, except the hook that went under the back fin. This was a fair sized moveable single hook, instead of the moveable treble, the end hook being exactly the same in both cases, and the method of baiting identical. The improved Bickerdyke tackle, shown in the accompanying illustration is, according to all reports of my pike fishing customers who have used it, a very good one indeed. The end treble has the small hook reversed with the shank lengthened considerably, the object of this long shanked hook being so that when a pike seizes the bait the hook can be drawn free from the bait, allowing a much better chance of hooking your quarry. The moveable single hook shown in the illustration is stuck firmly under the back fin, the double hook with the long shank reversed hook goes under the skin of the shoulder, so that the two hooks lay on the bait exactly in the position shown for baiting the ordinary "Jardine," and the treble hook that hangs free, is simply put over the bait on the opposite side to the other shoulder hooks and allowed to hang free without being stuck in the bait at all, or the point of one hook can be, if the angler likes, just hanked under the skin towards the belly if he does not like to see it swinging loose, but it may be a source of danger when

Fig. 15. The Bickerdyke Snap.

striking a fish if it is made fast in the bait. There are many more snap tackles made for use with live bait, such as saddle snaps that have two sets of hooks that straddle over the bait, and others too numerous to mention here, all more or less efficient for the work they are made to do; but taking things all round I don't think the old fashioned Jardine can be beaten. The working man pike fisherman, who has not got much money to spare for his tackle, may rest contented very well with them. One of my friends used to bait the Jardine somewhat different to the plan just described, instead of putting the end hook into the root of the shoulder fin, he used to put it fair on the top of the back, close behind the head; he would have it that, with a pike having eyes on the top of his head he was generally looking upwards, and could not see the hooks so well when fixed on the top of the back of the bait. There may be

H

something in this, but I don't think it matters much, as that old friend never had much better luck, and sometimes not so good as I had when adopting the ordinary plan. I don't recommend very large hooks unless the baits are extra big, No. 3 or 4 being ample for all ordinary purposes. For exceptional circumstances, where you know there is a very large pike, and you are trying him with a half-pound bait, or even a small jack which, by the way, is often a splendid bait for those large cannibal pike that inhabit a quiet cutting or isolated pool, it will be as well to have an extra large and strong snap tackle made up with some No. 1 trebles. In snap fishing when the water is only moderately clear, it does not matter so much about the tackle; oo copper gimp will be quite good enough for both trace and tackle, but if the water has run down very fine indeed, then a good strong gut trace will be less visible to the fish. The hooks themselves should be dressed on six or seven inches of gimp, then a single strand of strong salmon gut with a loop at each end, fixed between the gimp of the hooks and the buckle swivel on end of the trace, and finally a two or three feet trace of the strongest gut the angler can afford. Tackle for live livebaiting should always, if possible, be finer than spinning tackle, because in the latter case the bait revolves swiftly through the water, while in the former it is, comparatively speaking, stationary. The best colour for a float would be green with a white top, some anglers like them dark blue with a red top; but a good deal of this is only fancy. In snap fishing down a current that runs into an eddy, it is the best to fix the float so that the bait is some two-thirds of the distance down, that is, within eighteen inches or two feet from the bottom; if this distance can anyhow be guessed, if not, a heavy plummet hung on the buckle swivel and quietly sunk to the bottom will soon tell the proper depth; this mind, is for fishing clear running rivers that have pikey looking corners and eddies, into which a current gurgles and glides, with a bottom, comparatively speaking, clear and free from weeds, and an overhanging row of bushes or sedges lining the side. In this method of snap fishing, fix the small pilot float about a foot above the larger one, for reasons that will be given presently. In live-baiting a quiet lake or similar still water, the pilot is principally used to keep the line on the surface. In stream fishing this does not matter as the line is generally played out from the reel tight, but still a pilot is useful in detecting a proper run from a pike, or only an extra spurt from the bait when he pulls the first float under. In fishing a corner or eddy such as just described, the angler should stand right at the head of the swim, and just drop his bait on the outer edge of the stream, and let it work down the current at the further side of the eddy, letting it go just fast enough to prevent it from being swept too near the bank on which he stands. When the floats reach the eddy proper, by being slightly held back, the bait will work in a semicircular direction round the edge of the eddy towards the bank, and perhaps again take an outward direction towards the centre of the curl, if that eddy is of the shape known to Trent men as an umbrella; pike very often lay on the outer edge of these eddies, just between the sharp current and the curling water. The quieter parts of a streamy river, where a nice little current glides into an eddy and then seems to divide into two, with a wedge shaped pool between, should always be well tried, even if the bait has to be twenty-five or thirty yards away from where you stand. A little careful observation and manipulation of the floats and bait, by being dropped on one of the streams that glides down and across into these wedge shaped eddies, will result in reaching them without much trouble. In live-baiting distant places like that, it is rather difficult to hit the exact depth, and to be right, in my opinion, the bait should be about eighteen inches from the bottom; but the worst of these streams and eddies is the fact that the depth might vary. The best way to try the place is to put the float at what you consider to be the right depth with only the leaded trace, and throw it as near as you can to the spot you wish to fish, if the lead is on the bottom the float will bob about, and you want to be a lot shallower; if, on the other hand, the float rides quietly, you are not deep enough. If after a careful trial you find there is, say, an uniform depth of eight feet, the bait will want to be about six and a half feet from the float, and so on, always allowing this distance, that is, eighteen inches between the bottom of the river and the bait, no matter how deep the place is, because I believe in streamy eddies like those, the jack lay as near the bottom as possible. Sometimes the place may be very deep, say sixteen or eighteen feet, and you cannot manage very well with a fixed float, for this you must fish the float as a slider, a good deal after the plan I described in fishing a deep hole for barbel in Vol. 1; the small pilot can be dispensed with, and instead of having the larger float with the slit down the side, a plain one of the same shape will be best. Remove the plug altogether, so that the float will slip up and down the line easily, and knot into the line at the right depth a bit of indiarubber or something similar, of such a size and shape that it will easily run through the rings on the rod without jerking or catching, and yet will not go through the small hole down the centre of the float. In fishing holes of considerable depth this float drops down the line and is out of the way of the rod point when the bait is withdrawn; but when lead and bait sink in the water the float rises until stopped by the obstruction knotted into the line. Some anglers may say that places like those could be much better fished with the paternoster or the ledger tackle, but I would point out that the character of the streams down some of these running rivers, between the bank and the eddies, would be all against ledgering or paternostering; the strong current might drown the line and sweep the bait anywhere but where it was wanted, and a float on the surface, be the only plan of keeping the bait in the required position. Another question that anglers don't seem to be agreed on, is the time that should be allowed between the jack taking the bait and the striking, when snap fishing; this in a great measure depends on the nature of the water operated on, in stream fishing the pike generally takes a bait very quickly, and can be struck almost immediately. In lake or still water fishing the pike seem to me to be much more deliberate in their actions, and should be allowed a few seconds, say five or six, after the float disappears. In the stream fishing that we have just now been discussing, and the bait is of a fair size and lively, the float will now and again bob clean under, making the inexperienced think he has got a run; it was for this purpose of detecting a good run that I recommended the bait to be some eighteen inches from the bottom, and the small float or pilot about a foot from the larger one. As soon as ever both floats disappear under the surface, and sometimes they will follow one another like a flash, the line can be tightened with a slight jerk. Heavy striking is not necessary in this snap fishing, in fact, it is to be condemned; you see, when fishing in this manner down the streams and eddies you have rod in left hand with finger on edge of reel, and the line, comparatively speaking, tight between the finger and thumb of the right hand. A good run from a pike could very often be felt before it was even seen. If the finger is pressed tight on the edge of reel, and the point of the rod raised smartly, the plunge of the hooked fish would be quite sufficient to drive the hooks well home, without risking a broken line by striking heavily at a large pike when making his first plunge. If the place has a clear bottom and is free from obstructions, it is an easy matter to play the hooked fish, easing the pressure slightly on the edge of reel as he runs, and winding in whenever you have a chance, taking care, however, that the line is always taut; always play a pike as heavily as you can, and don't allow him to run all over the place more than you can possibly help. If it is an awkward place, full of weeds and obstructions, you will have to be guided by the circumstances of the case, as to how you play him, but keep him away from danger at any cost by putting on all the pressure the tackle will bear, and with a little luck he will be yours. In snap-fishing with a float in a lake or very quiet river, the bait cannot be manipulated into the eddies and streams like it is in stream fishing, you can only throw it out and wait for a run, of course, winding in a yard of line every now and again until the bait travels across the open water from the full extent of the cast, unto nearly the rod point, but each place will have to be fished according to its own peculiarities. It is a good plan sometimes when fishing a lake or other sheet of water that has a lot of reed beds all round the margin, to take a boat, if one is handy, and kick up a good big row by splashing a pole right in the middle of those reed beds. Large jack very often lay hidden deep among those reeds, and it is just possible you may startle them out and into the open water beyond, where later on they would have a much better chance of seeing one of your baits than they would while in the middle of that fortress. This dodge has scored more than once during my experience. A live bait can be thrown a considerable distance without injury; a gentle swing from the rod point in the manner described in Chap. 3, being sufficient to get out thirty yards without jerking the bait from the hooks; but a live bait on snap tackle must be carefully thrown. In snap fishing with a live bait the line should always be well greased, so that in still water it will float on the surface—many a fish has been lost by having a sunk line between the floats and rod point. Another point of interest to the would-be pike fisherman is whether the live bait should be near the bottom, or nearer the surface; my own opinion and experience favours the former, especially in deep, quiet waters. If the place is twelve or fourteen feet deep, I always found it to be the best to have the bait within a couple of feet of the bottom at the outside, that is if you wanted the larger fish. During the winter time they are, as a rule, much too sluggish to rise up to within three feet of the surface to take a bait; a few small ones may be got, but the larger ones lie low as a rule, and like the immortal Mr. Micawber, wait patiently for something to turn up. Another point is whether a large bait or a small one is the best, and here again the peculiarities of each place must decide the matter. If the jack only run small, then a dace from two to three ounces will be quite large enough; but if the place is a deep, quiet lake, tenanted by very large pike, then taking things all round large baits will stand the best chance. Once I remember getting a fourteen pounder on a dace that only weighed half an ounce; but the balance of opinion favours the large bait taking one time with another. I had a very curious illustration of these last two points some time ago: A gentleman got a day in a private lake, that was strictly preserved, and only occasional leave granted; the lake swarmed with pike of all sizes. He fished all day in deep water with the bait (small dace averaging two ounces each), about a yard from his float, and successfully landed ten fish weighing altogether forty-one pounds, largest 5¾lbs. Another gentleman whose ticket was dated for a week later, took down a can of dace that must have gone on the average half-a-pound each; he fished deep down, and landed nine fish weighing altogether 132½lbs., the largest 24½lbs, the smallest 7lbs; a vast difference, which could only be satisfactorily explained by the different methods the two anglers had of going to work, as the conditions were similar on both days. If the place is in a very awkward position and weeds are pretty plentiful, but not sufficient to stop a bait from working about at all, it will be as well to use a live gorge tackle instead of a snap; the hooks of the latter might catch among the weeds, whereas the gorge hook lies flatter on the side of bait, and is less conspicuous. The live gorge is simply a double hook, whipped firmly on the end of a foot or so of fine gimp, and threaded until the hooks lie on the side, close up to the gill covers; the loop of the gimp being brought out just behind the dorsal or back fin. Care must be taken in threading the bait that the needle and gimp only just goes under the skin, and that the points of the hook project well above the side, and are not buried in the bait at all. The same trace and float will do for this as for snap-fishing, the only difference in using a gorge bait, is that the pike must be allowed five or six minutes to swallow the bait, instead of striking at the disappearance of the floats. When the pike seizes the gorge bait you must let him go where he likes, even if he threads right through a bed of weeds, don't check him in the slightest, but pay out line until he stops, and then quietly lay down the rod in such a position that he can take more line off the reel if he wants it, and wait five or six minutes. If before this time expires the float comes to the surface, you may know he has rejected the bait, but if it keeps down unless it gets fast among the weeds, you may hope that he has got it swallowed, and tighten on him, extricating him from among the weeds in the best manner you can. I don't like gorge fishing at all, but still it is useful under some circumstances. A live bait can be worked by it among the weeds much better than with a snap. The bait can be hurled much further without so much danger of throwing off; and, finally, when a pike is fairly hooked, the hooks are down its belly, and not hanging from its jaws to catch in every weed-bed that comes handy. The pike fishermen of the Welsh Harp almost always use a gorge tackle, the main reason for this being that the lake is very shallow, as a rule, all round the margin, and it is necessary to throw out a considerable distance from the bank in order to get any depth of water. The generality of these men have an addition to the ordinary live gorge hook, in the shape of a small wire hook about as big as a little roach hook, but without either point or barb, that is brazed at the back of the other two, and projecting slightly above them. After the hook is threaded in its proper position this very small back hook drops into the hollow under the edge of the gill cover, and takes firm hold of the hard gristle just there. This prevents the gimp from tearing away the skin when the tremendous long casts are made.

Paternostering is another very quiet and deadly method of taking pike, particularly large pike that live in holes and eddies, where the bottom of the river is very unequal in depth. The paternoster is simply a long trace of strong gut or gimp, with a fairly heavy pear-shaped lead at the extreme end, and one or more sets of hooks at intervals higher up. Personally, I consider one set of hooks plenty to use on a paternoster, and this should be fixed at least two feet above the lead. There are various methods of making a paternoster, the most common being a main line about four feet long, with two single sneck bend hooks fixed by bone runners about a foot from each other on the main line. These single hooks are on separate bits of gimp and project about seven inches from the gimp of the main trace. These single hooks are just put through both lips of the live bait, so that when a pike takes them, he must have time given him to get the whole lot in his mouth before he can be hooked. I don't think this single hook is sufficient. The way I made my paternoster was to get a length of good fine gimp for slightly clouded water, and a length of strong gut for very clear water, each about one and a half yards long. A good fair sized and well whipped loop is made at each end, one loop being to fasten the lead in, and the other for the reel line to be attached to. About two feet from the bottom loop a swivel was put in, one of those swivels that has an extra eye or ring projecting at right angles from its side. Into the eye the seven or eight inches of gimp on which the hooks were whipped is attached, swinging clear as it were from the main gut line, the swivel allowing the bait to go round and round the trace without twisting himself up with it.

If the angler uses gut for the main line of his trace, which, I may add, is better for very clear water than gimp. I don't know that it matters about using the very expensive salmon gut, very strong barbel legering gut will do, because it is a dead certainty that the same gut that will kill a 10 or 12lb. barbel will kill almost any pike we are likely to get hold of nowadays.

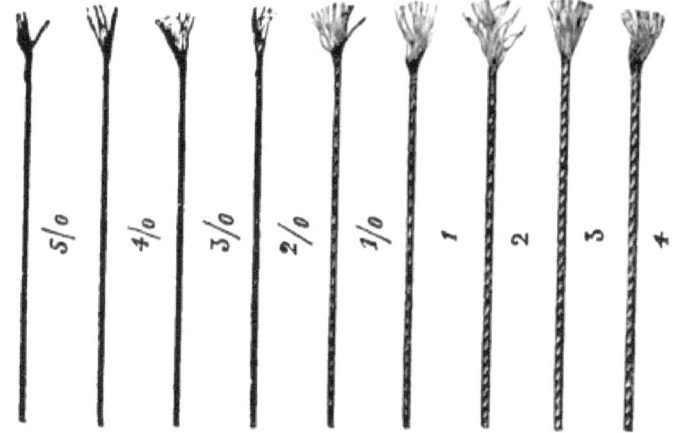

FIG. 16. SIZES OF GIMP.

The hooks should always be dressed on fine copper gimp or twisted flexible wire, it does not matter much which. A short length of very thick and stiff gut is also a very good thing to dress paternoster hooks on. I like a double hook with a small rider brazed at the back, a good deal like the hook of a Jardine snap, at the end of the gimp firmly whipped on, and a little distance above it a single moveable lip hook of a fair good size, say a No. 1 or 2. The double hook need not be very large, No. 4 or 5 being plenty big enough. In baiting this tackle the lip hook is shifted to suit the size of bait, so that when that lip hook is through both lips of the bait, the small hook at the back of the double one reaches to the root of the back fin, into which it is firmly stuck. This tackle enables a pike to be struck as soon as he runs off with the bait, and is much safer than the single hook only. In using a paternoster it is necessary to have a tight line, so as to be always ready when a pike attacks the bait, and work it into all sorts of eddies and corners, sometimes swinging it out like a pendulum to the far side of the river or open water, allowing the lead to rest on the bottom, and bringing it inch by inch to the bank on which you stand. In fact, it is in almost an endless variety of ways that a paternoster can be worked; holes can be tried where any other plan could hardly be adopted, open spaces among boughs and flags, eddies at the tail-end of a mill. You can hardly be wrong anywhere where jack are to be found, with a paternoster; but it is a question of practise and experience alone that will make a successful paternosterer. I might add that under no circumstances do I like a pike paternoster to have more than one set of hooks.

Legering for pike is another plan that, like the paternoster, requires no float, but is, during certain conditions of the water, a most deadly style to try. When a heavy flood or a break-up of the winter's frost causes a strong flush of water to come down the river, and it clears away sufficiently to see the bait when sunk a yard below the surface, then is the time to try the leger in the deep and quiet stretches away from the main current. Indeed, in some very deep and quiet rivers that have a gravelly and level bottom, the leger is as good a piece of tackle as can be tried. I like a fair sized bullet for my leger, one at least an ounce in weight, with a hole drilled through it sufficiently large to allow the line to pass easily through. This bullet is threaded on the line itself, with a bit of a stop, either a split shot pinched on, or a little bit of wood half an inch in length, and as thick as a match half-hitched in the line below it. This prevents the bullet from dropping down the trace and getting too near the bait. The proper distance between bullet and bait is about three and a half feet. Below the bullet, joined to the line, is a trace of either gimp or gut, with a small long barrel lead on it, and a buckle swivel at the end. The lead, as just noted, should be as thin as possible, say about one and a half inches long and no thicker than a goose quill, so that when a jack runs off with the bait the lead is no obstruction to him. Below the lead and buckle swivel is the tackle, and this can either be a double gorge hook or the tackle recommended in paternoster fishing. A tackle that I used to use sometimes in the deep waters of the Ouse, was an ordinary gorge tackle with the gimp threaded under the skin and brought out behind the back fin in the usual way, and an extra gorge hook mounted on a very short loop of gimp not more than a quarter of an inch long, with a very small hook whipped at the back. The eye or loop of this extra double hook was dropped over the gimp on the main tackle and brought right down to the back fin of the bait, and the tiny hook at back just stuck under the skin. This extra hook then laid flat to the side, and was not so liable to catch any obstruction on the bottom of river as the ordinary treble snap hooks. When a pike takes this tackle you can venture to strike or tighten him nearly as quick as snap fishing, the hanging hooks in the centre are bound to take hold if the pike gets the bait in his mouth at all. Anyhow, when you get a run, I should not allow him to go more than a couple or three yards before tightening on him. If you use an ordinary gorge tackle for legering, when you have to give the fish time to swallow the bait, you should see that the line can be easily drawn through the bullet, so that any amount of line can be taken off the reel without the bullet shifting at all. Every knot, loop, etc., on the line or tackle should be between the bullet and the bait. The long barrel lead that is on the trace some 18 inches above the bait is merely used as a weight to keep it from running too far about and getting so far away from the leger bullet. About 14 or 15 inches from the bait; in fact, close up to the buckle swivel of the trace, between it and the long barrel lead, it will be as well to put a rough bit of cork, any old bottle cork will do cut in half, with a nick in the flat side, into which the gimp can be stuck. This bit of cork will help the bait to swim some few inches above the bottom, and be more attractive than if the weight of tackle kept him flat on his side at the bottom.

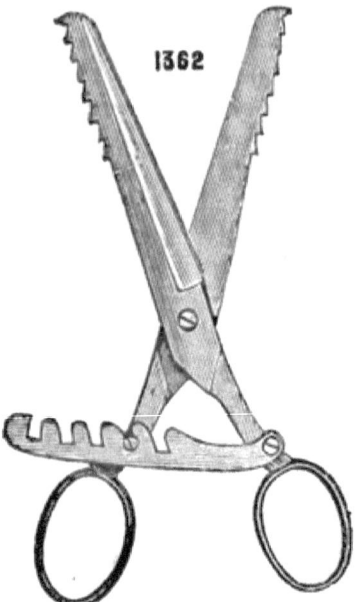

FIG. 17. DISGORGING SCISSORS.

I think I have said as much as I need say about live-baiting for pike; hooking and playing the fish have been carefully considered in another part of this volume; but I might just mention a peculiar thing that has often come under my notice, and that is that the pike of almost any river or stream prefers a live bait from a strange river in preference to those taken from the same stream in which he lives. It may be fancy, but a can of Thames dace seemed to be more attractive to the Ouse pike than baits taken from the latter river; while Trent dace were liked by Witham jack, and vice versa. I don't know if there is anything in this, but still during my career as a professional several like cases have cropped up that have been, to say the least, very peculiar. Pike are sometimes caught with very queer live baits, the two most noteworthy instances that

came under my own observation were a small jack over a
pound in weight, and a live blackbird with a broken wing.
In the former case we knew that a large pike tenanted a
pool some little distance from the Trent, but all efforts to
catch him by the ordinary baits proved futile. At last a
well-known Newark tradesman tried him with a small jack
that weighed at least a pound and a quarter. This fish was
threaded on a very large gorge tackle, and for nearly an hour
lugged four or five large live bait floats about manfully round
and round that pool. At last he took it, and we gave him
half an hour to swallow the bait, which he did. We
were disappointed over that fish, it was no less than 45 inches
long, and only scaled up to 16lb. The other case was also
in a pool away from the main river. We had noticed earlier
in the day a jack make a grab at a yellow wagtail that sat on
the edge of a weed bed. A small terrier we had with us
found a wounded blackbird with a broken wing under the
hedge bottom. This bird we carefully tied on a saddle
tackle, so that one set of hooks was on its back and the
other under its breast. Removing the trace, lead, and floats
this bait was thrown out like a huge fly. He flopped on the
water, making a rare commotion for a minute or so, when a
5lb. jack snatched him under and was safely landed. That
was the only time I ever fished with a live bird for a bait,
and I did not feel at all proud of the exploit, as it was a
cold-blooded job, to say the very best; but the pike snapping at the wagtail, and the dog finding the wounded bird
so soon afterwards, gave us a hint. But it was a strange
thing, as we had tried the same pool dozens of times before
and never landed a jack on a live fish out of it. Once I
got a brace of jack when chub fishing with a lump of pith,
and a friend of mine one afternoon landed four when bream
fishing with worms. A live bait kettle is also a necessity
of the pike fisherman as a receptacle to carry his live baits
about in. I have seen all sorts in use, from a square biscuit tin with a string handle, to Field's patent can, that has
an arrangement fixed to it to pump air among the water.
The accompanying illustration show the kinds that are generally in use; but perhaps the best of the lot is the one that
has an inner kettle of perforated zinc that can be lifted in

and out of the outer one. This arrangement is useful in a variety of ways, for one thing the baits can be got at without

FIG. 18. LIVE BAIT KETTLES.

putting the hand into the cold water—a consideration when the weather is nippingly cold—and another thing, the inner kettle can be set in the stream with the main stock of baits, so as to freshen them up if they got weak and sickly by being carried about too long. If the angler lives close to the water it would be as well to keep a stock of baits by him if he possibly can. The best thing is a strong hamper that has a closely fitting lid. Some men have a wooden box or trunk with a wire grating at each end, and the bottom and lid perforated plentifully with half-inch holes. In my opinion, based on a long experience with both, I am decidedly in favour of the wicker one sunk to the bottom, as the baits keep longer and in better condition in it than in a wooden one floating just under the surface. One of the best things I ever saw to keep live baits in was a stone trough that was fixed under a pump at the bottom of an old friend's garden. This trough was made out of a peculiar red sand stone, and had been there in all probability a good many years. It did not matter how sickly and weak the baits were when turned out of the can, they soon recovered in the trough. Perhaps there was some virtue or other in the old stone, anyhow I never knew any other pump trough that would keep baits so long and so well. I might also just tell the novice that it is not a good plan to keep live baits all night in a small bait can, as he would be bound to find some of them dead in the morning, and the rest not very lively. If you have nothing else, put them in a good sized pail with a landing net over the top, and let a tap drip into them all night; if no tap is available, use a good big tub three parts filled with water. A lump of ice put on the lid of a can will sometimes keep the baits alive for many hours.

Before I close this chapter I might just say that good silk gimp is better for pike traces than the twisted steel wire that is sometimes recommended. The latter is finer, and shows less in the water, but it will occasionally kink, and when it does kink it snaps very easily. Short lengths of twisted wire are extremely useful to dress the hooks of snap, etc., tackles on; but when a long trace is required I strongly advise either gimp or gut, for the reason just stated. Wire will kink and break very easily—at least this is my experience.

I think I have said as much as I need say on the subject of pike fishing that is likely to be of interest to the working man angler. Fishing with such items as a pike fly, or an artificial rat, or the thousand and one different tackles and artificials that are now put on the market would only be a slight variation not worth mentioning. The general principles I lay down in the foregoing pages would be the same in nearly all instances.

CHAPTER VIII.

THE PERCH.

PERCH AND PERCH FISHING.

The veteran and his first perch—Habits and haunts of perch—Perch packing in the winter—A cruel slaughter—Description of the perch—Weight of perch—" His eyes bigger than his belly "—Perch in the frying pan—Rod, reel, line, and tackle for perch fishing—Stream fishing for perch—Paternostering—Float fishing with a minnow—Fly fishing—Artificial baits for perch.

I find that I have gone into the subject of pike fishing at such a length that the space left at my disposal to treat of perch and perch fishing is only very limited, so I must be as brief as I possibly can in this chapter, only laying down the principal rules that must guide the novice who wishes to practice this branch of angling.

I wonder how many grey-haired veterans among the vast army of Britain's anglers who, looking back over a career spent by the side of river, lake, pond, and stream, cannot say that it was the capture of a small perch or two in some pond or canal that was the starting point of their angling experiences, and so fired them with enthusiasm for the sport that they have stuck to it till unable to get down to the waterside, and can now only sit by the fire and think of all the glorious days they have had since those boyhood's times, when the first perch snatched down their float so startlingly sudden that it nearly upset their nerves. There is no fish better adapted than small perch, that live in a pond or canal, to start a boy on his angling experiences. This class of perch is not particular what sort of tackle it is, neither does he care much about the bait—a worm freshly dug out of the garden, a slug picked at random from the cabbage bed, or a bunch of green and stinking gentles will all be greedily swallowed. And then again it does not matter about accurately plumbing the depth, or carefully ground-baiting a swim, or any one of the hundreds of minute details that go towards making, say, roach fishing such a fine art.

"Yes," some of you may say, "this is all very well talking about those ill-fed and hungry pond perch taking anything that is offered them, but what about a good well-fed river perch, that has a plentiful supply of small fry knocking about next door to him, as it were?" As the old saying goes, "this is a horse of another colour." A boy with a bent pin, a thick bit of gut, a heavy lead, and a rough home-made float, won't make much impression on him, he might catch one or two by accident during certain conditions of the water; but, say, during August, September, and October, when the rivers have run down very clear and bright, and even the knots on the tackle can be plainly seen deep down in the water, Mr. Perch is a particular wide-awake customer. To get them then you have to be as an old friend of mine put it, "as artful as a waggon-load of monkeys." You have got to use fine tackle, and you will have to use it far off. The bait also will have to be delicate and attractive, and mounted on the hooks in the most careful manner. During the early part of the season, that is, latter end of June and the first two or three weeks of July, perch are not quite so careful as they are a little later on. At that time they will very often take the small red worm or the cad baits when dace fishing down the shallow streams or run at a small artificial minnow. Just at that time they are picking up after spawning and cleaning, but a month or two later, when well fed and in good condition, they leave the shallow streams and seek refuge in deeper water, under the roots and hollows of an overhanging bank, in the deep and quiet eddies, round about the woodwork of an old bridge, in the deep and strong waters by the side of flags and rushes, and in the deep eddies by the side of the swirling water from a weir. It is then during the late summer and autumn that the big ones take some catching. The very worst time for poor Mr. Perch is after a sharp winter, when the ice and frost have broken up, and the river is tearing down in high flood. At this time they pack themselves together in large numbers, seeking the quiet corners, eddies, and even deep

I

dyke ends, out of the way of the raging flood water. Poor fellows, they have been most likely on very short commons during the long cold winter, and as a consequence very sharp set. When the water clears a little, and the angler drops across a corner in which a large shoal is packed, the execution is sometimes pitiful. A few handfuls of chopped-up worms are thrown in, and a red worm on the hook; and sometimes the sport (save the mark) continues until every perch is cleared out of the hole. Once only I can remember being in at the death of a whole shoal of packed perch, and even now I feel a little bit ashamed of the exploit. I found them at home in a deep hole at a dyke end that ran into the River Witham, not very far from where the county of Lincoln joined the county of Nottingham. It was during the early days of February, just after the frost of a long and severe winter had broken up, and the yellow floodwater was tearing down the river in high spate. A few yards up the dyke the water was, comparatively speaking, clear, and at least seven or eight feet deep. In about three hours I had landed three dozen fair good perch weighing a little over 20lb., and considered I had cleared every one out of the hole, as during the remainder of the afternoon I failed to add a single one to the bag. I have heard of as many as 200 being taken at one sitting under similar circumstances; but, thank goodness, whatever may have been my piscatorial sins, I have not one of that magnitude to answer for.

The perch is a member of the Percidæ family, and is a representative of the spinous-finned fish, that is, having spikes or prickles on the end of the rays of some of his fins. A great characteristic of this fish is the second fin on the back. His scientific name is Perca Fluviatilis, and he is a very handsome, well-made member of the finny tribe; in fact, I consider him a gem of the first water. Look at the beautiful scarlet of his fins, the golden rings of his eyes, the pale green of his sides, shaded and relieved by the darker bars that stripe his body from the shoulder to the tail. His scales are small, very hard, and extremely difficult to scrape off, but they are arranged in such perfect order; in fact, he appears to me to be about as perfect a fish form as it is possible to conceive. The dark stripes or bars down each side of this fish number, I think, never more than seven, although I have one here set up that has nine down one side; but I fancy this was only a lark of the preserver, who fancied he could improve on Nature.

Perch spawn early, say by the latter end of April or the beginning of May, and they choose peculiar positions for this operation. They deposit their ova on the submerged boughs, just under the surface of the water, and on the reed weed and flag beds, and sometimes over the stones on the shallows, spreading the ova all over everything handy, like long festoons of lace. Swans, ducks, and other water-fowl reap a merry harvest at this time, for nothing could be handier for them than perch spawn, which they speedily gobble up by the yard. Perch are wonderfully prolific, as many as three quarters of a million of eggs have been calculated to be in the ovum of a pound fish; and so there stands need to be, for perch spawn stands a very poor chance of coming to maturity, in all probability not more than one egg out of every thousand reaches the fish stage. This fish in favourable and well preserved waters will reach a very fair size, odd ones have been taken that exceeded 4lb. I should say that four and a half pounds would be the very outside weight of this fish in British waters. We have heard of English perch reaching the extraordinary weight of six, eight, and even one of nine pounds, but there does not appear to be any evidence in existence that such can now be seen preserved, so I am afraid we must take these gigantic perch with a good deal of caution. A two pounder is a good one, while as for a three pounder, they are not often caught. I have seen them taken from various rivers when they tipped the beam at from two to two and a half pounds, and probably twice when they scaled nearly three pounds; but never yet have I landed one or seen one landed that went over the three pounds. In some of the Scandinavian lakes we hear of them reaching extraordinary dimensions, and in the Danube there are some that go into the teens of pounds. The perch is blessed, or perhaps he would call it cursed with a very large mouth, and sometimes it is wonderful the bait he will go for, he must regulate the size of his quarry by the size of his mouth, and not by the size of his stomach at all, for some odd times it would be an utter impossibility for him to swallow the bait he ran at. The most extraordinary case that I ever heard off, was a little perch of only five or six ounces running at and getting hooked on a gigantic spoon, that a friend had purchased to use for large pike in one of the Irish lakes. He laid the fish in the bowl of the spoon, like a herring on a dish; whatever that perch took a six inch spoon to be, is merely a matter of speculation. I have taken half and three quarter pounders on pike baits, that it was utterly impossible for him to swallow; they seemed to me to be like the boy in the nursery rhyme, whose eyes were bigger than his belly. As a fish for the table perch are A1, being remarkably firm, white, and sweet in the flesh. It is not much good trying to scrape the scales off; the best plan to prepare them for the table is to cut off the head, tail, and fins, remove the insides, and wash them well inside and out, dry them thoroughly with a cloth and drop them in a frying pan among a liberal supply of boiling lard. As soon as they are cooked sufficiently on one side turn them over, and repeat the dose on the other. The skin and scales will all slip off together as soon as the cooking is completed. I am wonderfully fond of a dish of good river perch, and consider them better than a good fresh haddock, and equal to a lemon sole. With regard to the rod, reel, line, and tackle necessary for perch fishing, there is no need for anything very special, except an odd item or two, for extraordinary purposes. A good strong roach rod, eleven feet long, or a decent chub rod with an extra short top for occasional spinning, will be plenty good enough without running to the expense of a special rod for perch. The reel also can be a plain, easy going Nottingham, three and a half inches in diameter, or the centre pin reel I so carefully described in the vol. on barbel and chub fishing. The line also can be the stout roach or the chub line, say a No. 7 or No. 6 at the outside, and of undressed plaited silk, in fact, you cannot do better than use the rod, reel, and line I describe in Vol. I for chubbing down the streams. Perch tackle should be fairly fine, I don't recommend the very finest, four or five x drawn gut for stream fishing, although it should not be any stouter than the finest refina, undrawn quality. Hooks should be nearly as large as recommended for chub, say, Nos. 6, 7, and 8, and they can either be round bends, crystals, or sneck bends, according to fancy or the bait in use. Floats can be swan quill, some six or seven inches long, capable of carrying half-a-dozen B.B. split shot for use down lighter streams, and a pelican quill or small Nottingham curved cork float, capable of carrying ten to a dozen shots for work down the deeper, heavier waters. A small pilot, say about three quarters of an inch in diameter, a good deal like the one recommended in live-baiting for pike, will also be extremely useful in fishing the holes under the boughs or roots with a single minnow. Tackle for worm fishing need not be much longer than a yard, anyhow, I should say a gut line a yard long with a loop at each end, and stained either a dark blue or a yellowish brown will be capable of fishing nearly any place that contains perch. Hooks to suit all purposes can be carried securely whipped to fine single lengths of gut stained the same colour as the main gut line. By having your hook lengths separate, you can easily change the hook should a different size or pattern be required for special baits or purposes. The food of perch consists principally of the small fry of most sorts of fresh-water fish. Although he will take worms of various sorts, from a huge lobworm down to a tiny cockspur; I look upon him as being a fish eater generally. Nor is he by any means confined to worms and small fish, for he will sometimes go for a lump of cheese paste intended for a chub, a bit of bread crust when roach fishing, or a bunch of gentles or cad-baits when fishing the streams for dace, and even when raking the bottom for gudgeon perch will take the tiny scrap of worm intended for the smaller fish. But still, as I said before, I don't look upon those baits as being his staple food. I have dozens of times seen large perch on the feed, he gets on the track of a bleak, chasing it right across the river and all over the place, all the time close to the surface, chopping at it with a splash a dozen or more times until the poor bleak gets too exhausted to jump for freedom any more, it is almost sure to fall a victim at last, as I never yet saw a bleak in the deep, quiet stretches of the Ouse succeed in escaping from a perch, and I have watched the contests some scores of times. I don't know as I need say anything about fishing down the streams for perch with a worm, except that the worm, be it the tail end of a lob or the succulent marsh worm, or the red cockspur, should be clean and well scoured, and swum down very near the bottom, and let the swims be as long as possible, for it is a good deal like roach fishing when water is clear; fine and far off must be the order of the day. The instructions given for roach fishing down the streams in Vol. 2 will fit in for perch fishing exactly; a few scraps of clipped up worms thrown in from time to time in the track of the float is all that is required by way of ground bait. The only difference between roach and perch fishing in this style, and in the summer and autumn months, is that in roaching we generally stick to one place during the day, especially if it is a well ground-baited swim, whereas in perch fishing it is the best to rove about, throwing a few scraps of groundbait into every fresh place tried. A small fish, say a minnow or a tiny gudgeon, in fact, anything not over two inches long, will be found as good as anything that can be tried during the autumn months, and these can be fished on either a float tackle or a paternoster. The most common paternoster in use is generally made of stout gut, with a couple of bone runners at intervals in it; fastened to these bone runners are single sneck bend hooks dressed on short lengths of pig's bristles, while at the bottom is a pear shaped lead of a size to suit the requirements of the stream. Some anglers say that nothing else is so good as pig's bristles to dress the hooks on, as they always stick out straight from the main gut line at right angles, whereas a bit of gut collapses and hangs downwards. I don't know, I am sure, because I never used a bristle in my life; I always found a bit of stiff gut, about four inches long, plenty good enough for me. The way I like a paternoster to be made, is to have a gut line, fairly fine, about one and a half yards long, with a couple of those swivels (very small size, with an extra eye in the side, same as recommended in the chapter on pike fishing), about eighteen inches from each other, the bottom swivel to be eighteen inches above the lead. Into each of these swivels a stiff bit of gut, somewhat thicker than the main line, is firmly whipped in such a manner that they stick out at right angles; a bit of gut about five inches long for each will do very well. On one of these bits of gut a single round bend hook is whipped on the extreme end for worms or similar baits; some anglers only use a single hook for minnows, but I don't consider it hardly sufficient. I like a tiny treble, one of the smallest that is made whipped on the end, and a moveable lip hook several sizes larger, say a No. 8 single, above it. In baiting a minnow or tiny gudgeon, the moveable lip hook is put through both lips of the bait, and the tiny treble is stuck fair into the root of the tail, just where the flesh ends and the tail fin begins. By having the lip hook moveable, it can be adjusted to suit any sized bait. In using a small fish on a single hook baited through both lips, you are obliged to give a perch time to get it well into his mouth, or you will fail to hook him. A perch generally seizes his prey by the tail, and so by having a treble fixed there you can safely tighten on him, as soon as you feel the first pluck. Don't use a large treble that looks so awkward and clumsy against the bait's tail, but get the smallest you can; you may lose one or two runs by failing to hook firmly with the little hook, but then, on the other hand, you get more bites. I like one hook for minnows on my paternoster, and the other for worms; the bottom one, in my opinion, is the best for the former, and the top one for the latter. The lead on the end of the paternoster should be no larger than you can comfortably swing out, say fifteen yards on the fine line you are using, and should be worked or dropped into every available space in which you think a perch is lurking; if the place is open water and fairly deep, swing the lead and baits out as far as you can and allow it to touch the bottom, pause a few seconds, and then raise the rod point, winding in a foot of line, and so on until you have searched all the water between the furthest extent of your cast and the rod point. But whatever you do, don't let the baits go down too deep, only let the lead rest on the bottom and always keep the line as tight as possible. All sorts of places can be searched by a paternoster, but more particularly those places where the stream is deep and strong, with a clear and wide expanse of water. When fishing among the roots and under the boughs I prefer a float tackle with only one set of hooks on, and this float can either be a stout pelican quill or a small Nottingham cork, or the little pilot as before mentioned. Three or four fair sized shots are distributed on the tackle at intervals, the lowest one a foot or so from the hook. For hooks themselves I have a preference for the same as described on the paternoster, and baited exactly the same way. The float tackle is arranged so as to suit the depth of water, but I should say if you can anyway hit it, if the bait is a foot to 18in. above the bottom, you stand the best chance. The minnow is swum down by the edge of the boughs, or quietly insinuated into any opening large enough among the roots, and the draw or strike should be made as soon as you feel the first pluck of the fish.

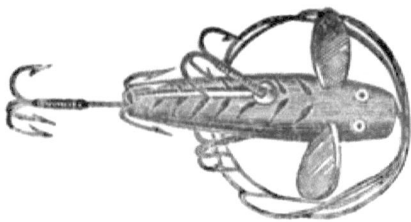

FIG. 19. THE DEVON MINNOW.

One of the best day's perch fishing I ever had was down the Witham, fishing the boughs in this manner. I got fifteen perch going nearly a pound apiece on the average, and three very decent chub, besides losing a few owing to some very awkward places I tried in. A very simple plan of carrying live minnows down to the river is by putting them in a bottle among some clean cold water, one of those sodawater bottles "without a bottom," as Andy called them, is as good as anything that can be employed; a half-pint bottle will accommodate two dozen minnows very well. Cork them down and slip the bottle in your side pocket; they will live very well corked down in a bottle. I suppose

the jolting about during carriage keeps the water well
aerated; but still if two or three small triangular nicks are
cut into the cork, the chances of them living longer will be
all the better. It is a nuisance carrying a bait-can with a

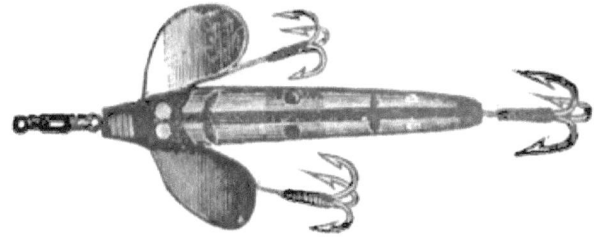

FIG. 20. THE QUILL MINNOW.

few minnows in, a bottle is far handier, you are not so liable
to empty the water into your pocket as you are with a can.
Small perch are sometimes taken with an artificial fly. A
little Zulu with a red tag appears to be the favourite; but
it is very little good, or, indeed, I should suppose hardly
any anglers go after perch specially with the fly. When they
are captured it is generally when dace fishing across the
shallows and streamy backwaters, and looked upon as
merely an accident; but still I have known as many as a
dozen perch to be landed during a single evening on the
fly.

With regard to spinning for perch, this, in my opinion,
is only a very sorry business, and not so safe as either worm
fishing or paternostering. It is true a few odd ones are
got now and again by that plan, but this game is apt to be

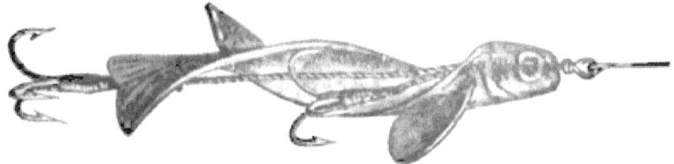

FIG. 21. THE SPIRAL MINNOW.

a little expensive. You are in all probability using an artificial that cost from one to two shillings, and small jack will
persist in running at them and quietly severing the gut with
their teeth, and if this happens two or three times during

a day, why the game is hardly worth the candle. It is as well where small jack abound to have four or five inches of fine gimp close up to the swivel of the minnow, or whatever else you are using. Almost any small artificial from one to two inches long will do for perch, such as spoons, Devons, phantoms, spirals, Caledonians, etc., and once I saw a spinning arrangement on which a lob worm was fixed. This, I fancy, was named "The Jigger," and was a pretty fair success. I give here two or three illustrations of arti-

FIG. 22. THE PHANTOM MINNOW.

ficials that are about as good as anything that can be tried for perch, but I say again that it is not a very brilliant plan to fill a bag with large perch.

I must now bring this part of my experiences and instructions to a close, and trust I have made myself perfectly understood, so that no one, however inexperienced, who is anxious to learn, can possibly make a mistake.

BY THE SAME AUTHOR.

BARBEL AND CHUB.

A Concise and Practical Work on How and Where to Fish for Barbel and Chub.

Price One Shilling.   Post Free, 1/2.

"ANGLER" OFFICE, SCARBOROUGH.

ROACH, RUDD, & BREAM.

Every angler should add this little work to his library. It is full of useful hints.

Price One Shilling.   Post Free, 1/2.

"ANGLER" OFFICE, SCARBOROUGH.

JUST PUBLISHED.   SECOND EDITION.
"AN ANGLER'S PARADISE."
(ILLUSTRATED.)
By J. J. ARMISTEAD.
The Best Book on Fish Culture.   Post Free, 7s. 10½d.

"ANGLER" OFFICE, SCARBOROUGH.

JUST PUBLISHED.   FIRST EDITION.
"GRAYLING, AND HOW TO CATCH THEM,"
(ILLUSTRATED.)
By F. M. WALBRAN.
A Cheap Concise Description of Grayling Fishing.   Post Free, 2s. 6d.

"ANGLER" OFFICE, SCARBOROUGH.

HOUGHTON'S "BRITISH FISHES."
(ILLUSTRATED.)
A Cheap Reprint of this Standard Work.   Post Free, 6s. 10½d.

"ANGLER" OFFICE, SCARBOROUGH.

JUST PUBLISHED.   FIRST EDITION.
"ANGLING DAYS."
(ILLUSTRATED.)
By JONATHAN DALE.
Post Free   -   -   -   -   -   2s. 6d.

"ANGLER" OFFICE, SCARBOROUGH.

"THE OLD CRONIES' ANGLING CLUB"
By EDGAR S. SHRUBSOLE.
Price 1s. 6d.   Post Free, 1s. 7½d.
EDITION LIMITED.

"ANGLER" OFFICE, SCARBOROUGH.

"The Angler"

ISSUED ON FRIDAY MORNING,

IS THE SMARTEST PENNY PAPER PUBLISHED.

BRIGHT, RACY, READABLE.

If you are a fisherman it is invaluable.

will interest you if you don't fish.

Publishing at present a series of Coloured Fish Plates— No Angler's Den should be without them.

ONE PENNY WEEKLY—From any Newsagent or Fishing Tackle Dealer.

COLOURED PLATES
OF BRITISH FISHES.

Lovely Plates in from Ten to Fifteen Colours, of

BRITISH

FRESHWATER FISHES.

WORKS OF ART.

POST FREE, 3D. EACH.

"ANGLER" OFFICE, SCARBOROUGH.

LIST OF FISH PLATES,

As Issued in the "Angler."

PRICE THREEPENCE EACH.

Perch, Pike, Roach, Chub, Bull Trout, Salmon Trout (Var), Tench, Common Trout, Carp, Eels, Ruffe and Miller's Thumb, Salmon Trout, Golden Tench, Sticklebacks, Loch Leven Trout, Grilse (or young Salmon), Barbel and Gudgeon, Sturgeon, Rainbow Trout, Bronze and Golden Carp, Bream, Silvery Salmon, Burbot, Black-Finned Trout, Bleak Loach and Minnow, Loch Killin Char, Pomeranian Bream, Salmon (Male), Dace and Graining, Windermere Char, Vendace and Grayling, Galway Sea Trout, Rudd and Azurine, Alpine Char and Torgoch, Gillaroo Trout, Pollan and Powan, Lampreys, Crucian Carp, Great Lake Trout, Sewen.

www.ingramcontent.com/pod-product-compliance
Lightning Source LLC
Chambersburg PA
CBHW021825230426
43669CB00008B/863